A practical guide to package holiday law and contracts

Tolley Publishing Company Limited

A practical guide to Package Holiday Law and Contracts

by

John Nelson-Jones and Peter Stewart
both of Field Fisher Waterhouse, Solicitors

Third edition

Foreword to the first edition by A. G. Kennedy, Deputy Chairman & Chief Executive of The Thomas Cook Group Ltd.

Tolley Publishing Company Limited
A UNITED NEWSPAPERS PUBLICATION

ISBN 0 85459 810 3

First published January 1985
Second edition June 1989
Third edition May 1993

Published by
Tolley Publishing Company Limited
Tolley House
2 Addiscombe Road
Croydon
Surrey
CR9 5AF
081-686 9141

Printed in Great Britain by
Hartnolls Ltd, Bodmin, Cornwall

Foreword to the first edition

by A. G. Kennedy, Deputy Chairman & Chief Executive of the Thomas Cook Group Ltd.

In the last two decades the inclusive tour holiday business has shown dramatic growth. In any developing industry mistakes will always be made and in the case of the travel industry the collapse of Court Line in 1974 and more recently the demise of Laker have focused attention on the legal aspects of those involved in the travel industry, be they tour operators, airlines or travel agents.

During this period of growth, consumerism has come to the fore with members of the public questioning their rights in regard to contracts with tour operators and the role of travel agents.

As far as I know, this book is the first to deal solely with package holiday law and contracts; it is certainly timely and, more importantly, I believe it is readable both by those engaged in the holiday and travel industries and others who are connected with it in their capacity as journalists or legal advisers.

The authors have had considerable practical experience on this subject and the book will be a most useful reference work, dealing as it does with relatively new statutes and the increasing volume of case law which has now arisen.

AGK
November 1984

Preface

Since 31 December 1992 package holiday law has been dominated by The Package Travel, Package Holidays and Package Tours Regulations 1992 ("the Regulations"). They implement the 1990 EC Directive on these subjects. This book focuses on *package holidays.* It is only incidentally concerned with the wide range of travel arrangements which also fall within the Directive's definition of "package".

In addition to the Regulations, the package holiday industry is affected by a wide range of common and statute law. This includes the common law of contract, agency, misrepresentation and tort; general legislation such as the Misrepresentation Act 1967, the Trade Descriptions Act 1968, the Unfair Contract Terms Act 1977, and Part III of the Consumer Protection Act 1987; specific holiday industry legislation such as the Air Travel Reserve Fund Act 1975 and certain provisions of the Civil Aviation Act 1982; and much else beside. In addition there are codes of conduct of relevant trade associations, and various codes of advertising and sales promotion practice.

This book aims to explain the relevant law and regulations in a concise and practical manner, and to describe and analyse the contracts which tour operators enter into with customers, travel agents, and the hoteliers, airlines etc whose services are featured in package holidays. In pursuing these aims, the authors seek to provide guidance both to holiday makers and their legal advisers and to those engaged in the holiday industry and their legal advisers.

Before examining the law relating to package holidays in detail, it would be beneficial for those readers who are not already familiar with it to have a general idea of how the holiday industry works, the overall structure envisaged by the Regulations and of the anticipated roles of various trade associations and regulatory bodies in light of the Regulations. Chapter 1 is devoted to this.

It is critically important for readers to appreciate the essential difference between tour operators and travel agents. It is the tour operator who actually arranges the component facilities, such as hotels and flights, which comprise a package holiday. It is the travel agent who sells, as agent for the tour operator, the operator's package holiday. The holiday maker's contract is with the tour operator, and allegations of breach of contract should usually be directed against the tour operator, not the travel agent. Chapter 2 deals in some detail with the nature of the contract between a holiday maker and a tour operator and the obligations imposed on tour operators by Regulations 4–14. Chapter 3 discusses the extent of the tour operator's responsibility for the acts and omissions of hotels, airlines etc which he does not own and over which he has no control. The law here has been radically altered by Regulation 15.

A key feature of the Regulations is the provisions for protecting holiday makers against the collapse of a tour operator contained in Regulations 16–22. These are explained in Chapter 4.

Travel agents have a dual role in relation to package holidays. The first is that of sales or booking agent for the tour operator. It involves displaying brochures, taking bookings, the subsequent servicing of bookings, and dealing with cancellations. The second is that of travel consultant to the customer, especially when a customer asks questions to try to establish whether a particular holiday will meet his requirements. Chapter 5 considers both these roles, and their attendant duties in law.

Allegations of misrepresentation can arise through, for example, the failure of a hotel to live up to its description, or through an inaccurate oral representation made by a travel agent about particular facilities offered by a tour operator. Misrepresentation can result not only in civil proceedings but also in criminal proceedings under section 14 of the Trade Descriptions Act 1968, Part III of the Consumer Protection Act 1987 and Regulation 5. Chapter 6 examines the law relating to misrepresentation and misleading descriptions.

The landmark decisions in *Jarvis* v *Swan Tours* and *Jackson* v *Horizon Holidays* established that disappointment and vexation form a legitimate head of damages when, in breach of contract, a holiday goes wrong. Chapter 7 surveys the damages which a wronged holiday maker might expect to receive in view of recent case law. It also deals with a holiday maker's duty to mitigate his loss.

Chapter 8 seeks to summarise the position when a holiday maker has a complaint about his holiday. Should he use the ABTA Arbitration Scheme, or should he issue proceedings? What difficulties does a tour operator face in defending claims and how can they be minimised?

In creating a package holiday the tour operator enters into a range of contracts with, for example, airlines, coach companies and hoteliers. Chapter 9 examines these contracts, and also the international conventions which limit the liabilities of carriers.

When a tour operator becomes insolvent, a host of difficult questions arise. Are there limits on the use to which bond monies can be put? Does it matter if a holiday maker paid by credit card? What happens to monies held by travel agents but not passed over to the tour operator before the financial collapse? These, and other issues, are considered in Chapter 10.

This book concentrates on the primary legislation, common law and ABTA regulations affecting the package holiday industry but the reader should also be aware of the following statutes which can be relevant:

(a) The Restrictive Practices Act 1976 requires trade associations, such as ABTA, to register restrictive provisions in their articles of association etc for approval, and reduces the scope for certain restrictive practices which might otherwise be adopted by tour operators and travel agents.

(b) The Resale Prices Act 1976 contains, *inter alia*, provisions prohibiting trade associations from imposing minimum price requirements upon their members.

(c) The Fair Trading Act 1973 contains various provisions for protecting consumers.

(d) The Competition Act 1980 enables the Office of Fair Trading to take action against anti-competitive practices.

(e) The Consumer Credit Act 1974 is applicable if a travel company provides consumer credit facilities for the purchase of holidays etc.

(f) The Transport Act 1980 lays down various requirements concerning, for example, the operation of coach services.

Because so little has been written about UK package holiday law this book would not have been possible without advice and assistance from many sources. The authors take this opportunity of thanking all of them. In particular, the authors wish to thank Linda Nightingale and Tina Sivyer for their research assistance, and Samantha Carter and Sharon Oliver for their invaluable typing help.

The law is stated as at 31 January 1993.

John Nelson-Jones and Peter Stewart
Field Fisher Waterhouse
41 Vine Street
London EC3N 2AA

Contents

Table of cases

Table of statutes

Table of statutory instruments

Chapter 1

The structure of the holiday industry

1. Package holidays

Package holidays, traditionally, are holidays the elements of which are packaged together to form a whole which is sold at an inclusive price. The creator of the package is the tour operator who makes arrangements for transport companies, hotels etc to provide the travel, accommodation, meals and other items which together constitute a particular holiday. In some cases the tour operator, or companies under common ownership and control, will own the airlines and hotels which feature in the package. But many substantial operators do not own any airplanes or hotels and are not members of a group of companies which does. And even operators who own hotels and planes will often use some which they do not own.

People normally think of package holidays as involving a flight to some sunny resort, a comfortable hotel by the sea and a few excursions. But the range of package holidays is truly astonishing: ski holidays, cruise and coach holidays, self-catering holidays, sporting and adventure holidays, Holy Land and other special interest holidays and many more.

A tour operator normally sets out in a brochure the package holidays which he is offering for a particular season. As well as containing the basic factual information regarding each holiday, and items such as the operator's booking conditions and booking form, the brochure contains a battery of photographs and titillating prose – "the stuff that dreams are made of".

"Tailor-made" package holidays have become increasingly popular since the late 1980s. These are holidays where the tour operator's brochure describes the constituent parts but leaves it to the holiday maker to ask for the constituents to be packaged into a whole which best satisfies the requirements of the holiday maker.

It has also become more common for holiday makers to supplement or vary holiday arrangements described in a tour operator's brochure with elements of which the holiday maker has personal knowledge. Usually, this applies where a holiday maker has been to particular accommodation before and wishes to substitute that for the tour operator's accommodation or to tack on to the end of the holiday arrangements some extra days in an area known to the holiday maker. Arrangements of this type will be referred to as "unbrochured elements".

Most tour operators sell their holidays through travel agents. Travel agents are the retailers of the travel industry. Between them they man travel shops in virtually every high street in the land. An agent will stock the brochures of the operators for whom he acts, answer questions about them, assist customers to complete the booking form and forward it to the operator for acceptance. Thereafter he performs a number of administrative functions. His role is totally different from that of the tour operator and an awareness of this is essential to a proper understanding of the legal responsibilities of each.

It is the tour operator who arranges the various facilities and services which make up the package holiday. For example, the tour operator who puts together a two-week package holiday at the Hotel Luxury, Utopia, will normally:

(a) arrange for a representative to be at the airport from which the holiday makers depart to deal with any queries or problems on check-in;

(b) arrange with the carrying airline that either a whole plane or a certain number of seats on a plane will be available for his customers on the given departure date;

(c) arrange for representatives to meet the plane on arrival at its destination and assist the holiday makers in assembling on the coach that is to take them from the airport to the hotel;

(d) arrange for the coach to attend the airport on the given date;

(e) arrange for the hotel to make available the appropriate number of rooms and the appropriate meals for the two-week period;

(f) arrange for his representatives to be available during the two-week period to deal with any queries, sell excursions etc;

(g) arrange for a coach to collect the holiday makers and take them to the airport on the date of return to the UK;

(h) arrange the required number of seats on the airplane returning to the UK on the appropriate day.

Normally the cost of the package holiday will include all the above facilities and services (with the possible exception of the cost of excursions) and sometimes more, such as travel insurance.

Unless he also arranges some package holidays of his own, a travel agent has no part in arranging or providing the facilities and services set out above. He is concerned solely with the business of selling package holidays, train tickets, airplane tickets, traveller's cheques, holiday insurance etc. It must be borne in mind that a travel agent sells not only package holidays but, in his capacity as booking agent for airlines, coach companies, hotels etc, sells the individual components which can provide a tailor-made holiday for those who do not like their holidays in packages. A travel agent will also give advice about which holiday to choose or the facilities available on a particular holiday.

The roles and responsibilities of tour operators and travel agents are totally separate and the public often deal exclusively with travel agents. Many of the large travel companies are both tour operators and travel agents but proper consideration must always be given to the capacity in which such a company acts on a particular occasion. It frequently happens that, in its capacity as travel agent, a travel company will sell a package holiday provided by itself as tour operator, in which event its respective functions and responsibilities should be analysed separately.

Certain companies sell their own package holidays direct to the public without the services of a travel agent. In theory, they can provide holidays at a lower cost by avoiding having to pay sales commission to travel agents. They will not be travel agents, however, unless they also sell to the public holidays provided by other tour operators.

2. The Regulations

The Package Travel, Package Holidays and Package Tours Regulations 1992 ("the Regulations") came into force on 23 December 1992. Their genesis was the EC Directive on Package Travel, Package Holidays and Package Tours (90/314/EEC) ("the EC Directive").

The EC Directive was adopted on 13 June 1990. It is a result of the EC's general aim to complete the internal market and harmonise laws. The EC identified the tourist sector as an essential part of the internal market.

The EC Directive required member states to introduce national laws implementing it by no later than 31 December 1992. The UK had a number of options as to how to implement it. Despite a considerable body of opinion that a statute would be most appropriate to consolidate all legislation relating, directly or indirectly, to the package holiday industry, the UK Government did not pursue this path. Instead, through the DTI, regulations were chosen as the appropriate method of implementation.

The Regulations, on their face, represent UK law. However, their purpose is to implement the EC Directive. This leaves it open to disputants to argue before the courts that any ambiguity in the Regulations should be resolved by studying the EC Directive. Additionally, those who consider that the Regulations do not satisfactorily implement the EC Directive can challenge the Regulations on this basis. It is, however, beyond the scope of this book to consider any inconsistencies between the EC Directive and the Regulations.

The Regulations apply to "packages" (see page 6) sold or offered for sale in the United Kingdom. Those of them which deal with aspects other than financial protection for consumers apply only to packages sold or offered for sale after 31 December 1992. Accordingly, there is an overlap for the early part of 1993. A package purchased, for example, on 20 December 1992 but due to commence on 4 April 1993 will be subject to the law which existed before the Regulations; an identical package purchased on 2 January 1993 and due to commence on 4 April 1993 will be subject to the Regulations.

Following the coming into force of the Regulations, the DTI published Guidance Notes. Their stated purpose is "to assist those approaching the Regulations for the first time". They give the DTI's views on terms used in the Regulations and the meaning and impact of some of the Regulations.

The DTI Guidance Notes do not have the force of law. As a matter of practice, however, they are likely to have considerable effect. Breaches of many of the Regulations are a criminal offence. The Regulations are enforced by Trading Standards Officers, who are part of the local Weights & Measures Authorities in Great Britain. The counterpart in Northern Ireland is the Department of Economic Development. It is unlikely that Trading Standards Officers will accuse a travel company of infringing the Regulations if it has complied with the DTI Guidance Notes.

Where the Regulations are interpreted by the courts, there can be less certainty about the weight they will attach to the DTI's views. High Court judges, in particular, will no doubt feel free to ignore the DTI Guidance Notes.

The law which existed before the Regulations will, so far as statutory provisions are concerned, continue to be in force. Common law principles and case law will survive only to the extent that they are consistent with the terms of the Regulations. In the event of inconsistency, the Regulations will prevail.

As explained at the outset, it is the tour operator who puts the package holiday arrangements together. It is the tour operator with whom the holiday maker contracts. The travel agent is the agent through whom many package holidays are sold. The Regulations do not use the terms tour operator and travel agent. Instead, they refer to, respectively, "organiser" and "retailer". Since this book deals primarily with package holidays, and not any other form of package (see next section), it will continue to use the terms "tour operator" and "travel agent" and will substitute these terms for "organiser" and "retailer".

3. Definition of a "package"

Regulation 2(1) defines a package as "the pre-arranged combination of at least two of the following components when sold or offered for sale at an inclusive price and when the service covers a period of more than 24 hours or includes overnight accommodation:

(a) transport;

(b) accommodation;

(c) other tourist services not ancillary to transport or accommodation and accounting for a significant proportion of the package".

It supplements this by saying that:

"(i) the submission of separate accounts for different components shall not cause the arrangements to be other than a package;

(ii) nothing in this definition shall cause a combination which is arranged at the request of the consumer and in accordance with his specific instructions (whether modified or not) to be treated as other than pre-arranged".

In addition to traditional package holidays, the definition encompasses a whole range of travel, accommodation etc which would never be thought of as package holidays. Examples are business travel, residential conferences, hotel theme weekends, residential tennis coaching, many camping holidays, theatre trips to Stratford. The range of possible packages is legion. Many of them would not be arranged through tour operators but through travel agents and one of the inevitable consequences of the Regulations is that travel agents in many cases will, for the purposes of the Regulations, become organisers.

The DTI Guidance Notes acknowledge the all-embracing effect of the definition of a package. Perhaps the most difficult term to interpret in the definition is "pre-arranged". Any arrangements which are made before departure can be viewed as pre-arranged. This would have the effect of making packages of virtually all travel arrangements which include the requisite components. The DTI Guidance Notes recognise this, stating that pre-arranged "does not mean only packages which can be bought off-the-shelf but includes all packages put together before the conclusion of the contract".

It is clear that traditional package holidays fall within the terms of the Regulations. It is also clear that tailor-made holidays do. In the writers' view this will even be the case where a tailor-made holiday includes unbrochured elements.

The Regulations apply to the whole "family" of packages but their practical implementation will vary substantially between different categories. In addition, there is a significant body of law and practice which applies exclusively, or in some cases primarily, to the package holiday industry. This book focuses on the law and practice relating to *package holidays, including tailor-made holidays and unbrochured elements, sold or offered for sale by tour operators.* It is vital for the reader to bear this in mind at all times. Much of what it says also applies to other types of packages but that is incidental. Because of the above, the writers do not dicuss the interesting questions regarding the meanings of "significant proportion" and "occasionally" in the definitions of "package" and "organise".

4. Financial protection for holiday makers

It is a feature of package holiday contracts that the customer pays money to the tour operator long before the holiday begins. Usually he pays a deposit at the time when he books his holiday and then pays the balance of his holiday price about eight weeks before departure. If he books within eight weeks of his departure, he will normally be required to pay the full price when he makes his booking.

This pattern of payment gives rise to special problems in cases where a tour operator ceases trading. Before he does so, he will, in the normal course of events, have received large sums of money paid by customers whose holidays have not commenced. He may have used some of this money to make advance payments to airlines and hotels, or to pay his other trade creditors. In any event, if the tour operator is insolvent, there is little chance of customers whose holidays have not commenced receiving a full refund in the course of its liquidation.

There is also the problem of holiday makers who are stranded abroad at the time of cessation of trading. In some cases, especially where the operator has paid the relevant hotels and airlines in advance, the holiday may continue as planned – albeit without the services of the operator's on-the-spot representatives. But often this will not be so, and there will be a need for urgent repatriation arrangements.

Hitherto, protection and assistance for holiday makers in the event of the insolvency of their tour operator has (in some cases) been provided via the Civil Aviation Authority's bonding requirements and those of trade associations such as the Association of British Travel Agents ("ABTA"). But there have been numerous gaps in the protection available. Some customers have paid for holidays which they have not received – one well-publicised example in 1992 being that of Land Travel. Others have found themselves stranded overseas.

The Regulations address this by requiring tour operators to make arrangements to protect and assist their customers in the event of the tour operator's insolvency.

These arrangements must take the form of bonding, insurance or the operation of a trust account.

It may be helpful to explain, at this juncture, what is meant by a bond. It is an irrevocable guarantee to pay a specified amount, or sums not exceeding a specified amount, given by a third party, such as a bank or insurance company, and which can be called upon in specified circumstances such as the insolvency of the company in respect of which the bond is provided. The person to whom the third party pays the specified sum is stated in the bond.

In theory, the Regulations ensure that purchasers of package holidays will receive a full refund if their tour operator goes bust before the start of their holiday and will be repatriated if it does so during their holiday. However, this will depend upon tour operators making the required arrangements and doing so by reference to correct projections of their turnover. The Regulations do not introduce any licensing or reserve fund arrangements. They rely on the honesty and reliability of all tour operators and the ability of Trading Standards Officers to make sufficient checks to ensure that tour operators maintain the required level of protection.

Regulations 16–22 set out the new financial security measures to cater for a tour operator's insolvency, and resultant offences where those measures are not observed. They are explained in Chapter 4. At this stage, there are only two points which should be noted. The first is that all packages which are covered by Civil Aviation Authority requirements are exempted from Regulations 16–22. The second is the concept of an "approved body" introduced in Regulation 17 dealing with bonding. It is defined as a body which is for the time being approved by the Secretary of State for the purposes of Regulations 17 and/or 18. Under those Regulations all bond payments on the insolvency of a tour operator must be made to an approved body. It will then apply them in providing refunds to consumers who have paid for holidays which do not take place and in making repatriation arrangements for those stranded abroad.

At the time this book went to print, the bodies which

have received for approval for the purposes of Regulation 18 are ABTA, the Association of Independent Tour Operators ("AITO"), the TOSG Trust Fund Ltd, the bonding arm of the Tour Operators' Study Group, the Bus and Coach Council and the Association of Bonded Travel Organisers Trust. Approval for all of them is expected very shortly. The Passenger Shipping Association has applied for approval for the purposes of Regulation 17 and also expects to be approved soon.

Additionally, discussions are continuing among ABTA, AITO, TOSG, the Bus and Coach Council and the Passenger Shipping Association about the establishment of the Travel Protection Association ("TPA"). The intention is that TPA will become a "bonding" organisation available to tour operators generally, including the members of ABTA, AITO, TOSG, the Bus and Coach Council and the Passenger Shipping Association. TPA, when established, will seek "approved body" status. Both ABTA and TOSG, at the time of going to print, have publicly stated that, when TPA becomes an approved body, they will cease to operate their existing bonding schemes. Instead, it will be a requirement of membership of ABTA and TOSG for members to be bonded through TPA. The other associations intend to continue with their bonding schemes unless the competition from TPA is such as to make it not practicable to do so.

The Government has given approval in principle to a levy being raised on customers by TPA. The purpose of the levy is to establish a back-up fund to repay customers, or pay for repatriation, if a bond proves to be insufficient. The back-up fund will apply only to tour operators bonded with TPA.

5. Association of British Travel Agents (ABTA)

The Association of British Travel Agents is a company limited by guarantee but not having a share capital which was incorporated in 1955. Its members comprise tour operators and travel agents all of whom pay annual subscription fees. As well as the rules laid down in its Articles of Association, ABTA also has Codes of Conduct for its tour operator and travel agent members (see respectively Appendix A and Chapter 5).

ABTA's rules provide that an ABTA tour operator can only sell its package holidays through an ABTA travel agent and that an ABTA travel agent can only sell an ABTA tour operator's package holiday. On its face, this is a restriction falling foul of the Restrictive Practices Act 1976. However, the restriction – known as "Stabiliser" – was approved by Lincoln J in the Restrictive Practices Court on 20 December 1982.

Stabiliser was approved because of the benefits which were perceived to exist for consumers through ABTA's rules. The two main benefits were perceived as being –

(a) financial protection – both ABTA tour operators and ABTA travel agents must provide bonds in favour of ABTA to provide protection for customers in the event of their insolvency, and additionally ABTA has back-up arrangements if the amount of a bond proves insufficient;

(b) standard of conduct – both ABTA tour operators and ABTA travel agents are subject to Codes of Conduct which impose certain minimum standards in relation to brochures, selling practices and responsibility for the holiday arrangements themselves.

At the time of Lincoln J's decision, there was no specific legislation regulating the travel industry. That remained the position until the Regulations came into force. The advent of the Regulations will undoubtedly bring the demise of Stabiliser, and this is something which ABTA itself has recognised. It is likely, though, that Stabiliser will remain until TPA is up and running, and the DTI has already indicated to ABTA that this would meet with its approval.

The present version of the ABTA Tour Operators' Code of Conduct was published in July 1989 and has been binding upon ABTA tour operators since 1 August 1989. It represents a considerable change from earlier Codes, particularly as regards the extent of the obligations which it requires tour operators to accept where something goes wrong with a package holiday. The changes had been made with a view to anticipating the EC Directive. However, in liability terms the EC Directive and the Regulations are considerably more onerous than the Code.

At the same time as the DTI was preparing the Regulations, considerable debate took place within ABTA about its future. There were a number of high profile financial collapses of ABTA members which emptied the coffers of ABTA's back-up arrangements and required special contributions by members to keep ABTA solvent. This led to speculation that, following the Regulations, ABTA would be split asunder. But, like Mark Twain, rumours of ABTA's death are greatly exaggerated. There is a strong feeling that the public recognition of, and belief in, ABTA's symbol more than justifies ABTA's continued existence and the payment of its membership fees.

At present, ABTA has certain criteria which must be fulfilled for a tour operator or travel agent to become, and stay, a member of ABTA. Some of these relate to finances and others to method of operation, experience of staff etc. The debate about ABTA's future may lead to substantial changes in its structure. Accordingly, this book does not deal with these membership criteria.

Equally, ABTA is in the process of re-examining its Codes of Conduct. Given this, and the supremacy and more stringent provisions of the Regulations, the Codes of Conduct are not considered in detail, although certain chapters refer to them.

Finally, reference should be made to ABTA's arbitration scheme which is discussed in Chapter 8. It operates on the basis of documents only (ie no oral argument at a hearing). It does not apply to claims of more than £1,500 per person or £7,500 per booking form or to personal injury claims. Nor does it apply to commercial disputes, that is where a tour operator and travel agent dispute who is responsible for the holiday maker's claim.

6. Tour Operators' Study Group (TOSG)

In 1967 the twenty largest tour operators within ABTA formed the Tour Operators' Study Group ("TOSG"). This association remains separate from ABTA but consists exclusively of ABTA members. One of its aims is to review problems of the trade, taking into account both trade and consumer viewpoints and to report its findings with a view to influencing standards and practices within the trade.

The TOSG is, perhaps, best known for its bonding system, under which its members arrange for banks or insurance companies to enter into bonds in favour of The TOSG Trust Fund Ltd, which bonds can be called upon in the event of a member ceasing to trade. These bonds are accepted by both ABTA and the Civil Aviation Authority as satisfying their respective bonding requirements. In the event of the collapse of a TOSG member, TOSG calls in its bond and applies the bond monies in repatriating stranded holiday makers and thereafter in reimbursing customers whose holidays were due to start after the collapse occurred.

7. Civil Aviation Authority (CAA)

The Civil Aviation Authority ("the CAA") is a statutory body, under the ultimate supervision of the Department of Trade, which is responsible for, *inter alia*, the administration of airlines operating within the UK or flying to and from airports within the UK. The principal enactments to be borne in mind for the purposes of this section are the Civil Aviation Act 1982, and the Civil Aviation (Air Travel Organisers Licensing) Regulations 1972.

Section 71 of the 1982 Act reads:

> "Provision may be made by regulations for securing that a person does not in the United Kingdom—
>
> (a) make available, as a principal or an agent, accommodation for the carriage of persons or cargo on flights in any part of the world; or

(b) hold himself out as a person who, either as a principal or an agent or without disclosing his capacity, may make such accommodation available, unless he is the operator of the relevant aircraft or holds and complies with the terms of a licence issued in pursuance of the regulations or is exempted by or under the regulations from the need to hold such a licence".

Regulation 2 of the 1972 Regulations provides that a tour operator who constructs holidays which have air travel as the principal means of transport will be required to obtain an Air Travel Organiser's Licence ("ATOL") from the CAA. Under Regulation 3 an application for the grant of a licence must be made in writing to the CAA and the CAA shall either grant a licence to the applicant on the terms requested in the application or in those terms with such modifications as the CAA thinks fit, or refuse to grant a licence. The CAA may refuse to consider an application unless it is accompanied by the appropriate fee and is made not less than six months before the beginning of the period for which the licence is proposed to be in effect.

Under Regulation 3(2) the CAA shall refuse to grant a licence unless it is satisfied that:

(a) the applicant is a fit person to make available accommodation for the carriage of persons on flights (and in determining whether the applicant is a fit person the Authority shall have regard to his and his employees' past activities generally and where the applicant is a body corporate, to the past activities generally of the persons appearing to the Authority to control that body, but shall not be obliged to refuse a licence on the grounds that it considers the applicant has insufficient experience in making available accommodation for the carriage of persons on flights); and

(b) the resources of the applicant and the financial arrangements made by him are adequate for discharge of his actual and potential obligations in respect of the activities in which he is engaged (if any) and in which he may be expected to engage if he is granted the licence.

One of the conditions of the grant of an ATOL is that the ATOL holder should be covered by a bond to protect its customers in the event that it becomes unable to perform its obligations to them. The CAA sets the level of bonds required for licensable activities (ie those activities for which an ATOL is required). The CAA will accept in satisfaction of its bonding requirements bonds granted in favour of TOSG and ABTA. Where an ATOL holder does not belong to either of these bodies, it must procure a bond in favour of the CAA, which will call in and administer the bond monies in the event of the ATOL holder ceasing to trade.

An ATOL may contain such terms as the CAA thinks fit, including terms as to the minimum charges which are to be made and the goods, services and other benefits which are or are not to be furnished by any person whatsoever under or in connection with any contract which includes provision for the making available of the accommodation to which the licence relates. A schedule of standard terms is incorporated in all ATOLs. The current standard terms are reproduced in Appendix B (see page 264).

Some of these terms are discussed in subsequent chapters but at this stage it is worth noting that standard term I requires a licence holder to include its exact company name and ATOL number in all advertising, brochures, and booking and confirmation of booking forms used for package holidays covered by its ATOL. In addition he is required to furnish to the CAA, as soon as it is published, a copy of any brochure in which he, or any agent acting on his behalf, quotes the prices at which he is prepared to make available accommodation for the carriage of persons on flights or to provide an inclusive tour which includes carriage by air, and a copy of any booking form relating to any such brochure.

If the holder of a current ATOL applies for the grant of another one in continuation of or in substitution for the current one and does so not later than three months (or in the case of a licence for a term of three months or less, half the term of the licence) before the expiration of the term of the current licence, then, unless the application is withdrawn, the current licence shall not cease to be in force by reason only of the expiration of that term until the CAA gives its decision on the application. The application must contain any information regarding fitness etc specified by the CAA and be accompanied by the appropriate fee.

An airline is not required to hold an ATOL, nor is an agent of an airline or an agent of an ATOL holder. Consequently a travel agent does not require an ATOL so long as he is selling tickets or holidays on behalf of airlines or tour operators who do hold ATOLs.

In *Jet Travel Limited* v *Slade Travel Agency Limited* ([1983] The Times 16 July) it was held that intermediaries who did not sell air tickets directly to the public but only to other tour operators were still required to hold an ATOL. The facts of this case were that the plaintiffs were a subsidiary of a German company, Jet Reisen GmbH, which did not hold an ATOL and which, in the summer of 1981, entered into a number of whole plane charters with Dan Air Services Limited to make flights between Gatwick and cities in Germany. Jet Reisen sold some of their surplus seats to the plaintiffs who, in turn, sold them to the defendants on terms that the defendants should pay for the seats fourteen days in advance. In breach of that agreement, the defendants did not pay for seats sold to them between 30 November and 11 December 1981. The defendants held an ATOL and sold the tickets to the public.

The defendants alleged that the plaintiffs required an ATOL to sell the seats in the first place, the absence of which rendered the contract illegal and unenforceable. Lord Justice May held that the words of regulation 2 of the 1972 Regulations were clear, and that they applied to the plaintiff's obligations under their contract with the defendants. He stated that although the requirement of a bond was no doubt an important and perhaps the most important protection afforded to the travelling public, it was not the only one. The CAA had always to be satisfied that an applicant was a fit and proper person to hold an ATOL and of sufficient financial stability.

The grant of an ATOL does not guarantee that the holder is financially secure but the licence must be renewed each year, the theory being that this will alert the CAA to deteriorating financial positions.

Finally, Regulation 16(2), which sets out compulsory alternative methods of providing financial protection, does not apply to package holidays which are subject to ATOL arrangements ("licensable turnover").

8. Air Travel Trust

The Air Travel Reserve Fund Act 1975 established the Air Travel Reserve Fund ("the Fund"). The purpose of the Fund was to provide assistance to the holiday maker if ABTA/TOSG/CAA bonds provide insufficient security. The Fund was dissolved by Order in Council on 27 February 1986 and its assets were passed to the Air Travel Trust ("the Trust") on that date. The Trust had previously been established by the Secretary of State for Transport by means of a Trust deed. It has been given wider discretionary powers than those enjoyed by its predecessor, the Air Travel Reserve Fund Agency. Like its predecessor, the trust fund extends the protection afforded to those who purchase *package holidays* involving *chartered* air seats offered by ATOL holders. It does *not* protect:

(a) customers who lose money when an airline fails where they have bought tickets from the airline or an agent of the airline; and

(b) customers who purchase holidays from someone who is not an ATOL holder; and

(c) customers who purchase from an ATOL holder a holiday (eg a coach holiday not involving air travel) in respect of which an ATOL is not required.

In 1975 the CAA in exercise of its powers under section 2 of the 1975 Act made the Air Travel Reserve Fund Agency Benefit Rules which contained detailed provisions concerning the application of the former Fund. These included provisions for determining the amount of a customer's loss and the conditions to be satisfied before payments are made out of the Fund. They were considered to be too restrictive and have been replaced by a Statement of Policies on the Administration of Tour Operator's Bonds issued by the Air Travel Trust, the CAA, ABTA and the TOSG.

9. Association of Independent Tour Operators (AITO)

AITO was set up in 1973 as a form of club representing the interests of smaller independent tour operators. Since then, its membership has grown – at present there are 126 members. It has become regarded as an influential and important trade body.

As a result of its growth, AITO decided in May 1991 to become incorporated as a company limited by guarantee. It also took two further, and more significant, steps.

The first was that it made it compulsory for all its members to have a bond. Many of them are not ABTA members, nor is their turnover licensable turnover. To assist them in making bonding arrangements, AITO set up its own bonding scheme in October 1990 through the medium of AITO Trust Ltd, in whose favour bonds are made. In addition, back-up insurance is arranged to cover any deficiency in the amount of a bond. AITO Trust Ltd follows similar practices to the CAA, ABTA and TOSG in administering and applying bond monies.

The second step taken by AITO was the introduction in September 1992 of a Quality Charter, which is akin to a code of conduct. It is a requirement for all AITO members who produce brochures after 1 October 1992 to include in those brochures a set statement referring to the Quality Charter and essentially incorporating it as a term of trading.

In conjunction with the Quality Charter came the inception of AITO's conciliation and arbitration scheme, which applies to package holidays booked with an AITO member after 1 October 1992. Further comment about this scheme is contained in Chapter 8.

10. Passenger Shipping Association (PSA)

The PSA was formed in 1958 (when it was known as Ocean Travel Development) as an association of passenger ship owners. At the time of its formation and throughout the 1960s and early 1970s, PSA concentrated almost exclusively on the promotion of holidays at sea. In the mid-1970s PSA started to become involved in liaison with Government authorities over matters affecting the business operations of its members.

In 1986, PSA adopted consumer protection methods similar to those practised by ABTA. In other words, PSA introduced bonding requirements and codes of conduct which applied to all its members including those selling package holidays. In addition PSA established an independent conciliation and arbitration procedure.

11. Bus and Coach Council (BCC)

BCC is a trade association which represents UK coach and bus operators. Before the Regulations, it operated a bonding scheme.

Chapter 2

Tour operators' pre-contract and pre-departure responsibilities

When a holiday maker books a package holiday in the United Kingdom, his contract is almost invariably with the tour operator who arranges the various component parts of the package, such as travel by air, sea or land, accommodation, guides etc. The travel agent who takes the holiday maker's booking does so in his capacity as booking agent for the tour operator and is not himself a party to the contract for the sale and purchase of the holiday. This chapter considers those obligations of tour operators (other than those involving financial security) which affect their conduct before a booking is taken and thereafter before the departure date. Chapter 3 considers the liabilities of tour operators for post-departure defaults including those of other persons whose services feature directly or indirectly in the holiday package. Chapter 4 explains the new financial security obligations imposed on tour operators.

The Regulations are the primary determinant of the contents of package holiday contracts and the brochures and other sources of information used by tour operators. The CAA's ATOL conditions and Part III of the Consumer Protection Act 1987 are also important, and there are still residual roles for the Misrepresentation Act 1967, the Trade Descriptions Act 1968, the Unfair Contract Terms Act 1977 and the ABTA and AITO Codes of Conduct. But all these pale into relative insignificance compared with the stringent and comprehensive requirements of the Regulations which apply to packages sold or offered for sale in the UK.

1. No misleading information (Regulation 4)

Regulation 4(1) stipulates that no organiser (the term used in the Regulations instead of tour operator) "shall supply to a consumer (ie holiday maker) any descriptive matter concerning a package, the price of a package or any other conditions applying to the (holiday) contract which contains any misleading information". The use of the words "supply" and "descriptive matter" suggests that Regulation 4(1) applies to written material, tapes, videos and other tangible vehicles for the transmission of information – but not to oral statements.

Tour operators already commit criminal offences under the Trade Descriptions Act 1968 and the Consumer Protection Act 1987 if they supply misleading information knowingly or recklessly. Regulation 4 renders them liable to a civil liability in respect of information which is misleading but not supplied knowingly or recklessly. In other words, there is no defence. The sole issue is whether or not the information is misleading. Potentially, this exposes tour operators to a considerable risk of claims for even minor inaccuracies.

If a tour operator breaches Regulation 4(1), it is liable to compensate the holiday maker for any loss which he suffers in consequence. This can include compensation for disappointment as well as direct financial loss. However, except in respect of disappointment, there is no need for a holiday maker to demonstrate reliance upon the information. He only has to show that, as a result of the misleading information, he suffered loss.

2. Brochure content (Regulations 5–6)

Regulation 2(1) defines a brochure as "any brochure in which packages are offered for sale". The DTI Guidance Notes amplify this by saying that "brochure" does not encompass advertising material which does not give, and is not intended to give, a comprehensive description of the components of the package. But the corollary of the DTI's statement, and it is a conclusion which the writers understand to have been reached by some Trading

Standards Officers, is that advertising material which does give a comprehensive description of a package is a brochure.

It is common practice for tour operators and travel agents to produce "leaflets" of under four pages which describe package holidays available at specially discounted prices. If such leaflets are to be regarded as "brochures", tour operators and travel agents will be in an impossible situation: it would not be practicable or economic for leaflets to include all the information required by Regulation 5 – see below. Equally, to have to include the stipulated information in newspaper advertisements would be a nonsense.

In the writers' view, a common-sense approach should be adopted in deciding what is or is not a brochure. A newspaper advertisement, display in a travel agent's window or a 1–2 page leaflet should not be regarded as a brochure. However, to avoid the risk of dispute, tour operators and travel agents should include statements in all advertising material which is not meant to be a brochure that the "advertisement" is not a brochure and does not give a full description of the holiday and that the customer should refer to the relevant brochure or tour operator/travel agent for full details.

Regulation 5(1) provides that no organiser shall make available a brochure to a possible consumer unless it indicates in a legible, comprehensive and accurate manner the price and adequate information about the matters specified in Schedule 1 to the Regulations (see below) in respect of the packages offered for sale in the brochure to the extent that those matters are relevant to the packages so offered. There is no requirement for package holidays to be sold through the medium of a brochure. But, where a brochure is used, it must contain the information specified in Schedule 1.

"A possible consumer" is an all-embracing term, which will cover anyone who makes an enquiry about a package holiday or is even simply browsing through brochures. It does not limit the category of recipient to someone who is definitely booking a holiday. Equally, "make available" goes considerably further than "supply". This will apply if a tour operator has arranged for brochures to be in a position where any possible consumer could collect one. Of course, Regulation 5 will also apply where a tour operator actually supplies a brochure.

Regulation 5(3) provides that an organiser who breaches Regulation 5(1) shall be guilty of a criminal offence and liable:

(a) on summary conviction to a fine not exceeding level 5 on the standard scale (currently £5,000); and

(b) on conviction on indictment, to an unlimited fine.

Regulation 5(4) provides that where a brochure was first made available to consumers generally before 31 December 1992 no liability shall arise under Regulation 5 in respect of an identical brochure made available to a consumer at any time. There is no requirement, therefore, for existing brochure supplies to be destroyed. But second editions require alteration, if the first edition did not comply with Regulation 5.

Liability under Regulation 5(1) is not absolute. Defences are available, and these are contained in Regulation 24. Essentially, a tour operator will have a defence if he can show that all due diligence had been exercised or that he had relied, reasonably, on information supplied by another. The defences are considered in detail in Chapter 6, as is the effect of Regulation 25 that an officer of a company may be prosecuted in addition to, or instead of, the company.

The above comments about Regulation 24 and 25 apply also to the potential offences for infringement of Regulations 7 and 8, which are mentioned below.

The basic obligation imposed by Regulation 5(1) is to ensure that any brochure made available by a tour operator covers clearly the holiday price and the other matters specified in Schedule 1 to the Regulations. These other matters are:

1. The destination and the means, characteristics and categories of transport used.

2. The type of accommodation, its location, category or degree of comfort and its main features and, where the accommodation is to be provided in a member state of the European Community, its approval or tourist classification under the laws of that member state.
3. The meals which are included in the package.
4. The itinerary.
5. General information about passport and visa requirements which apply for British citizens and health formalities required for the journey and the stay.
6. Either the monetary amount or the percentage of the price which is to be paid on account and the timetable for payment of the balance.
7. Whether a minimum number of persons is required for the package to take place and, if so, the deadline for informing the consumer in the event of cancellation.
8. The arrangements (if any) which apply if consumers are delayed at the outward or homeward points of departure.
9. The arrangements for security for money paid over and for the repatriation of the consumer in the event of insolvency.

Tour operators face a number of difficulties in deciding the extent of information required by Schedule 1. Listed below are just some of the problem areas.

(a) What is meant by "the means, characteristics and categories of transport"? Taking the example of a package which features air transport to the country in which the holiday is to be taken and a coach transfer from the airport to the hotel, the means of transport is both air and road. The category of transport, so far as air transport is concerned, would be economy, business or first class. But how is the category of coach transfer to be described? Additionally, what are the characteristics of either the air or road transport? The DTI Guidance Notes do not touch on this, although, in relation to Schedule 2, where the same words appear in a different context, they state that it would not be necessary to specify the type of aircraft in a package involving air travel.

(b) Where accommodation is provided in a member state of the EC, its approval or tourist classification under any mandatory laws of that member state must be provided. Member states, though, adopt different classifications and star ratings. In the Benelux countries – Luxembourg, Netherlands and Belgium – there is a star rating from 1–5, as there is within Spain, but there is no comparison between the two rating systems. On the other hand, France has ratings from 1–4, together with De Luxe, and Denmark has none at all. Tour operators will have to state the category but must also ensure that the overall description of the accommodation and its main features will make clear the standard rather than relying solely upon national classification systems.

(c) The brochure must describe the location of the accommodation. Does location mean the exact address? In the writers' view, it does not: the requirement will be satisfied by stating the resort in which the accommodation is to be found.

(d) Care will be needed in descriptions of itineraries. They will need to be specific. For example, in the case of coach tours, the itinerary will have to detail where the coach will visit on any particular day.

(e) General information must be given about passport and visa requirements, but only those which relate to British citizens. It would be inadequate simply to state that passports and visas may be required and that customers, when making a booking, should make enquiries with the relevant embassy. For each destination featured in the brochure, the information given should enable the customer to decide whether or not a passport and/or visa is required and, if so, the likely length of time to obtain the passport and/or visa.

(f) A tour operator is not obliged to provide assistance if there is delay at the outward or homeward points of departure. However, if no assistance is to be given, that must be stated in the brochure.

(g) Paragraph 9 is a reference to compliance with the financial protection requirements set out in Regulations 16–21. These are considered in Chapter 4.

Regulation 6(1) stipulates that subject to certain exceptions, the particulars in the brochure (whether or not they are required by Regulation 5(1) to be included in it) shall constitute implied warranties for the purposes of any contract to which they relate. This establishes all of them as binding terms in the contract, breaches of which will entitle the holiday maker to claim compensation. However, a holiday maker will be entitled to damages only if he can prove that he has suffered loss or injury as a result of the breach.

The exceptions are where:

(a) the brochure contains an express statement that changes may be made in the particulars contained in it before a contract is concluded, and changes in the particulars so contained are clearly communicated to the consumer before a contract is concluded. It is, accordingly, most important for tour operators to ensure that their brochures contain a booking condition to reflect this exception;

(b) the consumer and the organiser agree after the contract has been made that the particulars in the brochure, or some of the particulars, should not form part of the contract.

The particulars in a brochure which are converted into implied warranties by Regulation 6(1) are all those statements which relate to the holiday concerned other than the details relating to financial security and repatriation arrangements which are required to be included by paragraph 9 of Schedule 1 to the Regulations. Among other things, they include information about the hotel and its facilities and the resort. It is not clear whether pictures will be regarded as giving particulars. In the writers' view they will.

3. Contract terms requirements (Regulation 9)

As discussed earlier, Regulation 5 stipulates that brochures must indicate the holiday price and also the matters specified in Schedule 1 to the Regulations. Regulation 9(1) supplements this with provisions regarding the contents and form of the holiday contract. In the case of package holidays where booking is made by a holiday maker directly with a tour operator or through a travel agent which does not have a computerised booking system (Viewdata), the contract will normally comprise the booking form completed by the holiday maker, the booking conditions in the brochure, other relevant statements in the brochure and the tour operator's confirmation of booking. Where a booking is made via a travel agent which has Viewdata, there will be two forms of confirmation. The first is the initial confirmation printed by the Viewdata system, and the second is the subsequent confirmation invoice issued by the tour operator.

Subparagraph (a) of Regulation 9(1) requires the tour operator to ensure that, depending on the nature of the package, the contract contains at least the elements specified in Schedule 2 to the Regulations, namely:

1. The travel destination(s) and, where periods of stay are involved, the relevant periods, with dates.
2. The means, characteristics and categories of transport to be used and the dates, times and points of departure and return.
3. Where the package includes accommodation, its

location, its tourist category or degree of comfort, its main features and, where the accommodation is to be provided in a member state of the European Community, its compliance with the rules of that state.

4. The meals which are included in the package.
5. Whether a minimum number of persons is required for the package to take place and, if so, the deadline for informing the consumer in the event of cancellation.
6. The itinerary.
7. Visits, excursions or other services which are included in the total price agreed for the package.
8. The name and address of the organiser, the retailer and, where appropriate, the insurer.
9. The price of the package, if the price may be revised in accordance with the term which may be included in the contract under Regulation 11, an indication of the possibility of such price revisions, and an indication of any dues, taxes or fees chargeable for certain services (such as landing, embarkation or disembarkation fees at ports and airports and tourist taxes) whose costs are not included in the package.
10. The payment schedule and method of payment.
11. Special requirements which the consumer has communicated to the organiser or retailer when making the booking and which both have accepted.
12. The periods within which the consumer must make any complaint about the failure to perform or the inadequate performance of the contract.

Items 1–6 above wholly or partly duplicate the brochure content requirements of Schedule 1 to the Regulations, but items 7–12 are additional. Most of them are clear and comply with existing practice. The reference in item 3 to "compliance with the rules of that state" is somewhat cryptic. In the writers' opinion, a general statement that the accommodation complies with all relevant local rules (ie laws, regulations, etc) will suffice. This does, of course, impose potential liabilities upon the tour operator if the accommodation does not comply with the relevant laws. At the very least, tour operators should seek confirmation from the providers of accommodation that there has been such compliance.

As with Schedule 1, Schedule 2 poses a number of difficulties for tour operators. Item 2 refers to the "dates, times and points of departure and return". If anything other than approximate times are given, a tour operator could expose itself to potential liabilities. Further, on packages such as coach tours, it is well nigh impossible to give specific times of arrival and departure at each stopping point.

Item 4 refers to meals. But is it necessary to detail the meals which will be provided on board aircraft? The DTI Guidance Notes make no comment. However, as regards location of accommodation, they do state that there are cases where it is reasonable not to name the hotel. This would apply to "Square Deals", which are specially discounted arrangements detailing only the resort and type of accommodation – the holiday maker is allocated accommodation on arrival.

The reference in item 8 to supplying, where appropriate, the name and address of the insurer caters for cases where insurance against cancellation or the cost of assistance (including repatriation in the event of accident or illness) is effected under a scheme arranged by the tour operator.

Item 11 spells out something which is already established good practice. It covers matters such as the need of a disabled holiday maker for a ground floor room and arrangements regarding rooms with a view, extra beds for children, special food requirements etc.

Regulation 9(1) requires the tour operator to ensure that all the terms of the contract are communicated to the holiday maker before the contract is made. However, Regulation 9(2) provides that this does not apply when the time between the holiday maker making contact with the tour operator and the intended departure is so short that it is impracticable to do so. Three questions arise from these provisions. They are the time at which a contract is made between a tour operator and a holiday maker, the method of communication of the contract terms, and the relationship of Regulation 9 with general contract law.

In general terms, when a contract is made between a tour operator and a holiday maker will depend upon how the booking is made. Where it is made via a travel agent using Viewdata, confirmation of the booking is given by the Viewdata system. Application of general principles of contract law determines that the contract is made upon the issue of the Viewdata confirmation. Therefore, in this type of booking, the information required to be given under Regulation 9 must be given before or contemporaneously with the issue of the Viewdata confirmation. That means that the tour operator is dependent upon the travel agent giving the holiday maker all the requisite information at the time of booking.

There should not be any real difficulty in travel agents communicating the information where the relevant information is contained in the tour operator's brochure. To the extent that information is contained elsewhere – itinerary and some special arrangements may have to be set out and communicated in a rather different manner – tour operators will have to ensure that travel agents have the relevant information and are aware of the booking procedure which the tour operator expects from them.

Where a booking is made direct with a tour operator on the telephone, with payment being made over the telephone by credit card and oral confirmation of the booking being given simultaneously by the operator, the contract will be made in the course of the telephone conversation. The requisite information will have to be given not later than this time. This should not present difficulties where the holiday maker has a brochure which contains the requisite information, since the tour operator's booking clerk will be able to refer to the brochure.

If a holiday maker does not have a brochure, the tour

operator has two options. One is to give the information in full in the telephone conversation but that is commercially impracticable, and something which most holiday makers would detest. The other is to create a hiatus period, or option, at the end of which the contract is made. During this period the relevant information can be posted, and the holiday maker will be able to cancel the booking without penalty.

It is commonplace for tour operators' booking conditions to provide that the contract is only made when the confirmation invoice is issued. Such a provision should operate to overcome general principles of contract law in relation to a telephone booking, and the delay before the issue of confirmation invoice would create a time within which the operator could despatch the requisite information.

The DTI recognises the difficulties which may arise through telephone bookings, and its Guidance Notes give the following advice –

> "Frequently the consumer will when he makes a telephone booking be in possession of a brochure in which most and possibly all the terms of the contract are set out. Where this is the case the organiser or retailer may need to do no more than draw attention to this fact. Where this is not the case, the Department considers that the organiser or retailer will discharge his responsibilities under the Regulation if he ensures that the customer has been given, so far as is relevant, the information set out in Schedule 2 to the Regulations together with any special terms and conditions the organiser or retailer may impose (note that the information in Regulation 8 must still be provided but provision of this information is not linked to conclusion of the contract)".

The DTI advice is good so far as it goes. However, it does not recognise the impracticability of a tour operator's booking clerk, in the course of a telephone booking, orally reciting all the contract terms referred to in the Regulation.

Despite the provisions of Regulation 9, the impact of general contract law must be borne in mind. Contract law provides that the latest that booking conditions can be incorporated into a contract is at the time of making the contract. Failure to incorporate the conditions into the contract will result in their being inapplicable. For example, should anything go wrong during a holiday, the tour operator will not be entitled to rely on any post-contract attempt to limit or exclude liability.

In the writers' view, Regulation 9 adds nothing to the existing contract law requirement that contract terms must be incorporated in the contract before the contract is made. Further, Regulation 9(2) which appears to remove the need to communicate contract terms will not, in the writers' view, overrule the provisions of general contract law.

Many operators will already have in place systems for incorporating their booking conditions into the holiday contract before it is made. Maintenance of those systems should be sufficient to comply with Regulation 9. However, tour operators should bear in mind that the information required by Regulation 7 (see below) must also be given before the holiday contract is made.

Regulation 9(1) provides that the information to which Regulation 9 refers may be communicated "in writing or such other form as is comprehensible and accessible". If it is given in non-written form tour operators must subsequently give it in writing, provided that the period between the date of booking and the departure date is not so short as to render this impracticable. In the writers' view this will hardly ever be the case. If it is possible for tickets etc to be made available, it should be practicable for the information required by Regulation 9 to be made available in writing at the same time – if not before.

4. Pre-contract information (Regulation 7)

The preceding sections have considered the requirements of the Regulations regarding the contents of brochures and holiday contracts and the communication of holiday contract terms to holiday makers. Regulations 7 and 8 impose additional information provision obligations on tour operators. Regulation 7 requires the tour operator, before a holiday contract is made, to provide the following information in writing, or some other appropriate form:

(a) general information about passport and visa requirements which apply to British citizens who purchase the package in question, including information about the length of time it is likely to take to obtain the appropriate passports and visas;

(b) information about health formalities required for the journey and the stay; and

(c) the arrangements for security for the money paid to the organiser by the consumer and (where applicable) for the repatriation of the consumer in the event of insolvency.

The information specified in Regulation 7 must be communicated "before the contract is made". Where a tour operator uses a brochure to sell its holidays the information should appear in the brochure (Regulation 7 mirrors the requirements of paragraphs 5 and 9 of Schedule 1 to the Regulations). Accordingly, however a booking is made, Regulation 7 will not pose particular problems for a tour operator if all the requisite information is in a brochure and the holiday maker, or travel agent, has that brochure. Difficulties may arise where a holiday maker or travel agent does not have the operator's brochure. In that case, the DTI recognises that communication could be in 'some other appropriate form' including oral communication (eg by telephone) or projection on a visual display unit. Where there is a direct telephone booking, the tour operator has the choice of going through the detail in the course of making the booking or of creating a hiatus or option period before the contract is made (see the discussion of Regulation 9 on page 27).

The information specified in Regulation 7 must be given to an "intending consumer". This is slightly narrower than the term "possible consumer" used in Regulation 5.

In the authors' view, "intending consumer" means someone in the process of making a booking for a package holiday. If the term were to be extended to those who were simply making enquiries, the obligation under Regulation 7 would be particularly onerous.

A tour operator who breaches Regulation 7 is guilty of a criminal offence and liable:

(a) on summary conviction to a fine not exceeding £5,000;
(b) on conviction on indictment to an unlimited fine.

5. Pre-departure information (Regulation 8)

Regulation 8 supplements the pre-contract information and contract contents requirements of Regulations 5, 7 and 9 by stipulating that the tour operator shall supply the following information to the consumer in writing or some other appropriate form in good time before the holiday is due to start (whether before or after the contract is made):

(a) the times and places of intermediate stops and transport connections and particulars of the place to be occupied by the consumer (for example, cabin or berth on ship, sleeper compartment on train);
(b) the name, address and telephone number:–
   (i) of the tour operator's representative in the locality where the consumer is to stay,

   or, if there is no such representative,

   (ii) of an agency in that locality on whose assistance a consumer in difficulty would be able to call,

   or, if there is no such representative or agency, a telephone number or information which will enable the consumer to contact the tour operator during the stay;
(c) in the case of a journey or stay abroad by a child under the age of 16 on the day when the journey

or stay is due to start information enabling direct contact to be made with the child or the person responsible (for him/her) at the place where he is to stay; and

(d) except where the consumer is contractually required to insure against the cost of cancellation by him or the cost of assistance, including repatriation, in the event of accident or illness, information about an insurance policy which the consumer may, if he wishes, take out in respect of the risk of those costs being incurred.

Here again failure is a criminal offence rendering the tour operator liable to a fine up to a maximum of £5,000.

For a package holiday booked weeks or months before departure the DTI considers that the provision of information under Regulation 8 must take place at least a week before departure in order to be "in good time". But in the case of package holidays booked very close to the time of departure it could be when the consumer checks in at the airport.

The DTI considers that intermediate stops are those that significantly affect the nature of the package. Meal or refreshment breaks, etc , would not in its view need to be included unless they significantly affect the nature of the package. A common-sense approach dictates that stops by an aircraft do not need to be described. It is, however, probably good practice for tour operators in their brochures to make it clear that "direct flights" may well stop *en route*.

The reference to "transport connections" raises again the extent to which transfer details must be described. There are, potentially, so many variable factors that by giving times a tour operator could become a hostage to fortune.

Regulation 8(2)(c) is intended to apply to children on, for example, school or similar trips. It is not intended to apply to children who go on holiday with an adult who is not acting on a professional basis, voluntary or otherwise.

6. Transfer of bookings (Regulation 10)

Regulation 10(1) creates a new right for consumers to transfer their bookings. It does so by implying into the holiday contract a term that where the consumer is prevented from proceeding with the package he may transfer his booking to a person who satisfies all the conditions applicable to the package, provided that the consumer gives reasonable notice to the tour operator of his intention to transfer before the date when departure is due to take place.

The right to transfer a booking applies only where the consumer is prevented from taking his holiday. This will obviously cover sickness or accidents suffered by him and his close family, and mandatory matters such as jury service. It will probably also be interpreted as covering some work-related reasons which make it desirable for him not to go, as well as the insistence of an employer. A mere change of mind will not suffice.

The transferee must be someone who meets any requirements stipulated for people taking the relevant holiday. Somebody to whom an adventure holiday booking is transferred must satisfy the requisite health conditions. Somebody to whom a young persons' holiday booking is transferred must be reasonably young, etc.

If it is a condition of a holiday contract that if the consumer cannot go, the holiday should be offered first to people on a waiting list, the right to transfer the booking will not apply if there is a waiting list.

When a transfer takes place under Regulation 10(1), both the transferor and the transferee are jointly and severally liable to the tour operator for the holiday price, or the unpaid balance, and also for any additional costs incurred by the tour operator as a result of the transfer. It is not clear whether the latter is limited to the operator's administrative costs of arranging the transfer or whether it also includes cancellation charges imposed by suppliers. Particularly where air transport is on a scheduled airline APEX type of fare, the airline may well impose 100 per cent cancellation charges and demand the price of a replacement ticket. The DTI Guidance Notes are silent on this point. In the writers' view, additional costs such as these could be charged by the tour operator, provided that the operator's booking conditions make it clear that they may arise.

For the holiday maker to be able to transfer, reasonable notice must be given. The operator may have to contact a considerable number of suppliers to obtain new tickets, change names in rooming lists at hotels etc. Accordingly, it would be reasonable for an operator to stipulate that no request for transfer can be made within 21 days of the departure date. Again, this must be made clear in booking conditions.

In practice, this right may prove to be rarely exercised by holiday makers. Particularly where illness is involved, the holiday maker is unlikely to devote efforts to transferring his ticket. On the assumption that he has insurance, he is much more likely to rely on that. This will, of course, enable tour operators to levy cancellation charges. There is nothing in the Regulations which prevents tour operators imposing cancellation charges where a consumer cancels without putting forward a transferee. Any such charges will need to be clearly provided for in the holiday contract.

7. Surcharges (Regulation 11)

In contract law there is no objection to a supplier or arranger of future services reserving the right to increase the price of the services to reflect supervening increases in costs. Historically this is something which tour operators have usually done, though from time to time there have been spells when no surcharge guarantees were fashionable.

The need for some regulation of surcharging arrangements to protect the consumer was recognised many years ago. More recently, ABTA has regulated surcharges in its tour operator's Code of Conduct, setting out specific 'Standards on Surcharges'. Their principal requirements are reproduced in Appendix C. They still apply to ABTA members in so far as they add to the requirements of Regulations 11 and 12.

Regulation 11 renders surcharge terms void unless the contract provides for the possibility of upward or downward price revisions and satisfies the following conditions contained in Regulation 11(2):

- (a) the contract states precisely how the revised price is to be calculated;
- (b) the contract provides that surcharges may be made only to allow for variations in:–
  - (i) transportation costs, including the cost of fuel;
  - (ii) dues, taxes or fees chargeable for services such as landing taxes or embarkation or disembarkation fees at ports and airports; or
  - (iii) the exchange rates applied to the package.

Regulation 11(3) goes on to state that irrespective of what is said in the holiday contract –

- (i) no surcharge may be made in a specified period which may not be less than 30 days before the stipulated departure date; and
- (ii) no surcharge may be made in respect of variations which would produce an increase of less than 2 per cent of the price, or such greater percentage as the contract may specify ("non-eligible variations"), and that non-eligible variations shall be left out of account in the calculation.

It appears from the opening passage of Regulation 11(1) that a tour operator can, provided he satisfies the specified conditions, provide for an upward revision without also providing for a downward one where costs reduce rather than increase.

A holiday maker is under no obligation to accept a surcharge caused by alterations which the tour operator makes to a holiday.

No definition is given of "price", and the DTI Guidance Notes do not dwell on this. If an administration fee is agreed for an agreed improvement or addition to the holiday, is it taken into account or is any surcharge based only on holiday cost? The ABTA surcharges policy statement says that surcharges should be restricted to the initial holiday price and the writers consider that a similar view should be taken as regards the Regulations.

In the opinion of the DTI, the reference in Regulation 11(2)(b)(ii) to "dues, taxes or fees" is likely to extend to increases caused by a change in general tax rates (such as VAT) and not just those specific to travel or tourism.

There is no implied right of a tour operator to impose a surcharge. Surcharge terms must be spelt out in the holiday contract. A term which does not satisfy the conditions of Regulation 11(2) "has no effect".

8. Cancellation or alteration by the organiser (Regulations 12 and 13)

Holidays are often booked many months before their departure date. There is always the possibility of some supervening event, such as the closing of a hotel, which necessitates an alteration to, or possibly even the cancellation of, a holiday. There is also the possibility of a change after the holiday has commenced. These possibilities are catered for by terms implied into holiday contracts by Regulations 12, 13 and 14.

Subparagraph (a) of Regulation 12 implies into the contract a term that where the organiser is constrained before departure to alter significantly an essential term of the contract, such as the price, he will notify the consumer as quickly as possible. Subparagraph (b) of Regulation 12 supplements this by an implied term requiring the consumer to respond. He must do so by notifying the organiser or the retailer as soon as possible of his decision which may be to withdraw from the contract without penalty or to accept a variation of it which specifies the alterations made and their impact on the price.

Regulation 11 does not impose a limit on the amount of a surcharge. But if an increase is a significant one, Regulation 12 will enable the consumer to withdraw from the contract without penalty, and the provisions of

Regulation 13 would then apply. No attempt is made to define "significant" but in the opinion of the writers a surcharge of more than 10 per cent would be regarded as significant. Trading Standards Officers, however, have indicated that, in their view, a surcharge of more than 5 per cent could be "significant". This is, to say the least, draconian, particularly as that 5 per cent will include the initial 2 per cent to be absorbed by tour operators.

Where a consumer withdraws from a holiday contract under the implied right conferred by Regulation 12, or where the organiser for any reason other than the fault of the consumer cancels the holiday before the agreed departure date, Regulation 13 gives the consumer the following implied contractual rights:

(a) to take a substitute package of equivalent or superior quality if the organiser is able to offer him such a substitute; or

(b) to take a substitute package of lower quality if the organiser is able to offer him one and to recover from the organiser the difference in price between that of the package purchased and the substitute package; or

(c) to have repaid to him as soon as possible all the monies paid by him under the contract.

In addition to his rights under (a), (b) and (c) above the consumer will be entitled (if appropriate) to compensation for the organiser's breach of contract except where:

(a) the holiday is cancelled because the number of persons who agree to take it is less than the minimum number required and the consumer is informed of the cancellation, in writing, within the period indicated in the description of the package; or

(b) the holiday is cancelled by reason of unusual and unforeseeable circumstances beyond the control of the organiser, the consequences of which could not have been avoided even if all due care had been exercised.

It is expressly stated that overbooking shall not rank as an unusual and unforeseeable circumstance for the purposes of subparagraph (b) above. Compensation is to be paid "where appropriate". Provision of an alternative or repayment of all monies will not in themselves avoid the need for compensation. Factors to be taken into account will include the similarity of the alternative to the original and the length of time between intended departure and cancellation.

The implied obligations imposed on organisers by Regulations 12 and 13 are not as helpful to consumers as are some of the relevant provisions in ABTA's Code of Conduct for tour operators. In particular, ABTA tour operators – except for *force majeure* reasons – are not allowed:

(a) to alter materially a package holiday unless holiday makers and agents can be notified not less than 14 days before the departure date;

(b) to cancel a package holiday after payment of the deposit and balance of the holiday cost – normally 8 weeks before departure unless it is a booking within that period.

9. Post-departure changes (Regulation 14)

Although Regulation 14 deals with post-departure changes, it is more convenient to deal with it here. Regulation 14 implies terms into the holiday contract which apply where, after departure, a significant proportion of the services contracted for are not provided, or the organiser becomes aware that he will be unable to procure a significant proportion of them. The first is that the organiser will make suitable alternative arrangements, at no extra cost to the consumer, for the continuation of the package and will, where appropriate, compensate the consumer for the difference between the services to be supplied under the contract and those actually supplied.

The second applies where it is impossible to make suitable alternative arrangements, or they are rejected by the consumer for good reasons. In such cases the organiser must, where appropriate, provide the consumer with equivalent transport back to the place of departure or to another place to which the consumer has agreed. In addition, the organiser must, where appropriate, compensate the consumer. The two references to "where appropriate" are interesting and will no doubt give rise to disputes. It might well be appropriate for no compensation to be paid where the problem is caused by a genuine *force majeure* event such as an earthquake. This would be justified because Regulation 13 specifically provides that no compensation is to be paid where cancellation is because of "unusual and unforeseeable circumstances". An earthquake normally comes within this category.

In the opinion of the DTI (with which the writers agree) compensation for the consumer under Regulation 14(2) may take account of disappointment and inconvenience as well as monetary loss.

The provision of equivalent transport must of necessity depend on availability. If for example an organiser has transported a customer on a charter aircraft, "equivalent transport" could reasonably be interpreted as the organiser's next contracted departure.

10. Common and statutory law and ABTA's Code of Conduct

In addition to the Regulations, brochures issued by tour operators must have regard to the relevant provisions of the Misrepresentation Act 1967, the Trade Descriptions Act 1968, the Civil Aviation Act 1982, the Unfair Contract Terms Act 1977 and Part III of the Consumer Protection Act 1987. Also, the brochures of ABTA members must satisfy the requirements of Rule 2 of the Tour Operators' Code of Conduct, ABTA's Standards on Brochures and ABTA's Standards on Surcharges (see Appendices A and C).

In broad terms the main ways in which ABTA's requirements add to what is contained in the Regulations are (aside from the additions mentioned on page 39 in relation to alterations):

(a) No ABTA tour operator is allowed to impose surcharges unless the amount has been approved by ABTA. Set procedures are established under which the tour operator has to explain to ABTA exactly why a surcharge is required and how it is calculated.

(b) Brochures must contain a clause offering clients the option of ABTA's arbitration scheme in the event of complaints (see Chapter 8).

(c) Brochures must contain descriptions, in relation to package holidays featuring resorts, specifying any source of noise which might "reasonably be expected to cause offence to clients". This includes nightclubs, bars, discos, amusement parks and airports.

Chapter 3

Tour operators' post-departure responsibilities

A feature of the package holiday is that in most cases the tour operator does not himself provide the flights, accommodation, meals etc. which go to make up the holidays advertised in his brochure. But it is he who makes the arrangements which enable the holiday to be sold as a package, and it is he who enters into contracts with the airlines, hotels etc involved in the package. Usually the holiday maker has no contractual link with hotels and so is not in a position to make breach of contract claims against them. He may be able, in appropriate circumstances, to make non-contractual negligence claims against them but that depends on the law of the country concerned, quite apart from which an English holiday maker faces obvious difficulties in conducting court proceedings in a foreign country.

The fact that, in most cases, the tour operator does not himself provide the flights, accommodation, meals etc which feature in the package that he sells to his customers has been a source of interesting questions about the tour operator's contractual responsibilities to his customers. Was he responsible in damages for every accident suffered by holiday makers through the negligence of airlines which he employed, or for every bowl of boiling soup which hotel waiters accidentally dropped on the laps of his customers? Or was he only liable if he made what the French describe as a *mauvais choix*, namely a failure to choose good airlines, hotels etc.?

A. The law before the Regulations

No specific statute dealt with the nature of the contract between a holiday maker and tour operator, and the tour operator's consequent obligations when something went wrong with the package. It was a matter of applying the relevant general law, including precedents.

The seminal case was *Wall* v *Silver Wing Surface Arrangements Ltd (trading as Enterprise Holidays)* (1981 – unreported). In it, the plaintiff suffered serious personal injury due to a fire exit at the Marina Aparthol, Puerto de la Cruz being locked (to prevent burglars getting in). Two points, in particular, should be noted:

(a) In their booking conditions, Enterprise made no reference to liability for injury. They did not try to avoid responsibility for any fault of their own, nor did they say that they were not responsible for the acts or omissions of the airlines, hotels etc featured in the brochure.

(b) The fire escape was defective because the exit gate had been locked arbitrarily by the hotel management for security reasons. Had the gate not been locked, which it was not when Enterprise's representative inspected the hotel, the fire escape would have proved satisfactory.

The plaintiff's claim was based in contract and/or tort, the former being on the grounds that there was an implied term or condition in the contract that the plaintiffs would be reasonably safe in using the hotel for the purpose for which they were invited to be there. Hodgson J, in deciding in favour of the defendants, specifically rejected this contention. He made the following comments, *inter alia*:

- "In the normal way it is perfectly well known that the tour operator neither owns, occupies or controls the hotels which are included in his brochure, any more than he has control over the airlines which fly his customers, the airports whence and whither they fly and the land transport which conveys them from airport to hotel".

- "If injury is caused by the default of the hotel owners and occupiers, the airline, the airport controllers or the taxi proprietor, the customer will have whatever remedy (against them) the relevant law allows".
- ". . . I would find it wholly unreasonable to saddle a tour operator with an obligation to ensure the safety of all the components of the package over none of which he had any control at all".

This case supported the view that the contract between the tour operator and holiday maker was one whereby the tour operator undertook to exercise skill and care in making suitable arrangements with airlines, hotels etc. and that it was not liable for their negligence so long as it exercised sufficient care in selecting and instructing them.

That view of tour operators' liability was reinforced by the Ontario Court of Appeal in the case of *Craven* v *Strand Holidays (Canada) Ltd* (1982) 40 OR (2d) 186. In this case, the plaintiffs claimed damages for injuries received when the bus in which they were travelling overturned. They had booked a holiday in Columbia through the defendant tour operator which in turn had booked the bus transport with an independent bus company. The judge who heard the case found for the plaintiffs but the Court of Appeal reversed his decision and held that the defendant was not liable since it had exercised due care in the selection of the bus company. In giving their judgment, the Ontario Court of Appeal stated, *inter alia*:

> "If a person agrees to perform some work or services he cannot escape contractual liability by delegating the performance to another. It is his contract. But if the contract is only to . . . arrange for the performance of services, then he has fulfilled his contract if he has exercised due care in the selection of a competent contractor. He is not responsible if that contractor is negligent in the performance of the actual work or service, for the performance is not part of his contract".

"A person is not liable for the negligence of an independent contractor unless he has a primary obligation to carry out a non-delegable duty imposed upon him by law or by contract. It is clear in the evidence that Strand never undertook to perform the bus transfers but merely to arrange for this to be done by a third party".

B. The Regulations

1. Regulation 15(1)

Regulation 15(1) provides that the tour operator is liable to the consumer "for the proper performance of the obligations under the contract, irrespective of whether such obligations are to be performed by (the tour operator) or by other suppliers of services but this shall not affect any remedy or right of action which (the tour operator) may have against those other suppliers of services".

The aim of the EC Directive was that the tour operator would be responsible for all the elements of the package and that primary liability for anything which went wrong would rest with him. In other words, the tour operator should face strict liability for any of the services, facilities or goods to be supplied as component parts of the package and would not be able to mount a defence on the basis that the services, facilities or goods were supplied by others over whom he had no control. Regulation 15(1) seeks to implement that intention.

Regulation 15(1) refers to "proper performance of the obligations under the contract". Liability will depend upon exactly what the obligations under the contract are. As is explained in Chapter 2, the Regulations deal with cancellation, alteration, price increases, information to be contained in brochures and the elements to be contained in the contract. But there is no precise definition or categorisation of "the obligations" which exist as regards performance of the package itself.

It is the writers' view that the liability contemplated by Regulation 15(1) is strict liability for anything which goes wrong with the package, subject to the limited defences set out in Regulation 15(2). Should any tour operator seek to express his obligations as being merely in respect of arranging and monitoring, it is the writers' view that the courts would not support him.

2. Regulation 15(2)

Under Regulation 15(2) the tour operator is liable to the consumer for any damage caused to him by any failure to perform the contract or improper performance of it unless the failure or improper performance is due neither to the fault of the tour operator nor that of another supplier of services, because:

(a) it is attributable to the consumer;

(b) it is attributable to a third party unconnected with the provision of the services contracted for, and is unforeseeable or unavoidable; or

(c) it is due to:–

(i) unusual and unforeseeable circumstances beyond the control of the tour operator, the consequences of which could not have been avoided even if all due care had been exercised, or

(ii) an event which neither the tour operator nor the supplier of services, even if all due care had been exercised, could foresee or forestall.

Regulation 15(2) clearly establishes the primary responsibility of the tour operator for the proper and safe supply of all the services which are comprised in a package holiday. It is important to stress that none of the stated defences will apply unless there has been "no fault" on the part of the tour operator or any of his suppliers. But where does the burden of proof lie?

Take, for example, a claim by a holiday maker that, while in India, on a package holiday, he has suffered food poisoning. For the holiday maker to have a claim, he will have to demonstrate that there has been a failure to perform the contract: in other words, the holiday maker will have to prove that the food poisoning has been caused by the tour operator or one of the suppliers. It is only when the holiday maker is able to do this that the burden of proof – to demonstrate that there was no fault on the part of the tour operator or any of the suppliers – will arise. The initial burden of proof thus rests with the holiday maker, and then switches to the tour operator.

Continuing with the example, assume that the holiday maker can demonstrate that, while at a certain hotel, all guests there, within 24 hours of each other, suffered food poisoning. That would, in all probability, be regarded as proof of failure to perform the contract properly, and the burden would shift to the tour operator to show that there was no fault on the part of the hotel. Given that, by the time investigations are started, none of the food supplied at the material time is likely to be available for analysis, it may well be impossible for the tour operator to prove "no fault".

The difficulty for a tour operator to show "no fault" must not be underestimated, but that does not mean that every claim by a holiday maker is bound to succeed. Claims based on unreasonably subjective, or idiosyncratic, assessment of the standards to be expected will not succeed: the courts will consider objectively what the brochure promised would be provided.

In the 1989 case of *Odlin* v *Manos Holidays* (unreported), the plaintiff while on a package holiday in Lindos, Greece, fell from the roof terrace of his accommodation and suffered serious personal injury. It was accepted in the trial that, in general terms, the issue before the court was whether the accommodation was reasonably safe. It was held that it was, and the defendants' defence succeeded. Regulation 15, if it had been in force, would not have removed the defendants' ability to defend the claim.

(a) Holiday maker's failure

Regulation 15(2)(a) specifies a defence where the reason for the failure is the holiday maker's own actions. Easy examples are a holiday maker's failure to arrive on time at an airport or to obtain a visa which he has been told is necessary. But if a holiday maker is only told of the need for a visa two weeks before departure and it takes four weeks to obtain the visa, there will be no defence because there is clear fault on the part of the tour operator.

In *Dodgeson* v *Airtours plc* (1992), the plaintiff booked a package holiday with the defendants, commencing on 11 August 1989. On 12 August 1989, at approximately 10.00 am the plaintiff dived into the hotel swimming pool: unfortunately it was shallow and Mr Dodgeson sustained a laceration to his forehead. He claimed that Airtours' representative should have warned him about the pool, particularly since there were no markings or measurements.

The plaintiff's claim failed. The judge, in finding in favour of Airtours, said, *inter alia* –

> "I am afraid that I believe that it was really an imprudent thing to do – to launch oneself into a pool without taking a careful check to see that it was safe to do so. Any swimmer must know that pools vary in depth and it seems it was very unwise indeed to dive into it without first checking. I am afraid therefore that I find this case against Mr Dodgeson".

On the facts of this case, it appears that a defence under Regulation 15(2)(a) would have been available had the claim come before the court after the Regulations came into force.

(b) Defaults caused by unconnected third parties

Regulation 15(2)(b) caters for failures caused by unconnected third parties and which are unforeseeable or unavoidable.

Examples of unconnected third parties are other holiday makers, members of the public and the police. Other examples are local authorities and governments when not themselves suppliers of relevant services. Public utilities which supply gas and electricity to a hotel are not "unconnected with the provision of the services contracted for". The fact that, if it be so, that they are nationalised industries in the country concerned is neither here nor there.

Air traffic controllers are clearly connected with the provision of relevant services. But that does not mean that a tour operator is necessarily responsible for delays to, or even the total loss of, a holiday caused by industrial action by air controllers. Regulation 15(2)(c) may apply – see below.

Clearly the airlines, other carriers and hotels whose services and facilities feature in a package holiday are not unconnected suppliers of services. Nor are suppliers of goods and services to them such as airport catering companies, the butcher from whom a hotel buys its meat etc. Failures by any of these primary or secondary suppliers render a tour operator liable to the consumers who buy its holidays unless the failures come within the ambit of Regulation 15(2)(c). The operator may have a right to an indemnity from the hotel or carrier or it may have limited its liability as permitted by subparagraphs (3) or (4) of Regulation 15. But these are separate matters and do not derogate from the tour operator's primary liability to the consumer.

The mere fact that a default in the provision of a service is caused by a third party unconnected with the provision of services which form part of the package does not absolve the tour operator of responsibility to the consumer. It is also necessary for the default to be either unforeseeable or unavoidable.

In the abstract, there are very few things which are totally unforeseeable. It is perfectly conceivable that a fellow holiday maker will go berserk and sabotage the lifts, or poison the water in the hotel swimming pool. Likewise there is always a possibility, however remote, in certain parts of the world, of terrorists planting a bomb in a hotel foyer. In the writers' opinion, though, the fact that something is conceivable does not render it automatically foreseeable for the purposes of Regulation 15(2). "Unforeseeable" should be regarded as a legal term of art, and not in a colloquial sense. To prove that an event was unforeseeable, it should be sufficient for a tour operator to demonstrate that the event was outside his reasonable expectation. There must also be some reason for thinking that the event might happen to the particular holiday concerned. Accordingly, a terrorist attack might well be regarded as foreseeable in Spain but not in Switzerland.

The wording of Regulation 15(2)(b) suggests that, even if a failure caused by an unconnected third party is foreseeable, the tour operator will not be liable to the consumer if it is unavoidable. There may not be many occasions when this will help the tour operator because almost any foreseeable failure can be avoided by cancelling the holiday. Examples of failures which, although they may be unforeseeable, would probably be regarded as unavoidable are those caused by government restrictions on the use of water or electricity.

Some foreseeable failures can be avoided but only at considerable expense to the tour operator. If all pilots in the UK went on strike, advance notice having been given, other aircraft and aircrew may be available from outside the UK. The cost of taking such a step would be prohibitive to many tour operators. But, strictly speaking, this would not allow them to rely on the defence that failure to fly the holiday maker to his destination was unavoidable.

(c) *Defaults caused by force majeure*

Subparagraphs (a) and (b) of Regulation 15(2) absolve a tour operator from liability for defaults caused by people, companies, governments and other legal entities. Subparagraph (c) absolves it from liability for defaults caused by certain circumstances and events. Where the circumstance or event is caused by a natural or legal person, the tour operator may be protected by subparagraph (a) or (b) as well as by subparagraph (c). But there are various *force majeure* incidents which are not caused by natural or legal persons, or which, like a forest fire, cannot always be traced to one. Subparagraph (c) caters for these.

Subparagraph (c)(i) covers circumstances which are:

(i) unusual or unforeseeable;

(ii) beyond the control of the tour operator; and

(iii) the consequences of which could not have been avoided even if all due care had been exercised.

The word "unusual" in (i) above appears to be a case of overkill. If something is usual, it must be foreseeable. If it is not foreseeable, it must surely be unusual. In the writers' opinion, the test is one of foreseeability but, as indicated above, practical rather than conceptual foreseeability.

The unforeseeable circumstance must be one which is beyond the control of the tour operator. It is not easy to think of unforeseeable circumstances which a tour operator can control.

As well as being "beyond the control of" the tour operator, the unforeseeable circumstance must be one the consequences of which could not have been avoided even if all due care had been exercised. Thus a forest fire or a riot may well, depending on the holiday location, be an unforeseeable circumstance beyond the tour operator's control. But the tour operator will, in addition, need to demonstrate that the consequences of the fire or riot could not have been avoided "even if all due care had been exercised". This is a high burden. In the writers' view, the tour operator will not be able to rely on the defence if steps were not taken because of excessive cost. A tour operator will be under a burden to show that all that was possible was done.

The DTI Guidance Notes state that the DTI would regard unusual and unforeseeable circumstances as including "air traffic control delays, delays or diversion caused by bad weather and disruption caused by industrial action outside the control of the organiser". The writers agree. Simply because air traffic controllers, for example, are not persons whose actions would fall within the ambit of Regulation 15(2)(b) is no reason why they should not fall within subparagraph (c)(i).

The reference to due care and attention, in the writers' view, is confined to the exercise of such attention by the tour operator, or a supplier or sub-supplier of services which form part of the holiday package. For instance, the authors would not normally expect a tour operator to be held liable for injuries suffered by its customers merely because the police or fire brigade failed to exercise due care and attention.

Subparagraph (c)(ii) relieves a tour operator from liability for defaults caused by an event which neither the tour operator nor a third party supplier of services (e.g. a carrier or hotel) could foresee or forestall. Examples include an earthquake or a hurricane, though if sufficient advance warning is given of either to enable avoiding action to be taken, a court would presumably regard it as being capable of being foreseen, irrespective of whether it could also be forestalled.

But "foresee" and "forestall" are alternatives and, therefore, there would be a defence if the event could not be forestalled even if it could be foreseen. Again, these defences require a tour operator to prove that the event could not have been foreseen or forestalled "even with all due care".

(d) Summary

Once a holiday maker has proved a failure to perform the contract, the burden of proof to show that there was "no fault" on the part of the tour operator or any of the suppliers will rest with the tour operator. In many cases, this will not be easy – particularly where the tour operator has to show the exercise of "all due care".

In practice, the defences may prove to be illusory, rather than real. The need for tour operators to have adequate insurance to cater for their potential liabilities has never been more important. Operators should ensure that the terms of their insurance cover all potential liabilities. Insurance which is geared to liability based on negligence will be inapplicable in many cases since the liability introduced by Regulation 15(1) and (2) goes well beyond that which stems from the tort of negligence.

(e) Revisiting old cases

It is instructive to try to apply Regulation 15(2) to some of the former leading cases.

In *Wall* v *Silver Wing* the default, namely the locking of a fire exit, was that of the hotel. The judge held that this did not render the tour operator liable because the locking of the exit was outside its control. Under Regulation 15 the tour operator would in future be held liable in *Wall* v *Silver Wing* circumstances because tour operators are made responsible for the acts and omissions of the suppliers of services which form part of the package.

In the Canadian case of *Craven* v *Strand Holidays* the plaintiffs claimed damages for injuries received when the transit bus in which they were travelling overturned. The tour operator, Strand Holidays, was held not liable since it had exercised good care in the selection of the bus company. That was a good statement of the pre-Regulations law in the United Kingdom but is now overturned by Regulation 15(2).

What about the interesting county court case of *Kaye* v *Intasun* [1987] CLY 1150? In this case, the plaintiff's room was invaded by cockroaches during the first three nights of his family's holiday. He lost sleep and his daughter was badly upset. The evidence indicated that the hotel had not been afflicted by cockroaches before or after the plaintiff's stay, and that the tour operator had not failed in its monitoring or other responsibilities. The court held that the tour operator was not liable. This result would not be affected by Regulation 15(2), if a tour operator could establish that an invasion by cockroaches was an unusual or unforeseeable circumstance beyond its control, the consequences of which could not have been avoided even if all due care had been exercised.

In another Intasun case, *Gibbons* v *Intasun* [1988] CLY 168, the plaintiff's luggage was lost during transfer from airport to hotel. She lost all her, and her children's, clothes. They flew home without taking their holiday. She sued Intasun for breach of contract and negligence, but during the trial these allegations were withdrawn.

She also sued them for breach of an alleged duty as bailees. It was held that it is well known that tour operators employ local independent coach companies to effect transfers. The fact that the tour operator's representative works with the coach driver during the transfer process did not establish Intasun as bailees of the plaintiff's luggage. The claim failed.

As a result of Regulation 15 the plaintiff, in a repeat of the *Gibbons* case, would almost certainly be successful. The coach company which Intasun used to effect the transfer from airport to hotel was a supplier of services which formed part of the package. Accordingly Intasun would be liable for the supplier's default unless, which is unlikely, a defence could be established under subparagraphs (a), (b) or (c) of Regulation 15(2).

Another Intasun case to consider is *Usher* v *Intasun* [1987] CLY 418. Industrial action and technical problems resulted in the plaintiffs, a honeymoon couple, arriving a day late in Tenerife. The court held that a tour operator is not responsible for problems experienced in connection with a properly selected airline. However, it did accept the plaintiffs' claim that Intasun should have done more to reassure the plaintiffs. This was held to constitute a breach of an implied contractual term and the plaintiffs were awarded £50.

Here again the likelihood is that the plaintiffs would have succeeded with their primary claim if Regulation 15 had been in force at the time. The delay was caused by industrial action and technical problems suffered by the airline used by Intasun. Given the technical problems, it is most unlikely that Intasun would have been able to prove that there was "no fault" on the part of the air carrier, and thus the question of the application of any of subparagraphs (a), (b) and (c) of Regulation 15(2) would not even have arisen.

In *Davey* v *Cosmos Air Holidays* [1989] CLY 2561, Mr Davey booked a holiday for himself and his family for two weeks in October 1984, including accommodation at the Hotel Do Cerro, Albufeira at a cost of £726. On the third day of the holiday his daughter was taken ill and subsequently the remaining members of the family became ill. The symptoms included severe stomach pains and diarrhoea. Other holiday makers at the hotel suffered similarly. Earlier outbreaks of this illness had been reported, not only in the local press but also in the British press. The cause of the illness appears to have been that raw sewage was pumped into the sea fifty yards from the beach. The family sued for damages for breach of contract and/or negligence.

Cosmos were held to be negligent in that they were or should have been aware of the situation before Mr Davey and his family arrived, and had taken no precautions to reduce or eliminate the risk of injury to them. Cosmos were also taken to be in breach of an implied term of the contract "to take such steps as are reasonable taking all the circumstances into account to avoid exposing their clients to any significant risk of damage or injury to their health". The Davey family were awarded £1,000 "for breach of contract and for the ruin of their holiday"; Mrs Davey, who contracted dysentery, was awarded £500 for pain and suffering; Mr Davey and his daughter were each awarded £200 for pain and suffering; the young son was awarded £250. Special damages of £217.30 (for the cost of replacement of soiled clothing) were also awarded.

If the facts of the case were repeated now, it is almost certain that the Davey family would be able to rely on Regulation 15 in order to obtain compensation. This is because of the knowledge of the illnesses being suffered by other holiday makers before the arrival of the Daveys. If not, they would still be able to invoke their common law rights in the same way as they did before. It is worth emphasising that the case law which existed before the Regulations will continue in force unless it would remove an obligation imposed by the Regulations. Holiday makers who do not have valid claims under the Regulations can still invoke the pre-existing law.

An unreported 1980s case whose circumstances might not enable a future plaintiff to rely on Regulation 15 concerned a hotel whose guests during one fortnight included a large uncontrolled party of secondary school children. More as a result of boisterousness than malevolence they made life unpleasant for the other guests in the hotel. The county court judge held that in these circumstances the holiday maker who brought the proceedings was entitled to damages from the operator even though the operator was not responsible (in the normal sense of the word) for what had gone wrong.

This decision was based on a failure by the operator to notify the holiday maker in advance, and comments made in the course of the hearing indicate that a tour operator should notify its customers of potential trouble of any significant nature and give them an opportunity to withdraw from the holiday and take a refund. They also suggest that operators are under an obligation to make use of their local representatives to obtain early warning of trouble at a hotel – whether it takes the form of unruly guests, a breakdown of the air conditioning, or anything else calculated to diminish materially a holiday maker's enjoyment.

In the writers' opinion similar reasoning would probably be applied in post-1992 repeat circumstances to justify a similar outcome under Regulation 15. But what if the unruly guests arrive during the course of the holiday? Once a large party of them is installed at a hotel it may be difficult for the hotel manager – let alone the tour operator – to do much about it. Representations and pleas for better behaviour and control can be made but may not be of much avail. The local police may be called but perhaps neither attempt nor achieve anything particularly useful. In those circumstances, Regulation 15(2)(b) should give a tour operator a defence. Other holiday makers are persons unassociated with the provision of the services. Unless an aggrieved holiday maker can establish that the disruptive activity of the other guests was foreseeable, the tour operator will have a defence.

In *Wilson* v *Best Travel Ltd* [1993] 1 ALL ER 353, the plaintiff, while on a package holiday in 1986 booked with the defendants, stayed at the Vanninarchis Beach Hotel, Kos. On the morning of the second day of his holiday, the plaintiff fell through the glass patio door in his room suffering serious injury.

It was held that the defendant had a duty to exercise

reasonable care to exclude accommodation at any hotel whose characteristics were such that guests could not spend a holiday there in reasonable safety. That duty was discharged if the operator had checked that local safety regulations had been complied with, and the duty did not extend to excluding a hotel whose characteristics, as far as safety was concerned, failed to satisfy the current standards applying in England, provided always that the absence of the relevant safety feature was not such that a reasonable holiday maker might decline a holiday at the hotel in question, eg if there were no fire precautions at all. Since the defendants had inspected the accommodation, since the patio doors complied with Greek safety regulations and since the degree of danger posed by the absence of safety glass in the patio door was not such that the plaintiff would have declined to stay at the hotel, the defendants had discharged the duty of care owed to the plaintiff, whose claim therefore failed.

This case raises the difficult question of liability where standards in the country in which the holiday takes place are not as high as in England. If English standards were to be insisted upon, most accommodation in southern Mediterranean countries could not be featured by tour operators.

Where the hotel has complied with all local standards, it is difficult to see that the hotel could be regarded as being at fault. Equally, where the tour operator has seen that local standards are complied with, and in the absence of obvious dangers, it is difficult to see that the tour operator is at fault. However, for a defence to apply, more must be shown: one of the defences outlined in Regulation 15(2)(a), (b) or (c) must be available.

The evidence did not indicate that the accident was the plaintiff's fault – nor was the hotel "unconnected" with the services. If there is to be a defence, it will arise from Regulation 15(2)(c). However, the exercise of "all due care" taken to its extreme could have avoided, foreseen or forestalled the accident. Although, therefore, there are good reasons to suggest no fault, this is a case where there could well be liability under the Regulations. It provides a good illustration of the harsh new regime awaiting tour operators and their insurers.

3. Limitation of liability

Regulation 15(3) provides that in the case of damage arising from the non-performance or improper performance of the services involved in the package, the contract may provide for compensation to be limited in accordance with the international conventions which govern such services. At present the relevant conventions are:

(a) the Warsaw Convention on International Carriage by Air, as amended by the Hague Protocol 1955;

(b) the Berne Convention of 1961 on Carriage by Rail;

(c) the Athens Convention of 1974 on Carriage by Sea;

(d) the Paris Convention of 1962 on the Liability of Hotelkeepers.

Unlike Regulation 15(4) (see below), Regulation 15(3) permits compensation to be limited for personal injury as well as other types of loss and damage. Its purpose is to ensure that a tour operator can take steps to protect itself against having to pay a holiday maker more than the relevant convention would permit the tour operator to recover from the supplier responsible for the default. The limits imposed by the international conventions are discussed in Chapter 9. They only apply, though, to international travel. They provide no protection where the relevant flight, voyage or trip takes place within one country.

Thus, where a package involves internal air transport, journeys down the Nile etc., no convention will apply and the operator will have unlimited liability. A good example of the result of international conventions not applying is *Holmes* v *Bangladesh Biman Corporation* [1988] 2 Lloyd's Rep 120. In that case a Bangladeshi aircraft operated by the defendant crashed on a domestic flight in Bangladesh. The plaintiff, a passenger, was killed. The plaintiff's widow brought the proceedings in England under English law. It was held that the claim was not governed by English law applying international conventions but that the defendant was entitled to rely on its conditions of carriage which limited its liability to £913.

If, in the *Holmes* case, the deceased had been travelling on the Bangladeshi Airways flight as part of a package holiday, the claim could have been brought against the tour operator. The tour operator would not have been able to rely on any limitation of liability. The plaintiff would, therefore, have recovered considerably more from the tour operator. In the tour operator's claim for an indemnity from the carrier, the carrier would have been able to rely on its contract terms, thus leaving the tour operator to bear the bulk of the claim.

Tour operators must, therefore, ensure that such circumstances are covered by their insurance. Where tour operators utilise services not covered by international conventions, they must be certain that their insurance gives total cover.

Regulation 15(4) provides that in the case of damage other than personal injury resulting from the non-performance or improper performance of the services involved in the package, the contract may include a term limiting the amount of compensation which will be paid to the consumer, provided that the limitation is not unreasonable. The key points to note here are that Regulation 15(4):

(a) permits a package holiday contract to limit but not exclude liability (see also Regulation 15(5));

(b) does not permit limitation of damages for personal injury or death;

(c) requires that any limit imposed must be reasonable.

The question of what limits are reasonable for different types of loss will no doubt give rise to many law suits. In making their assessment English courts are likely to be influenced by the factors specified in Schedule 2 to the Unfair Contract Terms Act 1977:

(a) the relative strength of bargaining position of the parties;

(b) whether the customer could have entered into a similar contract with other operators without having to accept a similar term;

(c) whether the customer knew or ought to have known of the existence and extent of the terms;

(d) whether or not the customer received an inducement to enter into the contract.

In addition, however, the courts will take into account the normal basis on which damages are awarded. In the writers' view, any effort to limit damages in a way which falls far short of the amount likely to be imposed by the courts will be regarded as not reasonable. Chapter 7 deals with this in some detail, commenting upon different possible formulae to limit compensation for damage other than personal injury. It will clearly be of vital importance for tour operators to make full use of their rights to limit liability under both paragraphs (3) and (4) of Regulation 15. Limits on the amount of compensation will apply only if set out clearly in the tour operator's booking conditions.

4. Implied terms

Regulation 15(6) implies into every package holiday contract the provisions of paragraphs (7) and (8) of Regulation 15. Paragraph (7) says that in the circumstances described in paragraph (2)(b) and (c) of Regulation 15, the tour operator will give prompt assistance to a consumer in difficulty. This means that where a failure in the provision of services under a package holiday contract is caused by an unforeseeable/unavoidable act of an unconnected third party or by a *force majeure* event, the tour operator is required to provide prompt assistance to a holiday maker in difficulty even though subparagraphs (b) or (c) of Regulation 15(2) absolve it from liability to him.

Regulation 15(8) imposes a further obligation on the tour operator. It is that where a consumer complains about a defect in the performance of the holiday contact, the tour operator, or its local representative if there is one, will make prompt efforts to find appropriate solutions. This is a serious obligation and one which will need to feature prominently in tour operators' training programmes for their local representatives.

(a) Local representatives

This is an appropriate point at which to comment about tour operators' local representatives. The writers consider that the legal duties of a tour operator during the course of a holiday are greater than is often realised. One of the services which a tour operator normally agrees to provide is that of its local representative. The representative is usually an employee or agent of the operator over whom there is direct control, and so the operator will be responsible for any default on the representative's part. The main duties of the representative are to meet holiday makers on arrival at the resort, to assist in transportation to and from the hotel or their accommodation, to help holiday makers in settling in, and to be readily available to deal with any queries or complaints. In addition, the representative assists holiday makers to book excursions and helps with the final day departure arrangements.

It is natural for local representatives to become friendly with many of the hotel managers with whom they are in contact. It is also natural for them to shrug their shoulders about what they may regard as relatively minor (or totally insuperable) problems and to seek to avoid the more difficult type of holiday maker. But it is important for operators to train their representatives to overcome these temptations. In law, tour operators are responsible for the acts and omissions of their local representatives. It is the local representative who has to perform the operator's obligation to use all reasonable efforts to provide guidance and assistance to holiday makers and to help have any deficiencies at the hotel put right. Numerous county court cases bear witness to the heavy price which tour operators can pay for negative or unimaginative handling of complaints by their local representatives.

5. The consumer's communication obligation

Regulation 15(9) requires the tour operator to impose in the holiday contract an interesting obligation on the consumer. It is that he will communicate at the earliest opportunity, in writing or any other appropriate form, to the supplier of the services concerned and to the tour operator any failure which he perceives at the place where the services concerned are supplied. Read literally this is extremely demanding, particularly the requirement that notification should take place at "the earliest opportunity".

The authors doubt whether UK courts will construe this as requiring consumers to go out of their way to create opportunities but rather as requiring them to take the first opportunity which naturally presents itself. Thus, if something goes wrong in the hotel, the consumer should quickly report it to the hotel management and seize the first natural opportunity to report it to the tour operator's local representative.

Regulation 15(9) finishes with the words "at the place where the services concerned are supplied". In the opinion of the authors this restricts the consumer's communication obligation to defects which he "perceives" while on holiday. Its purpose is to ensure that the supplier concerned is given an early opportunity to put things right before it is too late and to enable the tour operator to encourage it to do so. If by the time a consumer has become aware of a defect it is too late to do anything about it, the complaint can follow at a more leisurely pace.

The regulations do not spell out the consequences of a failure by the consumer to report defects promptly. In the opinion of the authors they are akin to those which follow a failure to mitigate damage under basic contract law. The consumer will not forfeit his right to claim but the compensation which he is awarded will be reduced or, in extreme circumstances, extinguished, to reflect the lost mitigation opportunities.

6. Common law duties after a holiday

Does the tour operator have any implied common law duties after a holiday is over? In particular, is it under any obligation to assist a holiday maker in obtaining redress from a hotel for some accident or failing for which the operator clearly has no responsibility itself? The writers are not aware of any cases (even unreported ones) on this point. But, in their opinion, it is more likely than not that such a duty would nowadays be implied into the holiday contract. It is unlikely that this duty would require the operator to incur legal expenses on the holiday maker's behalf but it would require it in a clear-cut case to press the aggrieved holiday maker's claim actively and diligently.

7. ABTA's tour operators' Code of Conduct

Finally, mention should be made of ABTA's tour operators' Code of Conduct. There are two areas where it imposes liabilities more onerous than those under Regulation 15. The first is in relation to things which go wrong with a package holiday where no personal injury or death is involved. Clause 2.8(i) of the Code provides –

> "Tour operators shall include as a term of any contract for the sale of their foreign inclusive holidays or tours a provision accepting responsibility for acts and/or omissions of their employees, agents, sub-contractors and suppliers. In addition, tour operators shall indicate acceptance of responsibility should the services which the tour operator is contractually obliged to provide prove deficient or are not of reasonable standard save that tour operators shall not be responsible nor accept liability for death, bodily injury or illness caused to the signatory to the contract and/or any other named person on the booking form except as provided by Clause 2.8(ii) below. Where the services in question consist of carriage by air or by sea, the tour operator shall be entitled to limit his obligations and liabilities

> in the manner provided by international conventions in respect of air or sea carriers."

This does not provide for any defences unless international carriage by air or sea is involved. Thus, for example, in respect of complaints about hotel accommodation, absolute liability is imposed.

Also, Clause 2.8(iii) provides –

> "A tour operator shall include as a term of any contract for the sale of a foreign inclusive holiday provisions stating that, where appropriate and subject to the tour operator's reasonable discretion –
>
> (a) general assistance shall be afforded to clients who, through misadventure, suffer illness, personal injury or death during the period of their holiday arising out of an activity which does not form part of the foreign inclusive holiday nor or any excursion offered through the tour operator.
>
> (b) where legal action is undertaken by the client, with the prior agreement of the tour operator, initial legal costs associated therewith shall be met by the tour operator, always provided clients request such assistance within 90 days from the date of misadventure.
>
> (c) the aggregate costs for the tour operator in respect of Clause 2.8(iii)(a) and (b) above shall not exceed £5,000 per booking form. Furthermore, in the event either of there being a successful claim for costs against a third party or there being suitable insurance policies in force, costs actually incurred by the tour operator shall be recoverable from the clients."

This imposes much more specific obligations on tour operators to provide assistance where things go wrong in connection with activities unassociated with the package itself.

Chapter 4

Tour operators' financial security obligations

Chapters 2 and 3 focused on a tour operator's obligations to its customers as regards the description, sale and performance of a package holiday. There is, though, one further and all important obligation imposed on tour operators by the Regulations. This obligation, which is dealt with in Regulations 16–22, is to arrange "financial protection" for holiday makers, by ensuring that their monies will be refunded and/or stranded holiday makers will be repatriated should the tour operator become insolvent and cease trading.

The Regulations impose two separate requirements. Firstly, Regulation 16(1) requires a tour operator "at all times to be able to provide sufficient evidence of security for the refund of money paid over and for the repatriation of the consumer in the event of insolvency". Secondly, it goes on to stipulate three alternative arrangements by which tour operators are to safeguard their customers' money and pay for the cost of repatriation. The prescribed arrangements are a bond, an insurance policy or a trust account.

Breach of the financial security requirements is, like breach of Regulations 5, 7 and 8, a criminal offence. Enforcement is by Trading Standards Officers, who have wide powers under Schedule 3 to the Regulations to enter premises and seize documents to ascertain whether an offence has been committed.

If an offence is discovered, it is not just the tour operator company which risks prosecution. Regulation 25 sets out circumstances in which someone other than the tour operator can also be prosecuted for an offence. Under Regulation 25(2), where a company is guilty of an offence under the Regulations, any "director, manager, secretary or other similar officer" of that company, or any person who purported to act in one of those capacities, will be personally guilty of the offence if it can be shown that it was committed with his "consent or connivance", or that it was attributable to any neglect on his part. (An equivalent provision in Regulation 25(4) imposes potential personal liability on the partners of a Scottish partnership.)

Defences to a criminal prosecution are available under Regulation 24. These, and Regulation 25, are discussed in Chapter 6. This chapter considers, in turn, the obligations imposed by Regulations 16–21.

1. Regulation 16(1) – the requirement for sufficient evidence of security

Regulation 16(1) requires tour operators to be able at all times "to provide sufficient evidence of security for the refund of money paid over and for the repatriation of the consumer in the event of insolvency".

Regulation 16(1) does not state what will constitute "sufficient evidence" – nor does it say to whom a tour operator will have to "provide" it. The intention seems to be that all tour operators must have in their possession, or have access to, a means of proving to a Trading Standards Officer, or to any of its customers, that all holiday makers booking package holidays with it would be refunded and/or repatriated if it became insolvent. The simplest form of "evidence" would seem to be a copy of a relevant bond or insurance policy, or copy documents relating to a trust account. However, those documents taken alone can prove only that the tour operator has one of the prescribed arrangements in place. They cannot prove that the monies which would be available on the tour operator's failure would in fact be sufficient to ensure that all holiday makers would be refunded and/or repatriated. To ascertain that would require a detailed examination of the tour operator's accounts by someone with accountancy expertise. Trading Standards Officers are generally not qualified accountants.

In real terms, whether a tour operator's arrangements are sufficient to ensure the refund and/or repatriation of every customer on its insolvency will depend to a large extent on its honesty and integrity. A "cowboy" might decide to take the risk of trading without complying with the financial security requirements fully, or even at all.

The DTI Guidance Notes make it clear that the obligation under Regulation 16(1) is independent of the other obligations relating to financial security. They recognise that evidence of security against the costs of repatriation could be provided in a number of ways, including possession by customers of a valid return ticket for which the operator had paid.

2. Regulation 16(2) – the prescribed arrangements

Regulation 16(2) states that, in relation to all packages save certain specified exceptions (see below), a tour operator "shall at least ensure that there are in force arrangements as described in Regulations 17, 18, 19, 20 or (if the tour operator is acting otherwise than in the course of a business), as described in any of those Regulations or in Regulation 21".

The package holidays which are not required to be protected by one of the prescribed arrangements are holidays where customers are already protected by one of two means. The first is where the tour operator is established in another EC member state which has in force legislation which will protect the holiday in question. The second is where package holidays are covered by a bond taken out by the tour operator as a condition of holding an ATOL.

The requirements of Regulations 16(1) and 16(2) are complementary but separate. Both must be satisfied.

Although the primary purpose of making one of the prescribed arrangements required by Regulation 16(2) is to satisfy the requirement set out in Regulation 16(1), there may be occasions where the amount of a bond, or the sum insured, or the monies held on trust would not in fact be sufficient to ensure that all holiday makers were refunded and/or repatriated. The specific conditions which apply to each of the three prescribed arrangements relate only to the need to refund holiday makers but not to the need to repatriate them.

The DTI Guidance Notes expressly recognise this lacuna. The note on Regulation 16(2) states as follows:

> "It is expected that compliance with one of the options required by Regulation 16(2) (and set out in detail in Regulations 17 to 21) will normally meet the requirement for protection of pre-payments in the Directive which is laid out in general terms in Regulation 16(1). But this may not be so in all circumstances. This Regulation [i.e., Regulation 16(2)] is therefore worded so that it applies in addition to Regulation 16(1)".

This means that, if necessary, a tour operator must make supplementary arrangements to ensure that any holiday makers stranded abroad would be repatriated should the tour operator become insolvent and cease trading. The DTI Guidance Notes do not offer any assistance on how this should be done. They state as follows:

> "The Regulations do not specify how the requirement to have security against the costs of repatriation should be met. This is because there is a variety of ways in which this might be done, and to attempt to regulate for all possible circumstances could be over-prescriptive".

For the majority of tour operators, the most convenient way of ensuring full compliance with both Regulations 16(1) and 16(2) is likely to be to ensure that potential repatriation costs are included in the amount for which it is bonded or insured. However, if the prescribed arrangement chosen is a trust account, the tour operator may have to make a separate arrangement to cover repatriation costs, for example an insurance policy. This is because repatriation of holiday makers following an insolvency may give rise to costs over and above those originally included in the price of the package holiday. Some hoteliers may become hostile towards customers of failed tour operators, causing those customers to wish to cut short their holiday. Alternative flight arrangements will have to be made in these circumstances and these, of course, must be paid for. Also, there will be administrative costs associated with the arrangement of repatriation; depending upon the volume of holiday makers to be repatriated, these costs could be considerable.

The Regulations do not define "repatriation". In the writers' view, repatriation properly involves the return of a holiday maker to the country from which he originally departed, although not necessarily to the same airport from which he departed. Further, "repatriation" cannot apply in the case of package holidays taken entirely within the UK. This is endorsed by the DTI in its Guidance Notes:

> "Although the Directive is silent on the point, the Department does not consider that repatriation includes returning the consumer to his point of departure in the case of packages taken wholly within the UK".

3. Conditions to be satisfied by bonds – Regulations 17 & 18

Regulation 17 sets out specific conditions to be met where a bond is not reinforced by a reserve fund or insurance cover on which a call can be made should the amount of the bond prove insufficient. Regulation 18 sets out conditions to be met where a bond is supported by a reserve fund or insurance cover.

To satisfy either Regulation, a bond must be issued by an "authorised institution" in favour of an "approved body" and must not be in force for a period exceeding 18 months. An "authorised institution" is defined as a legal person authorised under the law of an EC member state to carry on the business of entering into bonds of the kind required by the Regulations. Typically, this will be a bank or insurance company. If one of the specified events occurs and the bond is called, the bond monies will be paid to the "approved body" in whose favour the bond is issued.

An "approved body" is defined in the Regulations as a body which is for the time being approved by the Secretary of State for that purpose. A body may not be approved for the purpose of Regulation 18 unless "it has a reserve fund or insurance cover with an insurer authorised in respect of such business in a member state of an amount in each case which is designed to enable all monies paid over to any member of the body of consumers under or in contemplation of contracts for relevant packages which have not been fully performed to be repaid to those consumers in the event of the insolvency of the member".

The Regulations do not say how a reserve fund should be created, although suggestions are given in the DTI Guidance Notes. These suggestions include membership fees levied from members of the approved body or a levy added to the cost of all holidays sold by the members of an approved body, whether as a fixed amount or as a percentage of the holiday cost. In the writers' view, the second suggestion is not practicable unless all tour operators were to levy their customers equally. Holiday makers often compare the prices in different tour operators' brochures. If, because of a levy, a package holiday featured in one tour operator's brochure is more expensive than an identical package holiday featured in another tour operator's brochure, holiday makers will simply book their holiday with the tour operator offering the lowest price. Reserve funds must be held "by persons and in a manner" approved by the Secretary of State. Alternatively, if bonds are to be reinforced by insurance, the policy must be effected with an insurer authorised in respect of such business in an EC member state.

Under Regulation 17 (bonds where there is no reserve

fund or insurance cover) a tour operator's bond must be for:

> "Such sum as may reasonably be expected to enable all monies paid over by consumers under or in contemplation of contracts for relevant packages which have not been fully performed to be repaid and shall not in any event be a sum which is less than the minimum sum calculated in accordance with Regulation 17(4)".

Regulation 17(4) states:

> "The minimum sum for the purposes of [Regulation 17(3)] shall be a sum which represents:–
>
> (a) not less than 25% of all the payments which [the tour operator] estimates that he will receive under or in contemplation of contracts for relevant packages in the twelve month period from the date of entry into force of the bond . . .; or
>
> (b) the maximum amount of all the payments which [the tour operator] expects to hold at any one time, in respect of contracts which have not been fully performed,
>
> whichever sum is the smaller".

Regulations 17(5) and 17(6) provide that, before a bond is entered into, a travel company must inform the approved body of which it is a member of the minimum sum which it proposes for the purposes of Regulations 17(3) and 17(4). The approved body must then consider whether, if the tour operator were to fail, the sum proposed would be sufficient to refund all monies paid by holiday makers for package holidays which had not been completed by the date of the failure. If the approved body does not consider that this is the case, it must tell the tour operator of the sum which, in its opinion, would be sufficient for that purpose. That sum will then become "the minimum sum" for the purposes of Regulations 17(3) and 17(4).

This procedure is designed to ensure that an approved body will effectively exercise a regulatory function over the amount of its members' bonds, limiting the extent to which the safety of holiday makers' money must depend on the integrity of the travel company. Indeed, Regulation 17(5) imposes an express duty upon an approved body to consider the adequacy of the amount of a tour operator's bond. Does this mean that, if a bond proves to be insufficient to refund all holiday makers, holiday makers will be able to sue the approved body?

Such a claim could arise either through breach of statutory duty or the tort of negligence. So far as the former is concerned, it is well-established law that to bring a civil law claim for breach of statutory duty the statute must provide for such a claim. The Regulations contain no such provision and, therefore, in the writers' view such a claim would not succeed.

A claim based on the tort of negligence would require a holiday maker to show that the approved body owed him a duty of care, that there was a breach of that duty and that, as a result of the breach of duty, he suffered damage. Clearly, an approved body has a duty to exercise proper and reasonable care in fixing bonding levels. An approved body should anticipate that holiday makers will rely upon proper care being taken to fix bond levels. It is certainly at least arguable that the duty of care is owed to all holiday makers who book packages with a tour operator bonded through a particular approved body.

If the duty of care exists, and there is a breach, the holiday maker will easily be able to demonstrate loss. Thus the most difficult issue will relate to the question of breach of any duty of care. To avoid such allegations, approved bodies will need to scrutinise vigorously the sales information of tour operators bonded through them and to make detailed enquiries of likely sales etc. Any failure to do so could well constitute a failure to exercise proper care and expose approved bodies to claims from holiday makers who are out of pocket.

The conditions to be satisfied by bonds which are reinforced by a reserve fund or insurance are set out in Regulation 18. The amount of such bonds is governed by Regulation 18(3) which states that they must be for:

"such sum as may be specified by the approved body as representing the lesser of:–

(a) the maximum amount of all the payments which the other party to the contract expects to hold at any one time in respect of contracts which have not been fully performed; or

(b) the minimum sum calculated in accordance with [Regulation 18(4)]".

The "minimum sum" must be at least 10 per cent of all the payments which the tour operator estimates that it will receive "under or in contemplation of contracts for relevant packages" during the twelve months immediately following the date on which the bond comes into force.

Regulation 18 does not impose the same obligation upon an approved body as Regulation 17; no express duty is imposed in the way that one is imposed by Regulation 17(5). This difference stems, no doubt, from the existence of a back-up fund which should, at least in theory, extinguish the risk of a holiday maker being out of pocket.

The DTI considers that the use of a back-up should be rare.

The EC Directive imposes the original obligation to provide financial security. Payments from back-up funds tend to be discretionary. Where, therefore, there is reliance on a form of "optional" payment to provide financial security, it is arguable that there has not been proper implementation of the Directive with its absolute requirement. It is, therefore, best to use a bond to provide "adequate" security. But the DTI itself has recognised the difference where there is a back-up fund by providing for lower minimum bonding levels!

4. Conditions to be satisfied by an insurance policy – Regulation 19

If a tour operator chooses to comply with the financial security requirements by taking out insurance cover, detailed conditions are set out in Regulation 19.

The insurance cover may be under one or more policies. In each policy, though, the insurer must agree that, if the tour operator becomes insolvent, the insurer will indemnify its customers for all money paid "under or in contemplation of" contracts for package holidays. The customers must be "insured persons" under the policy. In addition, the policy must not contain a term which would allow the insurer to avoid indemnifying holiday makers on the basis that:

(a) a particular action was or was not taken after the holiday maker became entitled to make a claim; or

(b) the tour operator had failed to make any payment in respect of another insurance policy; or

(c) the tour operator had failed to keep specified records or to allow the insurer access to information contained in those records.

If a tour operator chooses to safeguard its customers' monies by means of an insurance policy, it must include a term in its booking conditions stating that customers will acquire the benefit of a policy in the event of its insolvency. However, it may not be possible for the tour operator to be an insured party. Insurance law requires an "insured" to have an "insurable interest". That interest lies with its customers, and not with itself.

In general, the establishment of bonding systems may require more work than insurance schemes. However, once established, bonding arrangements will require less administrative work than insurance schemes, and may be slightly cheaper. Further, a bond provides a certainty of payment which may not exist in insurance to the same extent.

5. Conditions to be satisfied by a trust account – Regulations 20 & 21

The third prescribed option for protecting holiday makers' money is a trust account. The specific conditions which apply to trust accounts are set out in Regulations 20 and 21.

The conditions governing trust accounts set out in Regulation 20 may be summarised as follows:

(a) All money paid by a particular customer for a package holiday must be held by someone in the United Kingdom as a trustee for that customer until the package holiday has been fully performed, or the customer has cancelled the holiday and forfeited his money, or any money due to be repaid to the customer has been repaid.

(b) The tour operator must bear the costs of administering the trust account but will be entitled to any interest earned on customer monies while they are in the account.

(c) The trustee may only pay the tour operator trust monies held in respect of a particular holiday on his receiving from the tour operator a signed statement confirming that the package holiday has been fully performed, or that the customer has cancelled and forfeited his money, or that the tour operator has refunded money to the customer. The trustee may, in his discretion, require further information or evidence to substantiate such written statement.

(d) If the tour operator becomes insolvent, the trustee will use the monies in the trust account to refund customers. Any shortfall in the account will be borne on a proportional basis by all customers. Any excess over and above the amount due back to customers will be paid to the travel company's liquidator or receiver.

Regulation 21 applies where the organiser of the package "is acting otherwise than in the course of business". It is not uncommon for, say, a football club, a school or a trade association to organise a trip for its members, for example a football tour, a school skiing trip or a two-day conference at an overseas venue. The football club, school or trade association will only be an "organiser" for the purposes of the Regulations if it arranges such trips "otherwise than occasionally". In many cases, it will not do so. However, if it does come within the definition of an organiser, it will have to make prescribed financial security arrangements. Because it would be unrealistic to expect a school or association to comply with any of the alternative procedures set out in Regulations 16–20, less onerous requirements are set out in Regulation 21.

The Regulations do not define "acting otherwise than in the course of business". It is to be assumed that the phrase means as part of a trading activity and/or for profit. However, this construction could be challenged on the basis of the definition of 'business' contained in s. 47 of the VAT Act 1983 ("the 1983 Act"), which states that "business" includes "any trade, profession or vocation" and, further, that the provision by a club, association or organisation (for a subscription or other consideration) of facilities or advantages available to its members will be deemed to be "the carrying on of a business". However, these definitions are expressly stated to apply for the purposes of the 1983 Act, and it is to be hoped that a court would find that they have no application to Regulation 21. If they did, Regulation 21 would effectively be rendered redundant.

Regulation 21 has no application for tour operators organising package holidays. Brief reference should be made to the main difference between its provisions, and those of Regulation 20. It is that an organiser falling within the ambit of Regulation 21 is able to use holiday makers' monies to pay suppliers. That, of course, is the very thing that Regulation 20 prevents, and it is that prevention which renders the trust monies option unattractive to tour operators.

This is because a trust account involves paying all receipts from customers into a designated bank account and leaving them there until such time as the contract to which they relate has been fully performed or cancelled, or until something occurs which obliges the travel company to refund the customers' money. This procedure does not accord with standard travel industry practice. Many tour operators do not segregate customers' monies from other monies in their possession. Receipts from customers are likely to be held in a tour operator's general bank account, and may as easily be used to pay an electricity bill or staff salaries as an airline or hotel. Indeed, most tour operators need to use customers' monies as part of normal working capital.

Chapter 5

The travel agent

1. Introduction

The contract for a package holiday is between the holiday maker and the tour operator. *Prima facie,* the travel agent is the selling agent for the tour operator. It is the travel agent who provides the holiday maker with the tour operator's brochure, who takes from the holiday maker details of the holiday desired, who communicates these details to the tour operator and confirms with him the availability of a particular holiday, who collects payments from the holiday maker for despatch to the tour operator and who despatches the tickets to the holiday maker. This role imposes upon a travel agent liabilities and duties in law to the tour operator. These will normally be encapsulated in a written agency agreement between them—at least where ABTA members are involved.

Although a travel agent who sells package holidays for the tour operating companies who assemble them is clearly acting as their agent in certain respects and receives his commission from them, he is not a sales agent in the normally accepted sense of the term. He will usually be acting as agent for a large number of operators rather than just promoting the products of one. He will not often sally forth and call on potential customers. Although there are signs that this is beginning to change, he will not normally perform a positive selling role—at any rate not in the hard sell sense—on behalf of any particular operator. In general, his role as agent for the operators whose brochures he stocks is a less active one than that of the sales agent appointed by a manufacturer of goods. Historically, it has, in many respects, been more akin to that of a mere booking agent, such as those agencies through whom theatre tickets can be booked. However, there is now a tendency for some agents, mainly the larger ones, to concentrate in their brochures, window displays and staff recommendations, on promoting a few preferred tour operators.

Over recent years, polarisation in the retail travel trade has continued. A considerable divide has opened between the "multiples" (Lunn Poly, Pickfords, Thomas Cook etc) and the smaller, independent travel agencies. The multiples tend to promote primarily the large tour operators which has led to efforts at greater co-operation between small specialist tour operators and their retail counterparts. A recognised feature of the business dealings between multiples and the large tour operators is agreement on additional commission geared to sales levels and payments by the tour operator to support particular marketing efforts.

Although travel agents owe duties in contract to the tour operators they represent, it is submitted that they also have duties and liabilities in law to the holiday maker—the other principal to the package holiday contract. This chapter examines the relationships between travel agent and tour operator and between travel agent and holiday maker, and considers whether the travel agent is agent of both tour operator and holiday maker, something which, on the face of things, would be contrary to the general principle in agency law that an agent should not put himself in a position where he is purporting to act for both the buyer and the seller.

This chapter does not consider a travel agent's liabilities and duties in law when he is merely selling, for example, a train ticket. Nor is the position of "direct sell travel companies" specifically considered. Their duties and liabilities will be owed direct to the holiday maker, since there is no intermediary to take into account, and will encompass the duties and liabilities to the holiday maker of both tour operator and travel agent.

Before considering the contractual relationship between tour operators and travel agents, it is appropriate to indicate briefly some of the basic legal principles which govern relations between principals and agents generally.

2. Common law principles of agency

(a) Contractual relationships

The basic notion behind the present day English common law rules of agency can be expressed in the maxim "He who does an act through another is deemed in law to do it himself". In contractual terms this is traditionally expressed to mean:

> "The contract is the contract of the principal, not that of the agent, and *prima facie* at common law the only person who can sue is the principal and the only person who can be sued is the principal". (*Montgomerie* v *UK Steamship Association* [1891] 1 QB 370 per Wright J).

Accordingly, when a travel agent effects a sale on behalf of his tour operator principal, he is putting the holiday maker into a direct contractual relationship with the operator. If anything goes wrong with the holiday, the holiday maker must sue the operator and not the travel agent through whom the holiday was booked. This principle is affirmed in the International Convention on Travel Agents which was signed in 1970 but which to date only Belgium and Italy have incorporated into their national law. It states that a travel agent who merely arranges the provision of holidays by others will not be liable to the holiday maker provided that he has not been negligent in making the arrangements.

In modern times, most agency relationships involve an actual contract of agency between the principal and agent. In English law, there is no necessity for the contract to be in writing except where the authority given to the agent is to execute a deed (ie a document under seal which may subject a party to obligations for which he receives no consideration), in which case the agency must be created by a deed. However, the use of written agency contracts in the travel industry and elsewhere is increasing. The usual contractual stumbling blocks of fraud, duress, mistake or misrepresentation must be absent from any express agency appointment but it is not proposed to discuss these basic aspects of contract law in this book.

(b) Authority of agent

In the case of contractual agents, such as travel agents, the scope of the agent's authority will mainly be dealt with by the contract itself. In addition, authority may be implied from the nature of the business in which the agent is employed or by the custom in a particular trade. Generally speaking an agent has implied authority to do everything necessary for and ordinarily incidental to carrying out his express authority according to the usual way in which such authority is executed.

Where an agent is acting for his principal in a specific business, the agent is impliedly authorised to act according to the usages and customs of that business. The custom must be known to the principal or be so commonly known that he is taken to have knowledge of it. For example in the case of *Limako BV* v *Hentz & Co Inc* [1979] 2 Lloyds Rep 23, brokers in the cocoa trade were held to be agents even though in accordance with custom they had acted in their own name and made themselves personally liable to a third party. However, if the agent acts in accordance with an unreasonable custom, by which is meant one inconsistent with the nature of the transaction, the agent will not be taken to have authority so to act, unless the principal had notice, in which case he will be presumed to have consented.

An agent's implied authority supplements the authority which is expressly given to him and is another type of actual authority. Actual authority contrasts with apparent authority which arises where X by words or conduct represents to Y that Z has authority to act on X's behalf. In such circumstances X may be bound to Y by acts of Z even though Z did not have actual authority to bind X.

This apparent, or ostensible, authority arises because a principal allows his agent to appear to have more authority than he actually has, as where unknown to others a principal makes reservations in his agent's authority that limit the authority which the agent would normally have. For instance, in the case of *Watteau* v *Fenwick* [1893] 1 QB 346, Willis J stated that "the principal is liable for all the acts of the agent which are within the authority usually confided to an agent of that character (despite) ... limitations as between the principal and the agent put upon that authority".

Watteau v *Fenwick* involved an agent employed to manage a beer house by a firm of brewers. The agent was forbidden by the principal to buy certain articles for the business. Nevertheless, he ordered some from a third party who did not know of the limitation on the agent's authority. The principal was held liable to the third party on the basis that it was in the usual course of business for a manager to purchase this type of item and therefore he had ostensible authority to do so.

(c) Duties of agent

Where the agency is a contractual agency, it is the agent's duty to do what he has undertaken to do and to obey the lawful instructions given to him by his principal. These instructions may be contained in his express authority or may be implied from established trade customs. In circumstances which are covered neither by express instructions nor trade customs or usages the overriding considerations are that the acts of the agent must be lawful and for the principal's benefit.

An agent is bound to his principal to use reasonable care in the exercise of his powers. This is a comprehensive obligation which includes the duty to use customary diligence, care and skill. The agent will be responsible to his principal for any loss caused by a failure to observe these standards. The liability of an agent does not depend upon the success of his efforts but upon whether he has acted in as reasonable a manner as could be expected from an agent employed in such a capacity. Should the principal require a *higher* standard of care and skill to be exercised, he should provide for it by express terms in the contract.

It is a general rule of law that an agent must perform his undertaking personally and may not delegate the task unless specifically authorised to do so. The reasoning behind this rule is that the principal may well consider the personality of the agent to be essential to the relationship.

Under common law an agent is obliged to keep proper accounts of money and property received for and on behalf of the principal and to make them available for inspection by the principal. Further the agent must pay over to his principal all monies received on the latter's behalf. However in normal circumstances an agent is not obliged to bank his principal's monies in a separate bank account and if he does not, the principal has no preferential claim to "his money" if the agent goes into liquidation (*Henry* v *Hammond* [1913] 2 KB 515). In normal circumstances if a principal allows his agent to retain monies for more than six years from the date on which they should have been accounted for, the principal's claim to such monies becomes statute-barred.

(d) Duties of principal

The main duties of a principal are to pay his agent's commission and to indemnify him against liabilities properly incurred by him on behalf of his principal when acting within his express, implied or customary authority. In the absence of any express provision regarding when commission is earned an agent's entitlement in respect of a particular sale will normally vest at the time when the principal accepts the customer's order. Accordingly, if the principal subsequently repudiates his contract with his customer, he will still have to pay commission to the agent. However, if the principal's customer fails to complete the purchase, the agent will normally lose his entitlement to commission in respect of the "sale". This is because the agent's obligation is to introduce a purchaser ready and willing to purchase and able to purchase and to complete his purchase. Matters of this nature are normally dealt with in express terms in contracts between principals and agents and it is highly desirable that they should be.

3. Travel agency agreements

(a) Standard terms

Article 13(6) of ABTA's Articles of Association, which article is commonly known as "Stabiliser", provides that, in the absence of special permission, no ABTA travel agent should sell foreign package tours organised or promoted by a non-ABTA tour operator, and that no ABTA tour operator should sell foreign package tours through a non-ABTA travel agent. An ABTA tour operator can only sell such tours directly to the public or through an ABTA retail agent. But, as explained in Chapter 1, this restriction will disappear, probably towards the end of 1993/early 1994.

Further, ABTA requires that all ABTA tour operators dealing through agents establish formal agency agreements. Consequently, each ABTA travel agent should have a formal agency appointment agreement with every tour operator with whom he deals. In practice, though, it is not unusual for agreements to be so outdated as not to represent properly the actual trading practice between the agent and the operator or for there to be no agreement.

Normal terms to be found in these agreements are—

(a) the travel agent must stock and display the tour operator's brochures;

(b) he must use the operator's booking form when selling one of the operator's holidays;

(c) the agent must forward bookings to the operator and not purport to accept any booking without the express authority of the operator;

(d) the agent's responsibility for collecting cancellation charges;

(e) the rate of commission to be received by the agent and how and when it is to be paid;

(f) the time at which monies received from holiday makers are to be transmitted to the tour operator;

(g) a prohibition against the agent making representations or warranties on behalf of the operator;

(h) the agent's right to be indemnified by the tour operator and *vice versa*;

(i) the time from which any deposit or other monies paid by a holiday maker to the travel agent in respect of a booking are held by the travel agent as agent for the tour operator.

(b) ATOL requirements

As regards (i) above, standard term 9(1) of the Civil Aviation Authority's standard ATOL terms, requires all holders of Air Travel Organisers' Licences (ATOLs), which includes all operators offering holidays abroad which involve significant air travel, to make it clear to the travel agent and the customer in writing, that any money paid by the customer to the agent in respect of a holiday, the provision of which requires an ATOL, are held by the agent as agent for the operator from the date on which the customer receives confirmation of his booking from the operator. This only refers to ATOL holders. There are other tour operators who appoint travel agents whose holidays do not need an ATOL.

Standard term 9(2) also requires ATOL tour operators to make it clear in writing to travel agents whether monies collected by them from a customer in connection with a holiday booking are held by them as agent for the operator until the date on which the operator confirms the booking. The authors' research suggests that most ATOL tour operators notify their agents that monies held by them pending confirmation of a holiday are held by them for the customer. In addition, the authors believe that most ATOL tour operators include a statement to this effect in their booking conditions so that their customers are aware of the position.

(c) Discounting

On 1 August 1984 the Director General of Fair Trading asked the Monopolies and Mergers Commission to investigate the alleged practice whereby tour operators prevented travel agents from discounting the price of tour operators' holidays and bearing the cost of the discount themselves. The conclusions of the Commission can be summarised as follows:

(i) Tour operators did prohibit travel agents from supplying tour operators' package holidays at a discount from the price prescribed by the tour operator.

(ii) Tour operators had sought to prevent Ilkeston Co-operative Society from introducing a voucher system, and this prevented competition between travel agents.

(iii) Public interest was not best served by such restrictions of competition among travel agents.

As a result of the Commission's findings (readers who are interested in the details should refer to the Report, reference Cmnd 9879) the Restriction on Agreements and Conduct (Tour Operators) Order 1987 was introduced. It provides that:

(i) it is unlawful for a tour operator to make an agreement which prohibits a travel agent from offering "inducements" to the public; and

(ii) an inducement is defined as "a benefit, whether pecuniary or not, offered to a class or classes of persons or to the public at large by a travel agent expressly on his own behalf as an incentive to that class or those classes of persons or the public at large to acquire foreign package holidays through him rather than through another"; and

(iii) it is unlawful for a tour operator to withhold or to threaten to withhold the sale of package holidays through travel agents who offer inducements; and

(iv) it is unlawful for a tour operator to give any preference to a travel agent who does not offer inducements.

Tour operators are not prevented from specifying the prices at which their holidays are to be sold. What they cannot do is to forbid travel agents to offer cash discounts or other inducements at the agent's own expense.

4. Travel agent and tour operator

As previously stated, a principal is responsible to his customer for those acts of his agent which are within the agent's actual or ostensible authority. These normally include all steps necessary to process a holiday maker's booking. This is what the preface describes as the travel agent's "booking agent role".

If a travel agent, for whatever reason, incorrectly notes the dates on which a holiday maker wishes to travel and arranges the holiday contract on the basis of this error, will the tour operator be liable to the holiday maker, since this is clearly an act within the travel agent's authority? (Any liability of the travel agent to the holiday maker is considered later in this chapter.)

It is established law that an agent for reward (which a travel agent is) must exhibit such a degree of skill and diligence as is appropriate to the performance of the duties that he has accepted (*Lage* v *Siemens Bros & Co Ltd* (1932) 42 Ll.L Rep 252). A professional agent must show the degree of care to be expected of those in his profession. He is not responsible to his principal for a mere mistake or error of judgment not amounting to a failure to exercise proper care or skill (*Nitrate Producers' Co* v *Wills* (1905) 21 TLR 699). However, a failure to exercise proper care or skill will lose the agent his normal right of indemnity against his principal.

A form of agency agreement which is widely used provides for the operator to "keep the agent indemnified against all claims and liabilities relating thereto save to the extent that they are attributable to the acts and omissions of the agent" and that the agent should "keep the operator indemnified against all claims and liabilities attributable to acts or omissions committed by him in breach, or outside the scope, of this agreement".

A principal will be liable to a customer for mistakes by the principal's agents provided that the agent is acting within his actual or ostensible authority. In such circumstances the principal will normally be entitled to be indemnified by the agent. As a general rule a customer cannot sue an agent for a known principal for breach of contract. If incorrect departure dates have been noted by the travel agent and the error is not spotted by the holiday maker, the fault is that of the travel agent and not the tour operator. However, at the time of making the mistake the agent is acting within the scope of his authority. *Prima facie*, therefore, the tour operator will be liable to the holiday maker and entitled to a full indemnity from the agent.

The travel agent does not assume any contractual responsibility for faults in the package holiday provided by the tour operator. This is something for which only the principal to the contract can be liable. This is also the case where a holiday maker suffers personal injury and loss while on holiday, unless the circumstances were within the agent's control and attributable to his acts or omissions. It is normal for agency agreements to state that the agent will accept liability for any loss or injury suffered by a customer as a result of the negligent acts or omissions of the agent. This could happen where the agent gives a negligent answer to a customer's question or fails to deliver the customer's tickets or pass on information provided by the operator for onward transmission to the customer.

Chapter 3 commented upon the liability provisions of Regulation 15. It refers to "the other party to the contract", who is defined as the "organiser" or the "retailer" or both, as the case may be. Since the contract is between the tour operator and the holiday maker, the writers do not consider that any liability is imposed on UK travel agents by Regulation 15.

It is also necessary to consider the agent's position vis à vis the operator when the holiday maker fails to honour his contract with the operator, by, for example, failing to make payment in full or to take the holiday reserved. Normally this is catered for in agency appointment agreements by wording such as:

> "If the Agent has used his best endeavours to collect such balances, cancellation charges or other monies, but has failed to do so, the operator will release the Agent from his obligation hereunder, whereupon the operator will take steps to exercise his right at law to collect monies due . . .".

The Regulations set out in Chapter 2 impose considerable obligations upon tour operators to disseminate a variety of information to holiday makers. Where bookings are made through travel agents, many tour operators will expect travel agents to be responsible for giving the statutory information. Logistically, that would be the easiest method, particularly if the tour operator's brochure contains the information. Where a tour operator inserts the requisite information in brochures, or a combination of brochures and separate leaflets, it will be necessary to draw up a new, or variation, agreement specifying the agent's duties and containing specific indemnities for breach of them.

As discussed later in this chapter, there will be a quid pro quo. The Regulations impose potential liabilities on travel agents in respect of tour operators' brochures, and they should certainly seek to establish a revised trading *modus operandi* and obtain indemnities for brochures which fall foul of the Regulations. At the time of going to print, ABTA has indicated that it is reviewing its recommended standard agency agreement terms.

5. Whose agent?

Generally speaking, there is no contract or other written terms delineating a travel agent's responsibility to the holiday maker. Case law is not of much assistance and the travel agent's liabilities and duties must be derived from general principles of law and accepted practice in the holiday industry. Valuable guidance regarding the latter is given in ABTA's *Code of Conduct for Travel Agents.*

At the time of Clarkson's collapse in 1974 there was considerable controversy concerning for whom travel agents act. This was a matter of vital importance because if travel agents were acting as agents for customers, they would be able to refund deposits paid by customers rather than accounting for them to the liquidator. In the normal course of events this question would have been decided by the courts in the fullness of time. But it never was because the Government decided to put all Clarkson's customers out of their misery by compensating them out of the proceeds of a special levy imposed on people who booked holidays with ATOL holders in subsequent seasons.

Some lawyers who in 1974 advised that travel agents were the agents of the holiday maker and not of the tour operator regarded the position of travel agents as analogous to that of insurance brokers. It has been established in cases such as *Rozanes* v *Bowen* (1928) 32 Ll.L.R, 98 and *Anglo-African Merchants Ltd* v *Bayley* [1970] 1 QB 311, that insurance brokers, as distinct from insurance agents appointed to sell policies exclusively on behalf of a single insurer, are the agents of the insured and not of the insurer. And this is so notwithstanding that the broker is remunerated by commission paid by the insurer.

In certain respects travel agents engaged in selling package holidays are comparable with insurance brokers. They stock the brochures of numerous tour operators and do not normally seek to promote the holidays of any one operator in preference to those of others. They answer questions regarding holidays featured in a brochure and on occasions make comparative judgements regarding the suitability for a customer's purposes of different holidays. They assist customers in completing the operator's booking form and then forward it to the operator for acceptance.

On the other hand there are differences in the respective roles of insurance brokers and travel agents. Many more members of the public choose their holidays without asking questions than do people who take out insurance. The contents of a holiday brochure are much more intelligible to the average member of the public than those of an insurance policy. And the choice of a holiday is a much more subjective matter than the choice of an insurance policy. But these differences do not conclusively establish the agent as acting for the operator rather than the holiday maker.

At the time of Clarkson's collapse in 1974 the legal documentation employed in the holiday industry was rudimentary. Many tour operators did not even enter into formal agency agreements with the agents who stocked their brochures. And their brochures, instead of making it clear whose agent they were, used language which afforded great scope for litigation.

Since then there has been a considerable improvement. Nowadays all ABTA operators are required to enter into formal agreements appointing travel agents as their agents. By itself this is not necessarily conclusive because it is arguable that holiday makers have no knowledge of these agreements and so should not be prejudicially affected by their existence. However the formal agreement does create an initial presumption which may be difficult to displace. Furthermore the position regarding the main bone of contention, namely who owns deposits etc held by a travel agent, has to be made clear in brochures which feature ATOL holidays.

Although the matter is not entirely free from doubt, and in any particular case will be affected by the wording of the documentation employed, the authors consider that in most cases a travel agent is not acting as the agent of customers who book package holidays through him—not even where the operator's brochure refers to him as "your" travel agent. This is particularly so in the case of ABTA agents because of the wording of the agency agreements entered into between them and the ABTA tour operators whom they represent. Admittedly, the customer may be able to contest a position purportedly established by an agreement to which he is not a party and of which he is probably not aware. But the absence of any written or express oral agency agreement between a travel agent and its customers makes it difficult to override the written agreements entered into between ABTA operators and agents which, in the authors' opinion, establish ABTA agents as being booking agents for the tour operators whom they represent. In this respect there is an interesting contrast with freight forwarding agents who, like travel agents, do not receive any remuneration from their customers but who enter into written agreements with their customers which clearly establish them as agents for their customers.

In *Kemp* v *Intasun Holidays Ltd*, full details of which are set out on page 170, the issue of whose agent is a travel agent arose peripherally. This case concerned a casual conversation between Mrs Kemp and the travel agent, before the booking for the package holiday had been made, in which Mrs Kemp referred to her husband's asthmatic condition and whether that casual conversation was sufficient to put the defendant, through the travel agent, on notice of Mr Kemp's particular state of health. The Court of Appeal did not find it necessary to hold whose agent the travel agent was, Parker LJ stating:

> "I for my part would not be prepared without further consideration to make any pronouncement upon when, or in what circumstances, the travel agent is or is not the agent of the tour operator or is or is not under a duty to communicate information which he receives to the tour operator."

Kerr LJ did, however, state in the course of his judgment:

> "At the time of that conversation, *Thomas Cook* (the travel agent) *were not the agents of the defendants* . . . Whether they became their agents at a later stage and, if so, for what purpose, it is unnecessary to decide."

6. Monies held by agent

To some extent the question of whose agent a travel agent is is an academic one because of the protection afforded to holiday makers by the law of tort and misrepresentation discussed later in this chapter. However, it can assume great practical significance when a tour operator goes into liquidation and its liquidator claims that monies held by travel agents in respect of holidays which as a result of the liquidation will never take place belong to the tour operator. Because of the standard term 9 included in all ATOLs the position regarding monies held by travel agents on behalf of a collapsed ATOL holder will normally be clear. However, in other cases the ownership of monies held by an agent in respect of bookings taken for a tour operator who goes into liquidation may well depend on whose agent the travel agent is in law.

It was stated by Scrutton LJ in *Fullwood* v *Hurley* [1928] 1 KB 498 that:

> "No agent who has accepted an employment from one principal can in law accept an engagement inconsistent with his duty to the first principal . . . unless he makes the fullest disclosure to each principal of his interest, and obtains the consent of each principal to the double employment".

The writers consider that the problem of conflicts of interest does not arise in relation to the normal activities of travel agents engaged in selling package holidays. They doubt whether travel agents can be regarded as agents of customers as well as booking agents for tour operators. In any event the agent's role in helping members of the public to choose and book their holidays is, it is submitted, not inconsistent with his role as a mere booking agent (as distinct from promotional sales agent) for the tour operators for whom he acts. What would give rise to a conflict would be for an agent who is a party to an express written agreement to hold money received in respect of a confirmed holiday as agent for the operator to allow himself to get into a position in which he is under an obligation to hold the same money as agent for the customer. In the authors' opinion, most travel agents do not allow that to happen.

Although, in the writers' opinion, travel agents, when engaged in connection with package holidays, do not act as agents for "their" customers, this does not mean that they do not act for the customer in certain other matters. For instance, if a customer asks a travel agent to make bookings for a hotel in Paris, the agent may well be acting as agent for the customer even though he receives his remuneration by way of commission from the hotel. It is necessary in relation to any category of work undertaken by travel agents to consider a range of questions (eg is there a formal agency agreement? what role does the travel agent play? what is said in any relevant advertisements? how is the agent paid?) before arriving at a decision. But to do that for anything other than the sale of package holidays is outside the scope of this book.

7. The booking agent role

Brief mention has been made already in this chapter of the travel agent's role as booking agent for the tour operator. This involves the displaying of brochures, the taking of bookings, the subsequent servicing of bookings, and dealing with cancellations. In those cases, and there are some, where the holiday maker selects a holiday from a brochure and asks the agent to book it, the agent's role as the operator's booking agent may be his only role—albeit that in performing it he may owe duties to the holiday maker as well as to the tour operator.

The agent owes a contractual duty to the operator to transmit accurately all details given to him by the holiday maker, such as location, length of stay, departure dates etc. Although it is possible to imply a contract between a booking agent and a customer whereby in consideration of the customer agreeing to book through the agent the agent agrees to exercise all due care in processing the customer's booking, there must be doubts about whether an operator's booking agent, whose sole remuneration consists of a commission from the principal whose tickets, holidays etc he sells, has any *contractual* obligations to "his" customers. In particular it is difficult to formulate a contract which imposes duties in respect of answers to pre-booking queries. The only obvious consideration for obligations which it may be desired to impose on the agent at that stage is that the prospective holiday maker accepts a commitment to book his holiday through the agent. But nobody would seriously contend that an agent who gives advice to a prospective holiday maker is entitled to sue him if he decides to book his holiday through another agent. However, under the general principles of the tort of negligence, the holiday maker is entitled to assume that the travel agent will give accurate answers to questions and process his booking with due care.

In certain circumstances the courts may be prepared to treat a statement intended to have contractual effect as a separate contract or warranty collateral to the main transaction (eg *Esso Petroleum Co Ltd* v *Mardon* [1976] QB 801). Lord Denning MR in *J Evans & Sons (Portsmouth) Ltd* v *Andrea Merzario Ltd* [1976] 1 WLR 1078 stated—

> "When a person gives a promise or an assurance to another, intending that he should act on it by entering into a contract, and he does act on it by entering into the contract, we hold that it is binding".

Shanklin Pier Ltd v *Detel Products Ltd* [1951] 2 KB 854 established that a collateral contract could exist where the main contract was not between the plaintiff and the defendant but the plaintiff and a third party. The plaintiffs, owners of Shanklin Pier, wished to have their pier painted with suitable paint and the defendants, paint manufacturers, assured them that their paint would be suitable. In the plaintiff's contract with the contractors the plaintiffs inserted a term that the defendant's paint would be used. The paint was used, proved to be unsuitable and the plaintiffs sued. It was held that the assurance constituted a contract, collateral to the main contract, the consideration for which was the plaintiff's entry into the main contract on the condition that the defendant's paint was to be used.

A holiday maker's contract for a package holiday is with the tour operator but sometimes a travel agent, in response to pre-booking enquiries will give certain assurances about the standard of the holiday. If these assurances are not based solely upon information supplied by the tour operator, it is possible to contend that a collateral contract exists between the holiday maker and the travel agent. However, it is doubtful whether such a contract, if it exists, would impose liabilities upon a travel agent in excess of those imposed by common law and the Misrepresentation Act 1967.

Even in cases where a customer selects a holiday without asking any questions and then asks the travel agent to effect the booking, it is by no means certain that the agent is merely a booking agent for the operator. As a result of the promotional material employed by travel agents customers can be forgiven for believing that, at least up to the time the operator confirms a booking, the travel agent is acting as agent for them. Looked at in this way the holiday maker uses "his" agent to relay certain information and sums of money to the operator to secure a contract between him and the operator. Operators naturally regard the travel agent as their agent because he has entered into a written agency agreement with them but this does not preclude holiday makers from regarding the travel agents as their agent. That some do so can be seen from the fact that many dissatisfied holiday makers ask the travel agent to take their complaints up with the operator on their behalf, much as they would ask their insurance broker to pursue an insurance policy claim.

Paragraph 1 of ABTA's Code of Conduct for travel agents specifies numerous obligations which in any court case would provide persuasive evidence regarding the standards which a travel agent can reasonably be expected to achieve. Amongst them are:

(i) Travel agents shall maintain a high standard in serving the public and shall comply with all relevant statutory requirements.

(ii) Travel agents shall make every effort to ensure that accurate and impartial information is provided to enable their clients to exercise an informed judgement in making their choice of facilities.

(iii) Travel agents shall make every effort to ensure that their clients are sold tours holidays or travel arrangements compatible with their individual requirements.

(iv) When alterations are made to travel arrangements for which bookings have already been accepted, travel agents shall inform their clients immediately they are advised of the situation and act as intermediaries between their principals and clients in any subsequent negotiations.

(v) Travel agents shall ensure that their counter staff carefully study travel and other literature concerning the services provided in their agency so that they are able to impart accurate information to their clients and to sell more efficiently.

(vi) Travel agents shall ensure that booking forms are completed correctly in every detail. In particular they must ensure that any special requests related to disabilities or medical conditions are noted and passed on effectively to tour operators.

(vii) Travel agents shall draw the attention of their clients to booking and other published conditions applicable to their travel arrangements.

(viii) Travel agents shall draw the attention of their clients to insurance facilities and cover to suit the client's requirements.

(ix) Travel agents shall ensure that all travel and other documents received from principals are checked before delivery to their clients and that any points requiring clarification are explained to their clients.

(x) Travel agents shall advise clients of the health requirements and, as far as practicable, the passport and visa requirements for the journey to be undertaken and shall draw to their attention the availability of the Department of Health leaflet "Protect Your Health Abroad".

A travel agent will usually be liable to a holiday maker in tort if he negligently records, for example, the holiday maker's desired departure dates and effects a booking with the tour operator on the basis of such an error. What must be considered now is whether this means that liability for all resultant damages will attach to the travel agent. *Prima facie,* the answer to this must be in the affirmative. The holiday maker may regard the tour operator as being partly to blame but if the error arose solely through the travel agent's negligent recording of details which were passed on to the operator, the operator will be able to seek a full indemnity from the travel agent. This is because he acted in reliance upon the agent, as he was entitled to do, but the agent failed to exercise the proper care and skill reasonably expected of him. If the holiday maker issues proceedings solely against the tour operator, on the basis that the operator issued the actual tickets and it was presumed that the information given to the agent had been correctly relayed, the operator should join the agent as third party to those proceedings. If proceedings are issued against both operator and agent, the operator should serve a contribution notice upon the agent.

8. Contributory negligence

Would it be possible for the travel agent to allege that the holiday maker had been contributorily negligent through a failure to check the details on the tickets? Although it is perhaps cavalier for a holiday maker not to check his tickets upon receipt, it does not follow that it is incumbent upon him to do so. *Prima facie* he should be entitled to rely upon the travel agent and the tour operator who issues the tickets. This is particularly so if the booking is a late booking and the tickets are collected on the day of departure. Then the holiday maker's primary concern is to ensure a smooth departure and a certain disregard for things such as return dates must be expected.

When, though, the holiday maker has had the tickets in his possession for some weeks, he has had more than sufficient time to check their accuracy. To most people a holiday is still an annual event not to be treated lightly. This point is advanced most strenuously when complaints are made about a holiday but there is no reason to suppose that it should not apply in reverse. Thus, a holiday maker who has failed to check the accuracy of his tickets should, if he claims against the travel agent in tort, be regarded as contributorily negligent and have to bear at least a small percentage of any resultant financial loss. A nominal percentage, such as 10–15% will sometimes be appropriate, but where there is clear evidence that the customer was specifically asked to check his tickets, a significantly higher contribution would seem to be called for.

Obviously any holiday maker who could be shown to have been aware of an error and who relied upon it to obtain financial advantage from the travel agent should not be allowed to do so and should bear any financial loss himself. This would not be an example of contributory negligence. Rather it would be a case where the holiday maker acted in full knowledge of the mistake and any loss does not flow from the mistake but the holiday maker's deliberate actions.

On occasions a travel agent will make a mistake when helping to fill in a customer's booking form for him. The customer should spot it when he reads through the form before signing it. In those rare cases where he does not, there are further opportunities for doing so. Many travel agents provide receipts for deposits which summarise the essential details of the booking. In many cases the customer will at the same time also receive a computerised summary of his booking. About six days after signing and handing over his booking form he should receive a confirmation of booking which he can check. Subsequently he receives a final invoice and the tickets themselves at which time he is normally specifically asked to check them.

Rushed late bookings, sometimes involving collecting tickets at the airport, are a different matter and do occasionally give rise to mistakes which are not discovered in time. And, even with normal bookings, strange misunderstandings occasionally arise and persist. In such circumstances a minute dissection of what happened may be required to apportion responsibility.

On occasions flight times are changed after the initial booking of a holiday. It is then the duty of the tour operator to notify the agent, and of the agent to notify the customer. If the agent fails to pass on such information, or any other material post-booking information which he receives from the operator, he will be liable to make good any resulting loss suffered by the operator or the customer. If he notifies the customer, but in a manner which gives rise to misunderstanding, the apportionment of responsibility will depend on the facts of the particular case.

The subject of mistakes by travel agents in taking bookings is complicated by their role as booking agent for the tour operator. In legal theory the mistake of an agent made when he is acting within the scope of his agency duties is the mistake of his principal. Accordingly, in the circumstances outlined in the preceding paragraphs the customer should have a good claim against the tour operator—who in turn will have a good claim to be indemnified by the travel agent. The customer's claim against the operator could be presented as a claim in contract in which event the doctrine of contributory negligence could not be invoked to reduce it.

9. The agent's role as consultant

(a) The duty of care

Derry v *Peek* (1889) 14 App Cas 337, established that a duty of care in the making of statements did not exist unless the duty arose out of a contractual relationship. However, *Nocton* v *Ashburton* [1914] AC 932, decided that such a duty to take care could arise out of a fiduciary relationship, and that decision was greatly extended by *Hedley Byrne Co Ltd* v *Heller and Partners Ltd* [1964] AC 465.

The relevant facts of *Hedley Byrne* are that the appellants were advertising agents who had placed substantial forward advertising orders for a company on terms by which they were personally liable for the cost of the orders. They asked their bankers to inquire into the company's financial stability and their bankers made inquiries of the respondents, who were the company's bankers. The respondents gave favourable references but stipulated that these were "without responsibility". In reliance on these references the appellants placed orders which resulted in a loss of £17,000. They brought an action against the respondents for damages for negligence.

It was held that a negligent, though honest, misrepresentation, spoken or written, may give rise to an action for damages for financial loss caused thereby, apart from any contract or fiduciary relationship, since the law will imply a duty of care when someone seeking information from a party possessed of a special skill trusts him to exercise due care, and that party knew or ought to have known that reliance was being placed on his skill and judgement. In the *Hedley Byrne* case there was an express disclaimer of responsibility, so no duty of care was implied but travel agents do not normally publish or utter disclaimers of responsibility.

Lord Morris of Borth-y-Gest, in giving judgment, stated:

> "It should now be regarded as settled that if someone possessed of a special skill undertakes, quite irrespective of contract, to apply that skill for the assistance of another person who relies upon such a skill, a duty of care will arise. The fact that the services are to be given by means of or by the instrumentality of words can make no difference. Furthermore if, in a sphere in which a person is so placed that others could reasonably rely upon his judgement or his skill or upon his ability to make careful enquiry, a person takes it upon himself to give information or advice to, or allows this information or advice to be passed on to, another person, who, as he knows or should know, will place reliance upon it, then a duty of care will arise".

It is considered, applying the above and for the following reasons, that a travel agent does owe a holiday maker a duty of care when answering questions, despite the absence of a contractual or fiduciary relationship:

(a) Travel agents hold themselves out as experts in their particular field, and depth of experience is an aspect which large or specialised travel companies are anxious to impart to the public.
(b) Travel agents "take it upon themselves to give information or advice" to the general public.
(c) The public rely—and this is something of which travel agents are aware—upon the agent's skill and expertise, and trust that it will be properly exercised.

(b) Extent of duty of care

How extensive is the travel agent's duty of care? Clearly it applies where he answers questions which are put to him, or volunteers information or advice of his own accord. But is it his duty to advise, even if advice is not sought? To what extent is he entitled to rely upon warnings and advice given to the holiday maker by the tour operator (usually in his brochure)? Is he under a duty to disclose information known to him which could materially affect a particular holiday? If he is, it is also necessary to consider his position as regards the tour operator since disclosure by the agent of adverse information about a particular holiday may be tantamount to advising the holiday maker either not to contract with an operator or to break a contract already made.

The writers consider that travel agents are seldom under a duty to volunteer advice to a holiday maker who chooses a holiday without asking for guidance. If a holiday maker bungles his choice of holiday, he cannot blame the travel agent unless the agent gives a wrong answer to a clear and material question. If the faulty choice is the result of misrepresentations in the operator's brochure, the holiday maker will have a claim against the operator. However, civil liability under Regulation 4 for misleading "descriptive matter" is imposed upon travel agents, as well as tour operators. This new liability is discussed later in this chapter.

It is instructive to compare the agent's responsibilities when selling holidays with his responsibilities when selling air flight tickets. On the face of it they should be the same but, in the writers' opinion, there is a vital difference. Nowadays there are a wide range of special offers, Apexes, Super Apexes etc which provide opportunities for vast savings. The travel agent in his role as expert adviser to "his" customers should have some responsibility to advise them concerning the more obvious possibilities. For instance, if he lets his customer pay the full fare in circumstances where the normal agent would have known of a large (legitimate) discount, he must be vulnerable to a claim under the *Hedley Byrne* principle. But booking a holiday is different. It is a much more personal decision—not just a matter of getting from A to B quickly and cheaply. It is dominated by considerations of taste and personal preference. The agent has a responsibility to answer questions carefully—and to say that he does not know the answer where he does not. But it is doubtful whether more can reasonably be expected of him.

In the writers' submission there is a class of information which a travel agent is legally bound to communicate to holiday makers as a result of his supposed knowledge and expertise. The class is limited, and excludes information which is either highly specialised or commonplace. It is not, for example the travel agent's responsibility to point out to travellers that Beirut is not at present to be recommended for family holidays or that the Costa Brava in August will not afford quiet empty beaches. Nor is it his job to advise upon the circumstances in which an elephant will charge a Landrover. However, it is his duty to counsel the holiday maker about matters known to him but probably not known to the holiday maker which could prevent the holiday maker from reaching his destination or put him at risk once he has arrived.

In January 1983 the Sunday Times revealed that some holiday makers had died in self-catering apartments in the Algarve as a result of carbon monoxide poisoning. It was further revealed that the poisoning was a result of faulty gas heating appliances within the apartments. This was information which very quickly circulated within the holiday industry and caused great concern. The duty of tour operators to notify holiday makers who have booked with them about such a problem seems clear cut. What, though, is the position of a travel agent?

There are two basic types of travel agent whose positions must be considered—those which do not have a tour operations division, and those which do and whose tour operations division ceased to supply package holidays pending rectification of the problem.

There is also a third intermediate category, namely travel agents whose company does not have a tour operations division but which is a member of a group of companies one of which is a tour operator. In legal theory the knowledge of its tour operating affiliate company should not be imputed to such a travel agent but a court might be tempted to depart from that doctrine in the circumstances discussed below.

The same basic duty of care applies to both categories of agent. Customers who have booked through a travel agent rely upon his skill and knowledge of the industry. This reliance, and the agent's attendant duty, cannot be taken to end once the travel agent has effected the holiday maker's booking with the tour operator. It would be illogical and, in the writers' opinion, incorrect to state that a travel agent has a duty to advise a holiday maker of matters known to the agent which could endanger the life of the holiday maker before the operator confirms the booking but that thereafter no such duty exists. Such a duty must, it is submitted, exist up to the date of departure of the holiday maker—either under an extension of the *Hedley Byrne* principle or, more likely, as a result of the neighbourliness principle contained in the tort of negligence.

Accordingly, it is submitted that in the circumstances pertaining to the Algarve the travel agent, irrespective of whether or not he had a tour operations division, owed a duty to holiday makers to do the following:

(a) seek immediate assurances from those tour

operators whose brochures included self catering holidays in the Algarve that their holidays were free from risk and confirmation that such assurances were as a result of inspection by suitably qualified experts (preferably British);

(b) inform the tour operators that their holidays would not be sold pending receipt of the assurances and confirmation sought;

(c) advise those holiday makers who had already booked of the problem and suggest that they contact the relevant tour operator;

(d) advise the tour operators what steps were being taken.

A travel agent with a tour operations division which had withdrawn its own package holidays which utilised apartments thought to be dangerous but continued through its retail division to sell similar holidays provided by other operators would be placed in a particularly anomalous situation which would be difficult to justify either legally or morally.

Some travel agents have available for distribution booklets outlining various requirements for travelling abroad and details of conditions known to be prevalent in some countries. These do not purport to be extensive and usually refer holiday makers to embassies etc at which further detailed enquiries can and should be made. What they do is to put the holiday maker on notice of basic pre-requisites for travelling abroad and gaining entry to the country being visited. It is submitted that this adequately fulfils the travel agent's duty of care. Most travel agents do not have at their fingertips full details of the visa requirements for Outer Mongolia, nor would holiday makers expect them to have such knowledge. What holiday makers do expect is that travel agents will give general advice and put them on notice of, say, medical and visa requirements so that each holiday maker can make his own arrangements. Of course, this is exactly the obligation which is now imposed upon tour operators by Regulation 7 (see page 32).

The position of travel agents who offer specific services

regarding such requirements is different. A detailed consideration of the duties of travel agents offering such services is outside the scope of this book but, in general terms, it is submitted that those agents who take it upon themselves to offer services over and above the norm must assume duties and responsibilities over and above the norm.

A travel agent does not hold himself out as being responsible for the overall well-being of his customers while abroad nor is he so regarded. In particular, a travel agent cannot be presumed to know whether or not a particular individual has special health requirements. It is for the holiday maker to advise the travel agent of these and any failure to do so will absolve the travel agent from liability for any ill-health consequently suffered by the holiday maker.

It can be seen that the travel agent's duty to the holiday maker goes beyond merely conveying statements made by a particular tour operator. There is a wider duty, albeit in limited circumstances, to provide advice and information.

10. Impact of the Regulations

In general, the Regulations do not change the principles set out in the preceding sections. But there are two Regulations – 4 and 5 – which impose new potential liabilities on travel agents.

As discussed in Chapter 2 (page 21), Regulation 4 imposes liability on a tour operator to compensate a holiday maker for any loss or damage suffered as a result of the supply by a tour operator of any "descriptive matter" concerning a package holiday, its price or any other conditions which are "misleading". It also imposes that liability alternatively on a travel agent. The liability will arise if the descriptive matter is "misleading"; it matters not how it came to be misleading. Accordingly, a holiday maker will have a choice whether to bring such a claim against a tour operator or travel agent.

If a claim is brought against a travel agent, in circumstances where the misleading descriptive matter

– for example, a brochure, a leaflet or a video – has been supplied by the tour operator, the agent will wish to obtain an indemnity from the tour operator. Travel agents should ensure that their agency agreements contain specific provision for such an indemnity.

Regulation 5, which is also discussed in Chapter 2 (pages 21–27), imposes obligations in respect of brochure content. Regulation 5(2) provides that no travel agent shall make available a brochure "which he knows or has reasonable cause to believe does not comply" with the requirements of Regulation 5(1). In other words, the travel agent is also in the firing line in respect of brochure content. (Defences are available, and these are discussed in Chapter 6.)

The potential liability of travel agents raises a number of issues –

(a) the extent to which they should check brochures;
(b) systems for monitoring brochure changes;
(c) systems for monitoring brochure inaccuracies, which are brought to their attention by customers.

Particularly for multiple travel agents, it would be wholly impracticable to check that every brochure which they racked complied with Regulation 5(1). Indeed, so far as the accuracy of description of holidays is concerned, it would in practice be impossible – although theoretically possible – to ascertain whether or not a brochure contained every category of information stipulated in Regulation 5(1) and Schedule 1. In the writers' view, the extent of travel agents' obligations is to make random checks to ensure insertion of each category of information and to require from every tour operator a form of certificate, for each brochure, certifying that the brochure complies with Regulation 5(1) and Schedule 1.

It is not uncommon for tour operators to send out errata notices ("erratas"), correcting descriptions of holidays or their cost in brochures. Also, new editions of the same brochure, which may contain changes, are often used. A travel agent who receives errata notices or new editions which contain changes will have "knowledge" that a brochure does not comply with Regulation 5. Accordingly, systems will have to be devised by agents to ensure that the uncorrected brochures are not supplied to holiday makers.

The problem is particularly acute for multiple travel agents. It is impracticable to insert errata slips in every racked brochure. It is also impracticable to place a sticker on every brochure warning of the possibility of errata notices. In the writers' view, the most which can be expected is that –

- travel agents ensure that every retail outlet is fully aware of all errata notices, new brochure editions etc;
- clear and easily visible notices are displayed near the brochure racks advising customers of possible changes and that, before any brochure is removed, a customer should check with a booking clerk to see whether any changes have been made.

Such a system, aside from helping with defences, enables travel agents to argue that there is no "brochure made available" until checks have been made with booking clerks. This would prevent the commission of an offence, although if a booking clerk then failed to mention any changes, one would have been committed.

Finally, travel agents, through customer correspondence, may become aware of brochure inaccuracy/failure to comply with Regulation 5. Again, this would fix travel agents with "knowledge" or "reasonable cause" for knowledge, and lead to the commission of an offence through making available incorrect brochures. Two problems face agents here. One is the establishment of a system to enable centralised collation of such information and its dissemination to every retail outlet. The other is how to deal with the operator.

If there is a minor infraction, a tour operator may not wish to change the brochure. A small agent is in no position to dictate to any of the large operators as to what they should do and, equally, would not even contemplate taking their brochures off the racks. Every agent will have to take its own commercial decision, and ensure that as wide-ranging an indemnity as possible is contained in the agency agreement. The indemnity needs to be carefully considered, and it may be difficult for an agent to obtain a satisfactory one, because it is an indemnity against criminal liability.

11. Conclusion

The obvious conclusion is that a travel agent has different duties to different people, and indeed different duties to the same people. For this reason, although described as an "agent", he does not easily fit in with the general principles of agency law which apply to a "selling agent" and he is, in fact, something of a hybrid. Primarily the travel agent is the agent of the tour operator but there are several important points which distinguish him from a normal selling agent:

(a) Selling agents, when answering questions about their principal's products, can properly be regarded as answering them on behalf of their principals. This is particularly the case where the agent is precluded from selling competitive products—something which practically never occurs in the travel industry. Travel agents often answer questions in their own right, and incur the attendant liabilities for a false or misleading answer.

(b) Many holiday makers regard, and are encouraged to regard, the travel agent as their agent and certain of his duties are consistent with this.

(c) The travel agent has duties of care in tort which to some extent make him a consultant to the customer.

12. Sunday trading

The Shops Act 1950 provides that "shops" are to be closed for the serving of customers on Sundays. The case of *Erewash Borough Council* v *Ilkeston Consumer Co-operative Society Ltd* [1988] The Times 30 June, considered whether or not a travel agent's premises constituted a shop for the purposes of this Act.

The Queen's Bench Divisional Court held that a travel agent's premises did not constitute a shop for the offence of Sunday trading within the meaning of sections 47 and 74 of The Shops Act 1950. The following extracts from the judgment of Bingham LJ should be noted:

(i) "The travel agency was not a shop for no thing was in any ordinary sense offered or sold."

(ii) ". . . A travel agency business was not one where customers resorted to the premises in circumstances comparable with those in which the business of selling goods by retail to similar customers was carried on".

(iii) "The travel agent's business of booking hotel accommodation and issuing travel tickets was not at all closely comparable with or analogous to the typical retail shopkeeper's activity of selling goods across the counter or off the supermarket shelf."

The upshot of this case is that travel agents are at present free to trade on Sundays. The distinction drawn by the Divisional Court does seem somewhat semantic. Its implication is that services can but goods cannot be exchanged for reward on a Sunday.

Chapter 6

False and misleading statements

1. Introduction

Tour operators and, to a lesser extent, travel agents are frequently accused by customers of making false or misleading statements regarding the facilities available on a package holiday. In most cases the complaints relate to statements made in the tour operator's brochure, such as that a lift or a tennis court is available at a hotel when it is not, or that all rooms have a view of the sea when some do not, or that there is a good bus service to the nearest town whereas buses are practically non-existent. They can also be about oral statements made by either the tour operator or the travel agent. All such statements (whether oral or written) are usually referred to as representations.

Under common law a representation must be a statement of *fact,* past or present, as distinct from a statement of opinion (*Sanders* v *Gall* [1952] CPL 343), or of intention (*Angus* v *Clifford* [1891] 2 Ch 449), or of law (*Beesly* v *Hallwood Estates Ltd* [1961] Ch 105). Further, it must be a statement of fact made before the contract is entered into or be incorporated as a term of the contract. Civil liability in respect of erroneous statements will be on the grounds of misrepresentation, which is the subject of the Misrepresentation Act 1967, and also of breach of Regulation 4 and various common law principles. Criminal liability, in so far as the travel industry is concerned, will stem from breaches of s.14 of the Trade Descriptions Act 1968, of Part III of the Consumer Protection Act 1987 and of Regulation 5.

2. Criminal liability – Trade Descriptions Act 1968

(a) Section 14, Trade Descriptions Act 1968

Section 14(1) reads as follows:

> "It shall be an offence for any person in the course of any trade or business:
>
> (a) to make a statement which he knows to be false; or
>
> (b) recklessly to make a statement which is false;
>
> as to any of the following matters that is to say—
>
> (i) the provision in the course of any trade or business of any services, accommodation or facilities;
>
> (ii) the nature of any services, accommodation or facilities provided in the course of any trade or business;
>
> (iii) the time at which, manner in which or persons by whom any services, accommodation or facilities are so provided;
>
> (iv) the examination, approval or evaluation by any person of any services, accommodation or facilities so provided; or
>
> (v) the location or amenities of any accommodation so provided".

It should be noted that (i) to (v) qualify both subsections (a) and (b).

Various other passages from s.14 should also be noted:

> "For the purposes of this section—
>
> (a) anything (whether or not a statement as to any of the matters specified in the preceding subsection) likely to be taken for such a statement as to any of those matters as would be false shall be deemed to be a false statement as to that matter;
>
> (b) a statement made regardless of whether it is

> true or false shall be deemed to be made recklessly, whether or not the person making it had reasons for believing that it might be false". (s.14(2))

"In this section 'false' means false to a material degree . . ." (s.14(4)).

(b) *Enforcement of section 14*

Section 14 is enforced by Trading Standards Departments of local authorities. Local Trading Standards Officers work in liaison with the Department of Prices and Consumer Protection and the Office of Fair Trading and must report to the OFT any prosecutions brought under the Act. Although prosecutions are normally brought by Trading Standards Departments, it is open to an individual to bring a private prosecution.

For a successful prosecution to take place under s.14 the prosecution must show that a relevant statement of fact has been made; that at the time of making it was false; and that at that time the maker knew it to be false or was reckless as to its falsity. A relevant statement of fact may be one about services, accommodation or facilities to be provided by someone other than the persons making the statement. This proposition was categorically laid down in *Bambury* v *Hounslow Borough Council* [1971] RTR 1 (DC). Statements of fact made by tour operators about their package holidays and the services provided by, say, hoteliers do therefore come within the ambit of the Act.

Reported cases on prosecutions of travel companies under s.14 appear to involve only tour operators. If a travel agent makes a false statement about a package holiday, he will probably merely be repeating something which appears in the operator's brochure in which event it may be difficult for the prosecution to satisfy the court that the statement was made either knowingly or recklessly. It is possible for a travel agent to make a false statement of fact about services which he himself offers to assist customers in making their holiday arrangements but in practice it is not very likely.

(c) *Meaning of "false statement"*

It was established by *Breed* v *Cluett* [1970] 2 QB 459, that for the purposes of s.14 the false statement of fact need not induce the contract and that it can be made during the existence of the contract.

There have been no cases to date which have specifically reviewed the meaning of "false to a material degree". However, two cases in 1972/73 did indicate that the 1968 Act was not meant to cover what were in effect mere breaches of warranties. To create a criminal offence something more serious must have occurred. In *R* v *Clarksons Holidays Limited* (1972) 57 Cr App Rep 38, it was declared that "the count as framed converted what was at worst a breach of contract into a crime". The facts of this case involve a description of a hotel in Spain which was depicted in Clarkson's brochure by a drawing qualified by the words "Artist's impression of Hotel Calypso". The holiday maker requested a room with a balcony and Clarksons confirmed that this facility would be available. When the holiday maker arrived at the hotel, he complained that the balcony did not match its description in the brochure. Clarksons were convicted in the first instance but the Court of Appeal quashed the conviction making the comment mentioned above. It should be noted in passing that Clarksons were prosecuted on 10 counts in all and that the Court of Appeal upheld their conviction on the remaining counts. The 1973 case which reiterated this ruling was *Beckett* v *Cohen* [1973] 1 All ER 120.

(d) *Mens rea*

Section 14(1)(a) requires knowledge of the false statement of fact. Following the decision of the Divisional Court in *Wings Limited* v *Ellis* [1984] 1 All ER 1046 (the facts of which are set out later in this chapter) it had been thought that some element of dishonesty was required to impose liability. However, the view taken by the Divisional Court was the subject of an appeal to the House of Lords ([1984] 3 All ER 577).

The certified question for the opinion of the House of

Lords was "whether a defendant may properly be convicted of an offence under section 14(1)(a) of the Trade Descriptions Act 1968 where he has no knowledge of the falsity of the statement at the time of its original publication but knew of it at the time when the statement was read by the complainant". Their Lordships answered this question in the affirmative, holding that where a holiday company innocently issues brochures giving false information and takes steps to correct them immediately it discovers its mistake, it nevertheless commits a breach of section 14(1)(a) if a customer is subsequently issued with an uncorrected brochure, unless it can avoid strict liability by invoking one of the statutory defences specified in ss. 23 and 24.

The effect of the House of Lords decision is that unless a tour operator can successfully invoke one of the statutory defences, it will be liable under s.14(1)(a) for a false statement made in a brochure if, at the time the brochure comes into the hands of a customer it knows that a statement in it is false even though it believes that all copies held by its agents have been corrected.

(e) Recklessness

The question of what is or is not reckless as defined by the Act was specifically dealt with in *MFI Warehouses Ltd* v *Nattrass* [1973] 1 All ER 762. In this case the appellants issued an advertisement containing the words "folding doors gear (carriage free)" and offered folding door sets on 14 days approval. Two purchasers thought that the folding door gear sets could be bought separately without the doors. One of them found that he was expected to pay carriage on the gear set and the other discovered that he could not obtain it on approval without paying for it before despatch. The appellant's chairman had examined the advertisement for some 10 minutes before approving it but had not appreciated that it offered the gear set as an item which could be bought separately. The Divisional Court (Lord Widgery CJ, Ashworth and Willis JJ), in upholding conviction under s.14(1)(b), held—

(i) while the word "recklessly" in the context of section 14 did not involve dishonesty, it was not necessary to prove that the statement was made with the degree of irresponsibility which was implied in the phrase "careless whether it be true or false";

(ii) it was sufficient in this case for the prosecution to show that the advertiser did not have regard to the truth or falsity of his advertisement even though it could not be shown that he was deliberately closing his eyes to the truth, or that he had any kind of dishonest intention.

The criteria for deciding whether a statement of fact is misleading to such an extent as to come within the ambit of the 1968 Act were one of the matters considered in *British Airways Board* v *Taylor* [1976] 1 All ER 65. The following comment of Viscount Dilhorne should particularly be noted—

> "indeed, it is an essential feature of the Act that, when it has to be considered whether descriptions or statements are misleading, it is the meaning which they are likely to bear to the person or persons to whom they are addressed that matters, and not the meaning which they might, on analysis, bear to a trained legal mind".

Section 24(1) of the Act, which, *inter alia,* applies to possible offences under both paras. (a) and (b) of s.14(1), provides that:

> "In any proceedings for an offence under this Act it shall, subject to sub-section 2 of this section, be a defence for the person charged to prove—
>
> (a) that the commission of the offence was due to a mistake or to reliance on information supplied to him or to the act or default of another person, an accident or some other cause beyond his control; and
>
> (b) that he took all reasonable precautions and exercised all diligence to avoid the commission of such an offence by himself or any person under his control".

(Subsection 2 merely refers to the need to give notice to the prosecution that this defence will be relied upon.)

The difficulty with this defence is that if the court decides that the defendant has acted recklessly, it is difficult to see how he can successfully contend that he has taken all reasonable precautions and exercised all due diligence. A tour operator who is prosecuted under s.14(1)(b) for, say, failing to notify a holiday maker of a change of itinerary on a coach tour can plead not guilty, relying upon the provision of details about the operator's normal *modus operandi* in such circumstances and the fact (if it is true) that only one person out of, say, 50 had not been notified. If the court still considers that the operator has been reckless, he has ready-made grounds for a plea of mitigation. If only one person out of, say, 2,000 had not been notified, it is submitted that there are good grounds not only for proving the absence of recklessness but also for showing that all reasonable precautions and diligence had been exercised in an effort to avoid commission of the offence.

The standard of proof required to establish recklessness was refined and raised by the *Wings Limited* v *Ellis* case. The pertinent facts of this case are that on 13 January 1982 a Mr Wade booked, through travel agents, a holiday with Wings Limited for himself and his wife at the Seashells Hotel, Nogombo, Sri Lanka commencing on 3 March 1982. Mr Wade booked his holiday in reliance upon Wing's Brochure entitled *Wings Faraway Holidays Winter Oct 1981/Apr 1982,* which stated that the bedrooms at the hotel were air conditioned, and contained a photograph which purported to be of the hotel but was not. The photograph had originally been approved by the contracts manager and it was only someone with personal knowledge of the hotel, such as the contracts manager, who could have detected the error. Wings discovered the error in May 1981 and by a memorandum dated 1 June 1981 instructed their staff to amend their brochures, to inform travel agents of the error and to inform customers of the error when bookings were being made. Further, a letter was despatched to customers who had already booked holidays. When Mr Wade booked his holiday some seven months after discovery of the error, neither Wings nor the travel agents advised him of it. Wings were prosecuted, and convicted by a magistrates' court, of knowingly making a false statement contrary to s.14(1)(a) (this related to the statement in the brochure that the hotel bedrooms were air conditioned) and of recklessly making a false statement contrary to s.14(1)(b) (this related to the inclusion in the brochure of the incorrect photograph).

Wings appealed against both convictions. Various questions were referred to the Divisional Court in the case stated and some of those which it answered are set out below with the answers:

> "Whether the two facts (a) that the appellant's customer Mr Wade read the brochure containing the statement 'AC' (this refers to air conditioning) on 13 January 1982 and (b) that employees of the appellant discovered that the said statement was false before that date in about May 1981, by themselves suffice to support a conviction of the appellant under s.14(1)(a) of knowingly making a false statement, regardless of any other evidence, or of evidence that Mr Wade's travel agent in common with all other persons inquiring about bookings at the Seashells Hotel was told that it was not air conditioned?"
>
> *Answer: No (Reversed by the House of Lords)*
>
> "Whether to secure a conviction under s.14(1)(b) it was necessary for the prosecution to prove recklessness on the part of an employee of the appellant responsible for the publication of the said brochure?"
>
> *Answer: No*
>
> "Whether there was evidence on which the court could make the finding of fact made by it that the appellant was reckless?"
>
> *Answer: No*
>
> "Whether to secure a conviction under s.14(1)(b) it was necessary for the prosecution to prove recklessness on the part of a director or a controlling manager of the appellant who represents the

directing mind and will of the company and controls what it does?"

Answer: Yes

As regards liability for recklessness under s.14(1)(b), Mr Justice Mann, who read the judgment of the court, made the following particularly noteworthy comments:

> "A company cannot be guilty of an offence unless the specified state of mind was a state of mind of a person who is or forms part of the directing mind and will of the company . . . We can find nothing in the evidence which suggests that a person ruling the company was privy to the selection of the photograph. In particular, we reject the respondent's suggestion that Michael Stephenson who approved the photograph and who variously called himself a "long haul development manager" and the "contracts manager" could be inferred to be a member of the relevant class. The most that could be said for the respondent (ie against Wings) is that the members of this class, although establishing a system, failed to establish a system which would have prevented the mistake which occurred. That failure cannot, in our judgment, constitute "recklessness". There may be cases where the system is such that he who establishes it could not be said to be having regard to the truth or falsity of what emerged from it but that is not this case".

The Wings case indicates that tour operators who discover mistakes and take proper steps in accordance with an established system to notify customers of them cannot be successfully prosecuted under s.14(1)(b) merely because of an isolated failure in the system. But it will be paramount for there to be a well established and *provable* system. The absence of such a system, and of proof of steps taken to correct false statements, will render likely a successful prosecution under s14(1)(b).

In *Yugotours Ltd.* v *Wadsley* [1988] The Guardian 3 June, the Divisional Court heard an appeal by Yugotours against a conviction under section 14(1)(b). The relevant facts were that Yugotours' 1986 summer brochure advertised a holiday headed Adriatic Island Adventure with a photograph of a three-masted schooner and a description of the holiday offered, including the words "the excitement of being under sail on board this majestic schooner" and "lie back and enjoy the wind-filled sails". A letter dated 13 March 1986 to customers stated, *inter alia*, "your cruise will be a combination of sailing and motor sailing" and went on to state that the schooner had a minimum of two showers.

Two customers, who booked the holiday with Yugotours, complained that the schooner provided for them was not the one in the brochure, was not three-masted, had no sails and only had one shower. Trading Standards officers instituted proceedings against Yugotours on the grounds, *inter alia*, that the schooner provided was not the one depicted in the brochure, that it had one shower, not two, and that the cruise was not a combination of sailing and motor sailing.

Yugotours claimed, and this emerged from the evidence, that in September 1985 they had contracted with another company to provide a schooner with sails but, at some undetermined point, bookings became too great and Yugotours, in obtaining another vessel, arranged for a two-masted schooner to be provided. This was, though, before the letter of 13 March.

The Divisional Court upheld the conviction of Yugotours by the magistrates under section 14(1)(b). In the course of his judgment, Parker LJ stated that if a statement is false and is known to be false, and nothing whatever is done to correct it, the company making the statement can properly be found guilty of recklessness notwithstanding the absence of specific evidence. The state of mind envisaged by section 14(1)(b) is one which can only be a matter of inference and there was sufficient evidence from which such an inference could be drawn.

(f) Compensation

Prosecutions under the Act do not preclude civil proceedings. Although not widely invoked, it should be borne in mind that, under s. 35 of the Powers of

Criminal Courts Act 1973 (as amended by s.67 of the Criminal Justice Act 1982), the court can (if an application is made to it) make an award against the defendant in favour of the individual who first brought the matter to the notice of the Trading Standards Department if he has suffered any loss. In *R* v *Thomson Holidays Limited* [1974] 1 All ER 823, for example, Thomson Holidays were ordered to pay compensation to the original complainants. This order was upheld by the Court of Appeal which stated that the court had to consider under s.1(1) of the 1972 Act whether the loss or damage could fairly be said to have resulted from the offence for which the accused had been convicted. Compensation is presently limited to £5,000 per complainant in the magistrates' court, or "such amount as the court considers appropriate" in the Crown Court. The maximum fine under the Trade Descriptions Act is also £5,000 (on summary conviction – it is unlimited for conviction on indictment) but a prosecution can be brought on more than one count in respect of the same booking and it is each count which has a limit of £5,000.

The pertinent facts of the Thomson Holidays case mentioned above were that, following the distribution in August and September 1970 of two million copies of Thomson's brochure for the 1971 season, two complaints were made by unrelated individuals about the amenities described at a particular hotel in Greece. Separate prosecutions were instituted. At the hearing of the first, Thomsons pleaded guilty but at the second entered a plea of *autrefois convict*—ie that they could not be convicted twice for the same offence. The Court of Appeal held that this was not a valid plea. A false statement is made within the meaning of s.14(1)(b) when it is communicated to someone and each time a false statement in a brochure is communicated to a reader a fresh offence is committed. Thus, a tour operator whose brochure contains a false statement within the meaning of the Act could, in theory, have separate prosecutions brought against him by every person who reads his brochure.

(g) Time at which statement is made

The Court of Appeal in *R* v *Thomson Holidays Limited* held that a new statement was made on every occasion that an interested member of the public read it in a brochure published by a company engaged in attracting custom. It considered that communication was of the essence of making a statement. The House of Lords, in reaching their decision regarding the question referred to it in the *Wings* case, also considered the question of when a statement is made for the purposes of s.14(1)(a). Their decision is best summarised by the following extracts from the judgment of Lord Hailsham:

> "The Divisional Court used the authority of *R* v *Thomson Holidays* [1974] QB 592, 597 to establish the general proposition, taken out of context, that 'a statement is made when it is communicated to someone'.
>
> When, in the course of trade or business, a brochure containing a false statement was issued in large numbers through a chain of distribution involving several stages, and was intended to be read and used at all or some of the stages, it did not follow that it was only 'made at its ultimate destination'.
>
> It might be 'made' when posted in bulk, when the information was passed on by telephone or in smaller batches in the post, and when it was read by the ultimate recipient – provided that at each stage what happened was in accordance with the original intention of the issuing house.
>
> The statement in the present case was made when Mr. Wade read the brochure on January 13th 1982. It might also have been made at various other stages in the chain of distribution, and was certainly made to other recipients. On January 13th 1982 Wings knew that the hotel was not air conditioned, and therefore knew that the statement, if made in its uncorrected form (as it was), was false."

Lord Scarman stated in *Wings* v *Ellis* that it was unnecessary for the Court of Appeal in *Thomson* to hold that communication was of the essence of a statement. In his view, which is now the law, a statement in a brochure is originally made when the brochure is first published. But further statements to the same effect are made whenever persons do business with the operator on the strength of the uncorrected brochure.

(h) Statements of intention

The 1968 Act does not cover a statement of intention or future promise which is unfulfilled. This is because the statement is neither true nor false at the time it is made. The Court of Appeal, in *R* v *Sunair Holidays Limited* [1973] 2 All ER 1233, specifically held that s.14(1) of the Act had no application to statements which amounted to promises regarding the future and so which, when they were made, could not have the character of being either true or false. However it did state, *per curiam,* that a promise about the future may be within s.14 if it can be construed as an implied statement of present intention, means or belief which is false at the time of making and is made knowingly or recklessly. The case involved Sunair's 1970 brochure and *inter alia,* a statement that a hotel in Spain would have a swimming pool. The hotel's season began on 7 March 1970 and ended on 6 October. Its owners planned to improve it during the winter of 1969-70 and builders were instructed to construct a swimming pool on the roof immediately the hotel closed for the 1969-70 winter season. Building work progressed slowly and, when the brochure was read by the complainants — 7 January 1970 — the hotel was closed and the pool incomplete. Further, when the complainants arrived at the hotel on 27 May 1970, they discovered; that the pool could not be filled with water because it had not been properly completed. The Court of Appeal quashed Sunair's conviction under s.14(1)(b) on the basis that the comments in their brochure about the swimming pool related to the future but stated that, had the charges in the indictment been framed to the effect that the brochure impliedly represented that satisfactory arrangements had already been made for the provision of the facilities for services in the future and that such arrangements had not, in fact, been made at the time of the brochure, Sunair would have been convicted.

(i) Overbooking

This case should be contrasted with that of *British Airways Board* v *Taylor* [1976] 1 All ER 65. The facts were as follows. BOAC wrote on 14 August 1973 to a passenger, who had paid in advance, confirming his reservation for a specified flight on a particular date and at a particular time. Unknown to the passenger, BOAC operated a deliberate policy of overbooking whereby passengers were booked in excess of space on each flight. When BOAC wrote on 14 August 1973 the flight was not overbooked but it was at the time of the flight and the passenger was not allowed on board. The House of Lords held that the letter and ticket would be understood as a statement of fact that the booking was certain, which statement, in view of the overbooking policy, was false within s.14(1) of the 1968 Act since the passenger was exposed to the risk that he might not get a seat. It should be noted, in passing, that British Airways Board escaped liability on the grounds that the statement had been made by BOAC and not by British Airways Board which had replaced BOAC following BOAC's dissolution in 1974.

The question of overbooking will now be considered with specific reference to overbooking by foreign hoteliers. If a tour operator issues a confirmation invoice to a holiday maker that accommodation will be available at a particular hotel in, say, Greece but upon the holiday maker's arrival accommodation is not available at the hotel, will the tour operator be liable under s.14(1)(b)? It will be assumed for the purposes of this question that the tour operator had a contract for accommodation with the hotelier and that it was the hotelier who operated the policy of overbooking. The following are the material considerations:

(a) By analogy with the *British Airways Board* v *Taylor* case, the confirmatory invoice is a statement of fact. Subject to the wording of the particular invoice, it would not normally be a statement of fact that accommodation had been booked in a specific room at a specific hotel for a specific period but that accommodation had been arranged at a specific hotel for a specific period.

(b) At the time of the confirmatory invoice was the statement of fact false?

(c) Was the statement made recklessly?

(d) The facts which affect (b) and (c) above must be considered together since the same facts are material to each point. Whether or not a prosecution will be successful must depend upon the contractual arrangements between the tour operator and the hotelier. If, before the issue of the confirmatory invoice, the operator had concluded a contract with the hotelier to the effect that, say, twenty rooms would be available per day for the period June to September for occupation by clients of the operator, and if, at the time of the issue of the confirmatory invoice, the operator had not already confirmed bookings for twenty other rooms for the period during which the client in question was to stay, it is difficult to see how the operator can be said to be making a statement which is false—let alone be making a false statement recklessly. An arbitrary act of the hotelier, over which act the operator had no control, has created the overbooking.

(e) Most tour operators do have a system of making block bookings at apartments. So long as the operator's confirmatory invoice cannot be interpreted as stating that a specific room has been booked, and so long as the operator is not exceeding his allocation, it appears to follow that no false statement of fact has been made by the operator.

(f) The operator should be entitled to rely upon his contract with the hotelier. In normal circumstances it is unreasonable to suggest that at the time of making a booking with a holiday maker the operator should check with the hotelier that the accommodation contracted for is still available.

3. Criminal liability – Consumer Protection Act 1987

Part III of The Consumer Protection Act 1987 ("the 1987 Act") makes it a criminal offence for a business to give a misleading price indication to consumers about goods, services, accommodation or facilities. It came into force on 1 March 1989 together with regulations – the Price Indications Regulations 1988 – and a Code of Practice regarding its interpretation.

It is beyond the scope of this book to provide a detailed analysis of the 1987 Act. What follows is a brief summary of the relevant provisions.

The 1987 Act creates two offences. The first is contained in s.20(1) which provides that:

> "A person shall be guilty of an offence if, in the course of any business of his, he gives (by any means whatever) to any consumers an indication which is misleading as to the price at which any goods, services, accommodation or facilities are available (whether generally or from particular persons)."

This section will apply however the price indication is given – whether in a TV or press advertisement, in a catalogue or leaflet, or notices in windows or even orally (say over the telephone).

Section 20(6) defines price. It makes it clear that the total sum to be paid is to be regarded as the price. The Code of Practice advises traders to "make clear in your price indications the full price customers will have to pay for the product". For example, the price should include VAT. There is also a section in the Code of Practice which deals with "holidays and travel prices". The following points should be noted:

(a) If a variety of prices is offered, the brochure should make clear the basic price and what are optional additional charges.

(b) Any non-optional extra charges which are for fixed amounts should be included in the basic price.

(c) Details of non-optional extra charges which may vary, such as holiday insurance, should be made clear to customers in the brochure near to the information on the basic price.

(d) If there are any circumstances in which prices could be increased after customers have made their booking (for example a surcharge), this must be clearly stated with all indications of prices together with details of where in the brochure customers will find full information on the circumstances in which an increase could be made.

A price indication includes not only a statement as to price but also a comparison with another price. The Code of Practice deals at some length with price comparisons. The principal points to note are:

(a) Price comparisons should always state the higher price and the intended price. "Reduced to £50.00" is wrong: the price from which the reduction has been made should also be given.

(b) It should be made clear what sort of price the higher price is. For example, comparisons with something described in terms such as "regular price", "usual price" or "normal price" should say whose regular, usual or normal price it is (ie "our normal price").

The 1988 Regulations further qualify the position on price comparison. They make it clear that a comparison with an earlier price is only authorised where it has been charged for a continuous period of not less than twenty-eight days within a period of six months before the new price. It is also necessary that the earlier price related to the supply of the relevant item at the same premises.

The second offence under the 1987 Act is contained in s.20(2). It makes it an offence for a person in the course of his business to give a price indication which, after it was given, has become misleading unless he takes all reasonable steps to prevent consumers from relying on it. It is a prerequisite for this offence to have been committed that some or all of those consumers to whom the price indication was given might reasonably be expected to rely on it at a time after it became misleading.

The Code of Practice comments upon this offence with particular reference to the holiday industry. It recommends as follows:

(a) Tour operators who sell direct to holiday makers must make the correct price clear when a package holiday is being booked, indicating where the original price is misleading. This must be done before the holiday maker has entered into a contract for the package holiday.

(b) If a price indication becomes misleading while a brochure is current, all travel agents to whom the tour operator has distributed the brochure must be advised. Further, tour operators should be prepared to cancel any bookings made on the basis of a misleading price indication.

(c) Travel agents who are advised of a misleading price indication must ensure that the correct price is made clear to holiday makers before a booking is made.

The Code of Practice is most important. It provides guidance as to the interpretation of the 1987 Act. Breach of the Code will not in itself give rise to any criminal or civil liability (s.25(2) of the 1987 Act); but failure to follow it will be used as evidence of an offence.

The 1987 Act applies not only to tour operators but also to travel agents. For an offence to be committed it is not necessary for the person making the price indication to be the person providing the holiday.

There are various defences to prosecutions brought under s.20(1) and s.20(2). The five possible defences to a prosecution under s.20(1) are contained in s.24(1)–(4) and s.39. The three possible defences to a prosecution under s.20(2) are contained in s.24(1)–(3).

Section 25(2)(b) states that:

> "Compliance by that person (ie the defendant) with such a code (ie the Code) may be relied on in relation

to any matter for the purpose of showing that the commission of the offence by that person has not been established or that that person has a defence."

This makes it clear that the Code of Practice will be of immense importance in defending any prosecutions.

Section 24(1) provides that it is a defence for a defendant to show that the acts or omissions allegedly creating the offence were authorised by regulations made under s.26. Section 26 gives the Secretary of State the power to introduce regulations which, for example, govern the way in which price indications may be given. The Price Indications Regulations 1988 were introduced pursuant to s.26.

Section 24(2) provides that if the price indication complained of is published in any book, newspaper, magazine, film or radio or television broadcasts or in a programme included in a cable programme service, it will be a defence to show that the indication was not contained in an advertisement.

Section 24(3) is what could be described as the "publishers" defence. It applies if the defendant can show that, in the course of his business, he publishes advertisements, that he received the advertisement in question for publication in the ordinary course of his business, and at the time of publication did not know and had no grounds for suspecting that the publication would involve commission of the offence. The third limb of the defence is important. If the "publisher" becomes aware that there are persistent complaints about a particular advertisement, it may be difficult for him to show that he did not suspect the publication would involve the commission of the offence. The burden of proof will rest with the defendant.

Travel agents who give misleading price indications based on documentation, promotional literature etc from tour operators may well be able to take advantage of the defence in s.24(4). It provides that it is a defence if:

"(a) The indication did not relate to the availability from him of any goods, services, accommodation or facilities;

(b) A price had been recommended to every person from whom the goods, services, accommodation or facilities were indicated as being available;

(c) The indication related to that price, and was misleading as to that price only by reason of a failure by any person to follow the recommendation;

(d) It was reasonable for the person who gave the indication to assume that the recommendation was for the most part being followed."

Section 39 provides that it is a defence to show that "all reasonable steps" were taken and "all due diligence" exercised to avoid committing the offence. The burden of proving this lies with the defendant.

Where this defence involves an allegation that the commission of the offence was due to the act or default of another or to reliance on information given by another, it is necessary to serve on the prosecution a notice identifying the person who committed the act or default or who gave the information. If the defence involves an allegation of reliance on information from another, it will be necessary to satisfy the court that it was reasonable in all the circumstances to rely on the information having regard in particular:

(a) "to the steps which he (the defendant) took and those which might reasonably have been taken for the purpose of verifying information; and

(b) to whether he had any reason to disbelieve the information."

This sub-section also makes it clear that those who on the face of it may be unconnected with an offence but who have been put on notice of, for example, complaints or previous offences may not be able to escape a successful prosecution. The 1987 Act is enforced by Trading Standards Officers.

4. Criminal liability – the Regulations

Chapters 2, 4 and 5 have discussed the obligations imposed upon tour operators and travel agents by Regulations 5, 7,

8, 16 and 22. Breach of any of those regulations results in a criminal offence. Liability, however, is not strict. Under Regulation 24(1) there is the following possible defence:

> "Subject to the following provisions of this regulation, in proceedings against any person for an offence under Regulation 5, 7, 8, 16 or 22 of these Regulations, it shall be a defence for that person to show that he took all reasonable steps and exercised all due diligence to avoid committing the offence."

This defence is similar to those available under the Trade Descriptions Act and the Consumer Protection Act. It will be available if the tour operator or travel agent can show that he took all reasonable steps and exercised all due diligence to avoid committing the offence. It is not sufficient to demonstrate simply that all reasonable steps were taken. In addition, it must be shown that all due diligence was exercised. That due diligence test will have to be applied in two ways: the first is to show that all reasonable steps equate to the exercise of all due diligence; the second is to show that in carrying out the reasonable steps all due diligence was exercised.

In relation to Regulations 5, 7 and 8, it will be necessary for a tour operator or travel agent to demonstrate that –

(a) proper systems have been established to ensure proper compilation of brochures and of the requisite information, and their dissemination;

(b) procedures exist to monitor the above systems;

(c) steps have been taken to ensure proper addition, and notification, of corrections.

In an ideal world, these procedures will be contained in instruction manuals made available to all staff. Where procedures involve use of Viewdata systems it is possible to programme the systems to ensure that certain things, such as mentioning visa requirements, must be done before the booking clerk can move on to the next step. The essence of the defence is that a one-off, or inexplicable, error has arisen.

In relation to the financial protection offences under

Regulations 16 and 22, it is rather more difficult to see how the defence can arise. To evaluate an adequate level of security will involve taking the period of highest bookings/receipt of monies/customer travelling and arranging a bond level to cover that. If a lower bond level is arranged for economic reasons, it is difficult to see that the defence could be invoked. Equally, it is rather hard to see how a tour operator could allege that, through an oversight, no bonding or insurance or trust monies arrangements were put in place.

A refinement to the defence exists where the tour operator or travel agent alleges that the commission of the offence was due to the act of another or reliance on information supplied by another. But, to be able to use the defence in this way, the operator or agent, pursuant to Regulation 24(4), must be able to show that –

> "... it was reasonable in all the circumstances for him to have relied on the information, having regard in particular –
>
> (a) to the steps which he took, and those which might reasonably have been taken, for the purpose of verifying the information; and
>
> (b) to whether he had any reason to disbelieve the information."

As regards Regulation 5, in the writers' view it should, in general terms, be reasonable for travel agents to rely upon assertions by tour operators that their brochures comply with Regulation 5. It would be harsh to impose any duty to check. But if a travel agent does not even enquire of a tour operator whether or not a brochure complies, it may well be that the travel agent would not be able to rely upon the defence.

Regulation 7 deals *inter alia* with visas and health formalities. In the writers' view, the obligation rests with tour operators. Where a tour operator obtains information from an embassy, or from an organisation such as the World Health Organisation, or from Department of Health leaflets on health, a tour operator should be able to rely upon it. There will, however, be a need for tour operators to check on a regular basis that there have been no changes.

In many circumstances, a tour operator may rely on a travel agent to disseminate, or even provide, the information. In that case, for a tour operator to be able to rely on the defence, the authors consider that the tour operator will need to have established and expressly agreed with the agents the procedures upon which the tour operator relies. It may even be that the operator should make random checks to ensure that the agent is doing what the operator expects.

So far as Regulations 16 and 22 are concerned, again it is difficult to see how a tour operator could use the defence. Whichever of the bonding, insurance or trust monies alternatives are to be used to provide financial security, the onus must rest with the operator to check proper execution etc of the relevant documents. It is possible, however, that wherever professional advice has been sought as to the level of financial security or its method, and that advice was wrong, the operator would justifiably be able to claim reliance on the professional advice.

Where the defence involves allegations of default on the part of another etc, Regulation 24(2) contains the following procedural requirement –

> "Where in any proceedings against any person for such an offence the defence provided by paragraph (1) above involves an allegation that the commission of the offence was due –
>
> (a) to the act or default of another; or
>
> (b) to reliance on information given by another,
>
> that person shall not, without the leave of the court, be entitled to rely on the defence unless, not less than seven clear days before the hearing of the proceedings, or, in Scotland, the trial diet, he has served a notice under paragraph (3) below on the person bringing the proceedings."

The person to whom the notice must be given is the prosecution. The notice must identify or assist in identifying the person blamed for commission of the offence.

Where a tour operator or travel agent is other than an individual, Regulation 25 provides that "any director, manager, secretary or other similar officer of the body corporate" may be prosecuted as well as the body corporate. Such a prosecution will only take place if the offence is shown to have been committed with the "consent or connivance of, or to be attributable to any neglect" on the part of such person.

In cases of simple omission or false brochure description, it seems unlikely that there will be individual prosecutions. Where, however, deliberate decisions to flout the Regulations have been taken, it is much more likely; and this is particularly so in respect of any failure to arrange adequate financial security where the consequences of breach may well be especially severe for holiday makers.

5. Civil liability

Civil liability in respect of false or misleading statements can arise from written or oral representations by either tour operator or travel agent. The reader should keep in mind the two basic principles outlined at the start of this chapter, namely that a representation must be a statement of fact and that it must be made before the contract is entered into or form one of its terms. It should also be borne in mind that misrepresentation can give rise to actions based in contract or in tort. The contractual action will normally be between the tour operator and the holiday maker—they are the principals to the contract and it is generally only the principals who can sue or be sued upon the contract. Actions for tortious misrepresentation will normally be brought by the holiday maker against the travel agent, with whom alone the holiday maker is in personal contact.

This chapter merely considers the circumstances in which liability may attach to a tour operator and/or travel agent as a result of a misrepresentation made to a holiday maker. It also revisits Regulation 4. The remedies available to a holiday maker are discussed in Chapter 7. Contractual misrepresentation is considered first by relating specific legal points to a tour operator's *modus operandi* and then by an overall assessment of the operator's position.

(a) Contractual misrepresentation

To mount an action for contractual misrepresentation, the misrepresentation must have been made either by the other party to the contract (ie the tour operator) or by that party's agent acting within the scope of his authority (ie the travel agent relaying to the holiday maker information obtained from the tour operator). In either case, the holiday maker should sue the tour operator alone and, if proceedings are instituted against the travel agent, the agent will be entitled to claim an indemnity against the operator on the basis that he acted at all times within his authority and upon information supplied by the operator. If a travel agent has misrepresented the situation outside the scope of his authority he may be liable to the holiday maker in tort for fraudulent or negligent misrepresentation.

(b) Representee

The person commencing an action on the grounds of misrepresentation (ie the holiday maker) must be able to show that he is a representee. There are three classes of representee—

- (a) Persons to whom the representation is directly made. Holiday makers to whom a direct oral representation is made by a tour operator are in this category.
- (b) Persons to whom the representor intended or expected the representation to be passed. Holiday makers to whom a travel agent acting within the scope of his authority communicates representations made by a tour operator are in this class.
- (c) Members of a class at which a representation was directed, which includes the public at large. This covers anyone who reads a tour operator's brochure.

(c) Representation

As has already been emphasised, to constitute a representation a statement must be one of fact, past or present. A statement of opinion does not in general constitute a representation. However, this is not always so. If it can be shown that the person expressing the opinion did not honestly hold it, or that a reasonable man in possession of the same facts as the person expressing the opinion would not have held it, the statement may be regarded as a statement of fact which is actionable (*Smith* v *Land and House Property Corporation* (1884) 28 Ch D 7). Further, a statement of opinion published as if it was a fact may be regarded as a statement of fact (*Reese River Silver Mining Co Ltd* v *Smith* (1869) LR 4 HL 64). Statements in a tour operator's brochure regarding facilities available at a particular resort or hotel are usually made as if they were statements of fact and must, therefore, be regarded as such.

A statement of intention can be regarded as a misrepresentation of existing fact if, when made, it is not possible to give effect to it (*Edgington* v *Fitzmaurice* (1885) 29 Ch D 459). Accordingly, an argument by a tour operator that a statement made in his brochure was only one of intent will not enable him to escape liability if at the time of confirming a particular holiday maker's booking it was clear that the original intention was unlikely to be fulfilled. In this context it should be remembered that an invoice confirming the holiday arrangements to the holiday maker is regarded by the courts as containing an implied statement that the relevant statements included in the brochure are correct.

Chitty on Contracts (26th edition page 274 of volume 1) states, as regards statements of intention or opinion:

> "It is suggested that the fundamental principle which underlies the cases is not so much that statements as to the future, or statements of opinion, cannot be misrepresentations, but rather that statements are not to be treated as representations where, having regard to all the circumstances, it is unreasonable of the representee to rely on the representor's statements rather than his own judgment".

(d) Non-disclosure

Mere non-disclosure does not constitute misrepresentation (*Percival* v *Wright* [1902] 2 Ch 421), unless the contract is one *uberrimae fidei* (ie of the utmost good faith), in which case there is a fiduciary relationship between the parties and non-disclosure of a material fact creates a misrepresentation out of a representation. A contract between a tour operator and a holiday maker is not one of the utmost good faith, nor is there a fiduciary relationship between the parties. Nevertheless, there are circumstances in which non-disclosure may amount to misrepresentation. Suppose a picture in a brochure shows a hotel set against a luscious, verdant landscape and the accompanying literature elaborates the idyllic landscape. This would distort reality considerably if, in fact, a mere fifty yards to the west of the hotel is a power station continually belching out noxious fumes. Because most holiday makers have only the tour operator's representations to guide them in their choice of resort the circumstances hypothesised should, in the writers' opinion, impose a liability on the operator for non-disclosure of a material fact. But the duty to disclose can only be a duty to disclose facts which are contrary to what is implied by the brochure and which substantially and materially affect the package holiday.

A failure by the representor to inform the representee of a change in circumstances which has rendered an originally true representation false can be a misrepresentation (*With* v *O'Flanagan* [1936] Ch 575). This can apply to either tour operator or travel agent in circumstances such as a failure to notify a holiday maker that, for example, a particular hotel which used to have all-night discotheques every night of the week has stopped them and does not intend to recommence the facility.

In certain circumstances, a representation is treated as continuing until the contract is concluded, particularly when it was innocently made in the first instance but the representor, upon being made aware of the true position, does not inform the representee of the change in circumstances (*Davies* v *London Provincial Marine Insurance Co*

(1878) 8 Ch D 469). Under Regulation 12, tour operators are required to notify the holiday maker as soon as possible of a significant change in circumstances and offer a similar alternative holiday or a total refund. Regulation 13 provides, additionally, for the possibility of compensation. This reflects the legal position which existed before the Regulations.

The representation need not be material nor need it have been the sole inducement to enter into the contract. But, for the representation to be actionable, the representee must be able to show that it affected his assessment of the situation. So long as the holiday maker relied upon it, as the tour operator or travel agent should expect him to do, the misrepresentation will be actionable. However, its materiality will affect the relief available to a holiday maker.

At common law damages have always been recoverable for a *fraudulent* misrepresentation. The 1889 case of *Derry* v *Peek* decided that, in order for fraud to be established, it is necessary to prove the absence of an honest belief in the truth of what has been stated. In that case Lord Herschell stated–

> "fraud is proved when it is shown that a false representation has been made (i) knowingly, or (ii) without belief in its truth, or (iii) recklessly, careless whether it be true or false".

The onus of proof in this cause of action rests upon the representee.

(e) Negligent misrepresentation

The position of people who suffer as a result of misrepresentations which are not fraudulent was revolutionised by s.2(1) of the Misrepresentation Act 1967 which reads as follows:

> "Where a person has entered into a contract after a misrepresentation has been made to him by another party thereto and as a result thereof he has suffered loss, then if the person making the representation would be liable to damages in respect thereof had

> the misrepresentation been made fraudulently, that person shall be so liable notwithstanding that the misrepresentation was not made fraudulently, unless he proves that he had reasonable grounds to believe and did believe up to the time the contract was made that the facts represented were true".

The effect of this is that a tour operator will be liable in damages for a negligent misrepresentation (ie one made carelessly or without reasonable grounds for believing it to be true) unless he can show that he had reasonable grounds for believing the truth of the representation made by him. It must be stressed that the onus of proof rests with the tour operator.

(f) *Reasonable grounds for belief*

The case of *Howard Marine and Dredging Company Limited* v *A Ogden & Sons (Excavations) Limited* [1978] QB 574 is instructive concerning what constitutes reasonable grounds for belief. In this case, the plaintiffs misrepresented to the defendants the carrying capacity of two barges which the defendants wished to hire for carrying large quantities of clay out to sea and then dumping. The defendants entered into the contract in reliance on this misrepresentation and used the barges for some time before they discovered the true facts and returned the barges. The plaintiffs' misrepresentation was based upon their recollection of an entry in Lloyd's Register about the capacity of the barges but the entry was incorrect. The correct capacity could have been ascertained from the ship's documents in the plaintiffs' possession. A majority of the Court of Appeal held that the defendants were entitled to damages for breach of s.2(1) of the 1967 Act. It was held that to avoid liability the plaintiffs had to prove that they had reasonable grounds to believe and did believe up to the time the contract was made, that the facts represented were true and that on an analysis of the evidence that burden had not been discharged since the person making the representation had not shown any objectively reasonable ground for disregarding the capacity stated in the ship's documents and for preferring the Lloyd's Register incorrect figure. The following *dicta* in particular should be noted:

> "If the representee proves a misrepresentation which, if fraudulent, would have sounded in damages, the onus passes immediately to the representor to prove that he had reasonable grounds to believe the facts represented. In other words the liability of the representor does not depend upon his being under a duty of care the extent of which may vary according to the circumstances in which the representation is made. In the course of negotiations leading to a contract the statute imposes an absolute obligation not to state facts which the representor cannot prove he had reasonable ground to believe . . . But the question remains whether his evidence, however benevolently viewed, is sufficient to show that he had an *objectively reasonable* ground to disregard the figure in the ship's documents and to prefer the Lloyd's Register figure". (*per* Bridge LJ).

A point also arose regarding an exclusion clause upon which the plaintiffs sought to rely to exempt responsibility for negligent misrepresentation. Bridge LJ stated:

> "What the judge said in this matter was: If the wording of the clause is apt to exempt from responsibility for negligent misrepresentation as to carrying capacity, I hold that such exemption is not fair and reasonable. The judge having asked himself the right question and answered it as he did in the exercise of the discretion vested in him by the Act (section 3 of Misrepresentation Act 1967), I can see no ground on which we would say that he was wrong".

Two other cases which, although not directly relating to s.2(1) of the Misrepresentation Act, set out analogous principles are:

Greenwood v *Leather Shod Wheel Company* [1900] 1 Ch D 421. This case involved a misrepresentation by a company in its prospectus. Section 38 of the Companies

Act 1867 stated that no person is liable for a misrepresentation in a prospectus provided that he can prove that he had reasonable cause to believe and did believe that the statement was true; in other words that there was not notice of matters which would cast doubt on the veracity of any statement of fact in the prospectus. (These are the same criteria as in s.2(1) of the Misrepresentation Act.) Lindlay MR stated:

> "Notice in the section (ie s.38 Companies Act 1867) means not what is called 'constructive notice' but actual notice, that is notice which brings home to the mind of a reasonable, intelligent and careful reader such knowledge as fairly, and in a business sense, amounts to notice of a contract. In other words, liability under s.38 could be avoided provided that the person who had included the representation in the prospectus could show that he did so upon information which to a reasonable intelligent and careful person in a business sense would justify the inclusion of the representation."

Brown v *Raphael* [1958] 2 All ER 79 was a case which arose from a negligent misrepresentation at common law as to certain matters affecting the sale of a house. The vendor relied upon information provided by his solicitors but it was held that he could not rely upon this information. Lord Evershed MR stated—

> "The question then arises: was that information such as to justify a reasonable person who had any awareness of the significance of the matter, asserting as an inducement to a reasonable purchaser that the annuitant was believed to have no aggregate estate? . . . it is quite plain that that very meagre information formed no basis whatever on which a responsible person could put forward that view as an inducement for somebody to buy the reversion".

To obtain the protection of the proviso under s.2(1) of the Misrepresentation Act 1967 tour operators have two burdens of proof, one of which is subjective and one of which is both objective and subjective. The subjective burden of proof is to show to the court that it was believed that the statements in the brochure were true. The objective burden of proof is to show that there were reasonable grounds for this belief. Reasonable grounds will of course be subjective in that different people will come to different decisions based upon the same information. The starting point must, therefore, be objective. Adapting Lindlay MR's words—would a reasonably intelligent and careful person with knowledge of the travel industry be entitled to form the belief that was formed?

It is accepted practice in the travel industry that tour operators rely for their information upon inspections by their products departments, reports which they receive from their representatives, trade publications and information provided by hotels themselves. The *Brown* v *Raphael* and *Greenwood* v *Leather Shod Wheel Co* cases indicate that information from hotels alone would not provide a basis to justify the inclusion of representations in brochures. However, reports from products managers and representatives constitute actual notice and, in the writers' opinion, should be accepted as providing reasonable grounds for making representations.

Chitty on Contracts (26th edition page 292 of volume 1) states as follows (when commenting on the *Howard Marine & Dredging Co* case):

> "It was also stressed that the question was, strictly speaking, not one of negligence but that the Act imposed an absolute obligation not to state facts which the representor cannot prove he had reasonable grounds to believe. No doubt it is correct to say that it is not a question of negligence, as at common law, where a duty of care is in issue; and it is possible that circumstances may exist in which a person may make a statement without having reasonable grounds to believe it, in which case it would be held that he was not (having regard to all the circumstances) negligent. Nevertheless, for most practical purposes it will usually be correct to equate liability under section 2(1) of the Act with liability for negligence".

This statement reinforces the following *dicta* by Mr Justice Hodgson in the *Wall* v *Silver Wing* case (the *dicta* arose in connection with negligence)—"Before it (the representation) was included in the brochure the Martina was inspected and found not only to have adequate but admirable fire escape facilities. I think that that fulfilled any duty of care owed to the customers and I think it robbed of any suggestion of misrepresentation anything contained in the brochure. I do not think that there was any duty upon the tour operators to make routine inspections thereafter".

(g) Remedies

Section 2(2) of the Misrepresentation Act 1967 reads as follows:

> "Where a person has entered into a contract after a misrepresentation had been made to him otherwise than fraudulently, and he would be entitled, by reason of the misrepresentation, to rescind the contract, then, if it is claimed, in any proceedings arising out of the contract, that the contract ought to be or has been rescinded, the court or arbitrator may declare the contract subsisting and award damages in lieu of rescission, if of the opinion that it would be equitable to do so, having regard to the nature of the representation and the loss that would be caused by it if the contract were upheld, as well as to the loss that rescission would cause to the other party".

In the event of an innocent misrepresentation (ie an inaccurate representation which is not fraudulent within the meaning of fraudulent specified in *Derry* v *Peek*) the common law normally only entitled the representee to claim rescission of the contract. As discussed above, s.2(1) entitles the representee to claim damages in the event of a negligent misrepresentation and the effect of s.2(2) is to enable the court to award damages in lieu of rescission in the event of a misrepresentation which is neither fraudulent nor negligent. This remedy is only available at the discretion of the court in lieu of rescission and does not provide a right to claim damages.

(h) Exclusion clauses

At common law a representor could not exclude liability for fraudulent misrepresentation but could for innocent (including negligent) misrepresentation. Section 3 of the Misrepresentation Act 1967, as amended by s.8 of the Unfair Contract Terms Act 1977, states—

> "If a contract contains a term which would exclude or restrict:
>
> (a) any liability to which a party to a contract may be subject by reason of any misrepresentation made by him before the contract was made; or
>
> (b) any remedy available to another party to the contract by reason of such a misrepresentation;
>
> that term shall be of no effect except in so far as it satisfies the requirement of reasonableness as stated in s.11(2) of the Unfair Contract Terms Act 1977; and it is for those claiming that the term satisfies that requirement to show that it does".

The onus will be on the tour operator to show that the exclusion clause is reasonable. Given the terms of the Regulations, and particularly Regulations 4 and 15(5), it is most unlikely that a tour operator will be able so to prove.

It is the tour operator's brochure which contains the main body of representations about the facilities on a particular holiday and, if inaccurate, it will provide the holiday maker with a valid cause of action unless the operator can prove that he had reasonable grounds to believe and did believe up to the time the contract was made that the representation was true.

Misrepresentations by a tour operator are not necessarily confined to statements made in its package holiday brochure. Sometimes a holiday maker will ask his travel agent a question which will lead to the latter ringing the tour operator for an answer, which is then passed on to the holiday maker. For instance, the holiday maker may want to know whether there is a golf course in his resort or a casino. Some travel agents will know the answer but others will need to check with the operator. If the operator gives an answer which is false without having reasonable grounds for believing it to be true, the holiday maker should normally be in a position successfully to claim against the operator under the Misrepresentation Act.

(i) Tortious misrepresentation

As previously stated, claims of tortious misrepresentation will normally be brought by the holiday maker against the travel agent. It is not necessary to consider in any detail the legal basis of tortious misrepresentation since—

(a) the general principles regarding what constitute a representation are applicable; and

(b) the effect of the 1964 case of *Hedley Byrne & Co Ltd* v *Heller & Partners Limited,* which is discussed in Chapter 5, will mean that any proceedings brought will generally be for negligent advice rather than misrepresentation.

Some travel agents adopt the practice of specially recommending holidays offered by a particular tour operator by the endorsement of recommendation stickers on the front of the tour operator's brochures displayed in the agent's premises. It is suggested for the following reasons that such travel agents can be liable to a holiday maker who is justifiably dissatisfied, even if only with one aspect of the facilities offered:

(a) The effect of such a recommendation sticker must be that the travel agent, in his own capacity as a travel expert, is endorsing the holidays in the operator's brochure. In the absence of wording to the contrary this must mean every holiday detailed in the brochure. Obviously the wording of the sticker is most important but the writers have in mind those which merely say "Specially recommended by . . ."

(b) The agent must intend that holiday makers will rely upon his recommendation that the operator's holidays will be more than satisfactory—a classic example of an inducement to enter into a contract.

(c) Normally the travel agent has not actually inspected the operator's hotels etc and, therefore, will not be able to prove that he has taken reasonable care in the way that the operator may be able to.

Travel agents who use such stickers argue that it is not each and every holiday which is being recommended but rather that the sticker is a pointer towards a generally reputable tour operator. This is not likely to be the interpretation put upon it by members of the public and, in the writers' opinion, would not be how a court of law would see it. However reputable a tour operator may be, his reputation will not justify a travel agent in recommending a holiday of which he had no personal knowledge.

Whether or not the travel agent is entitled to obtain an indemnity from the tour operator will depend upon the background to the use of the recommendation stickers. If they are used pursuant to an agreement between operator and agent, it is likely that it will provide that the agent be indemnified in the event of complaints/court proceedings. If there has been no agreement, the operator may well consider that the agent has acted outside his normal scope and should bear the consequences himself.

(j) Regulation 4

Chapter 2 has already outlined the provisions of Regulation 4, and Chapter 5 has commented further. The Regulation renders a tour operator or travel agent liable to compensate a holiday maker for any loss or damage suffered as a result of any misleading descriptive matter about a package.

The use in Regulation 4 of the words "supply" and "matter" suggest that it does not apply to oral statements. If that is correct, Regulation 4 does not render the preceding sections on misrepresentation redundant.

Clearly, though, where Regulation 4 does apply, a holiday maker is much better placed by relying on it, rather than on the common law and the Misrepresentation Act 1967 outlined above.

6. Advertising standards

There is one further aspect of misrepresentation which must be examined and which is not associated with any of the foregoing. A brochure as well as being a source of representations and a contractual document in its own right is a promotional document which is required to observe the standards laid down by the Advertising Standards Authority.

The Advertising Standards Authority prepares the British Code of Advertising Practice. It establishes criteria for professional conduct by advertisers and indicates to the public the limitations accepted by those in advertising. The following aspects of the code should be noted in particular:

(a) All advertisements should be legal, decent, honest and truthful.

(b) All descriptions, claims and comparisons which relate to matters of objectively ascertainable fact should be capable of substantiation.

(c) Advertisements should not contain any statement or visual presentation likely to mislead the consumer either directly or by implication, omission, ambiguity or exaggeration.

(d) All comparative advertisements should respect the principles of fair competition and should be so designed that there is no likelihood of the consumer being misled.

It is open to members of the public or other travel companies to complain to the ASA about a breach of its code in a tour operator's brochure. The ASA's sanctions are, basically, the withholding of advertising space or time and adverse publicity due to the reports which they publish about complaints. They do, though, require a certain length of time to investigate the situation.

It is worth noting that comparative advertising is not much practised by ABTA members who are generally keen to avoid internecine strife. Where it does occur, an aggrieved operator may consider that the ASA are not the most effective body to deal with it and may prefer to complain to ABTA.

Other options which are available to an operator who is aggrieved by the contents of a competitor's brochure are to report the matter to the Trading Standards Department or to seek immediate relief from the courts by means of an injunction. In blatant cases there is considerable merit in involving the Trading Standards Department since they have the authority to enter upon an operator's premises, seize its records for examination and seriously disrupt trading. Relief by means of injunction can be difficult to obtain since, if it is a case of a minor operator at fault, there is a risk that the courts will decide that the threat to business is not sufficient to justify the grant of an injunction. Any situation of this nature will require that the operator and his legal advisers consider the circumstances peculiar to the case—it is not possible to set down hard and fast guidelines, and it is outside the scope of this book to review possible causes of action in any detail.

Chapter 7

Damages

Chapters 2, 3, 5 and 6 have considered the various obligations which a tour operator or travel agent has to holiday makers. The obligations now stem primarily from the Regulations. The law which existed before the Regulations continues in force only to the extent that it does not conflict with the effect of the Regulations.

This chapter assumes liability and examines the extent to which holiday makers will be able to recover damages. The relevant legal principles will be examined first, followed by the principal cases involving tour operators and travel agents. Before doing so, it is appropriate to examine the extent to which the Regulations deal with damages.

Neither the Regulations, nor the EC Directive before them, deal directly with damages. They both leave them to be decided by existing national law. However, the level of damages may be affected by whether a Regulation imposing civil liability gives a right in contract or in tort.

Regulations 6, 9, 10, 11, 12, 13, 14 and 15 deal with obligations to be implied into contracts for package holidays, and the consequences of failure to perform contractual obligations. These, therefore, will create a right in contract law to damages. Regulation 4, however, will create a right in tort.

Regulations 5, 7, 8, 16 and 22 create obligations which are enforced by criminal law sanctions. In certain cases breach of statutory duty also gives a right to bring a civil law claim in tort for damages. No such right exists under the Regulations. Regulation 27 specifically states that "no right of action in civil proceedings in respect of any loss shall arise by reason only of the commission of an offence under Regulations 5, 7, 8, 16 or 22 of these Regulations".

1. Meaning of damages

Lord Blackburn, in *Livingstone* v *Rawyards Coal Co* (1880) 5 App Cas 25, defined damages as—

> "that sum of money which will put the party who has been injured, or who has suffered, in the same position as he would have been in if he had not sustained the wrong for which he is now getting compensation".

This definition is equally applicable to damages in contract or in tort but it must be stressed that there is a basic distinction between damages in contract and in tort. In contract, the "wrong" to which Lord Blackburn refers is breach of the contract and, as stated by Parke B in *Robinson* v *Harman* (1848) 1 Ex 855, a plaintiff is entitled to be put into the position he would have been in if the contract had been fully performed. The claim, in essence, is for loss of bargain. In tort, on the other hand, the "wrong" is the doing of that which gives rise to the complaint and a plaintiff is entitled to have the position restored, so far as is possible, to the *status quo ante*.

2. Damages for breach of contract

(a) Causation

For damages to be recoverable for breach of contract there must be a causal connection between the defendant's breach of contract and the plaintiff's loss, *and* the particular loss must be within the contemplation of the parties. The first question to be considered is whether or not the defendant's breach caused the plaintiff's loss, in respect of which two alternative situations must be borne in mind—

(a) the defendant's breach *directly* causes the plaintiff's loss; or

(b) the defendant's breach *indirectly* causes the plaintiff's loss, ie a "new intervening event" occurs pursuant to the defendant's breach and causes the plaintiff's loss.

In either of these situations what must be determined is the extent of the plaintiff's loss for which the defendant, by reason of his breach, should be held liable. The question of causation can be somewhat complicated, and a detailed analysis is beyond the scope of this book. The writers do not propose to dwell on this subject, save to bring it to the reader's attention and comment briefly on "indirect" causation.

Indirect causation can stem either from the intervening act of a third party, or from an intervening act of the plaintiff. Regarding the latter, the effect of s.1(1) of the Law Reform (Contributory Negligence) Act 1945 is that damages *in tort,* will be reduced if the plaintiff "suffers damage as the result partly of his own fault and partly of the fault of any other person". There has been doubt whether or not damages in *contract* may be reduced by the application of this Act. In *Forsikringsaktieselskapet Vesta* v *Butcher* [1988] 2 All ER 43, the Court of Appeal held that contributory negligence will apply "where the defendant's liability in contract is the same as his liability in the tort of negligence independently of the existence of any contract."

Regulation 15(2) (see pages 48–59) means that a tour operator will not be able to make use of the defences unless it can first be established that there was no fault on the part of the operator or any of the suppliers. This, however, relates to liability. It does not render principles of contributory negligence inapplicable to the assessment of damages.

(b) Foreseeability

Assuming that the plaintiff's loss is attributable to the defendant's breach, what has to be considered is whether the loss was within the contemplation of the parties and was not too remote from the breach to merit compensation. The first definitive outline of what damages are or are not too remote is contained in the following words of Alderson, B in *Hadley* v *Baxendale* (1854) 9 Exch 341—

> "Where two parties have made a contract which one of them has broken, the damages which the other party ought to receive in respect of such a breach of contract should be such as may fairly and reasonably be considered either arising naturally, ie according to the usual course of things, from such breach of contract itself, or such as may reasonably be supposed to have been in the contemplation of both parties, at the time they made the contract, as the probable result of the breach of it. Now, if the special circumstances under which the contract was actually made were communicated by the plaintiffs to the defendants, and thus known to both parties, the damages resulting from the breach of such a contract, which they would reasonably contemplate, would be the amount of injury which would ordinarily follow from a breach of contract under these special circumstances so known and communicated. But, on the other hand, if these special circumstances were wholly unknown to the party breaking the contract, he, at the most, could only be supposed to have had in his contemplation the amount of injury which would arise generally, and in the great multitude of cases not affected by any special circumstances, from such a breach of contract. For, had the special circumstances been known, the parties might have specifically provided for the breach of contract by special terms as to the damages in that case; and of this advantage it would be very unjust to deprive them".

The above principle was restated by Asquith LJ in *Victoria Laundry* v *Newman* [1949] 2 KB 528 as follows:

> "(1) It is well settled that the governing purpose of damages is to put the party whose rights have been violated in the same position, so far as money can do so, as if his rights had been observed. This purpose, if relentlessly pursued would provide him with a complete indemnity from all loss *de facto* resulting from a particular breach, however improbable, however unpredictable. This, in contract at least, is recognised as too harsh a rule.
>
> (2) Hence, in cases of breach of contract the aggrieved party is only entitled to recover such part of the loss

actually resulting as was at the time of the contract reasonably foreseeable as liable to result from the breach.

(3) What was at the time reasonably so foreseeable depends on the knowledge then possessed by the parties, or, at all events, by the party who later commits the breach.

(4) For this purpose, knowledge 'possessed' is of two kinds; one imputed, the other actual. Everyone, as a reasonable person, is taken to know the 'ordinary course of things' and consequently what loss is liable to result from a breach of contract in that ordinary course. This is the subject matter of the 'first rule' in *Hadley* v *Baxendale*. But to this knowledge, which a contract breaker is assumed to possess whether he actually possesses it or not, there may have to be added in a particular case knowledge which he actually possesses, of special circumstances outside the 'ordinary course of things', of such a kind that a breach in those special circumstances would be liable to cause more loss. Such a case attracts the operation of the 'second rule' so as to make additional loss also recoverable.

(5) In order to make the contract breaker liable under either rule it is not necessary that he should actually have asked himself what loss is liable to result from a breach. As has often been pointed out, parties at the time of contracting contemplate not the breach of contract but its performance. It suffices that, if he had considered the question, he would as a reasonable man have concluded that the loss in question was liable to result.

(6) Nor, finally, to make a particular loss recoverable, need it be proved that upon a given state of knowledge the defendant could, as a reasonable man, foresee that a breach must necessarily result in that loss. It is enough if he could foresee it was likely so to result. It is indeed enough . . . if the loss (or some factor without which it would not have occurred) is a 'serious possibility' or a 'real danger'. For short, we have used the word 'liable' to result. Possibly the colloquialism 'on the cards' indicates the shade of meaning with some approach to accuracy".

Asquith LJ's use of the test of reasonable foreseeability was, however, qualified by the House of Lords in

Czarnikow v *Koufos* [1969] 1 AC 350. To use Lord Reid's words in that case the test should now be regarded as whether the loss is "of a kind which the defendant, when he made the contract, ought to have realised was not unlikely to result from the breach . . . the words 'not unlikely' denoting a degree of possibility considerably less than even chance but nevertheless not very unusual and easily foreseeable".

Asquith LJ's proposition that "foreseeability" depends upon both imputed and actual knowledge is still, however, regarded as correct in law. The question of "knowledge" is important since it establishes a holiday maker's duty to disclose material facts if he subsequently wishes to claim damages in contract for an unusual result occurring from the tour operator's breach of contract due to such material facts. If, for example, there is a particular health reason whereby air conditioning is a necessity for a particular holiday maker, the operator, in the event of a hotel not providing air conditioning in breach of the operator's contract with the holiday maker, will only be liable for damages which would ordinarily result, if the special circumstances have not been communicated to him by the holiday maker. He will not be liable for those damages which result due to the plaintiff's particular state of health. This principle is set out in the 1987 Court of Appeal case of *Kemp* v *Intasun Holidays Limited* (see page 170).

(c) Indirect damage

Reference was made earlier to a breach of contract which directly causes a loss and one which only does so indirectly (through a new intervening event). The writers submit that this distinction can be misleading in relation to damages and that it causes confusion in the drafting of exclusion clauses. For instance, does an exclusion clause which excludes liability for indirect or consequential loss exclude liability for every sort of loss which would not have occurred but for a new intervening event? This depends on what is meant by a new intervening event. In the case of *Saint Line* v *Richardsons Westgarth & Co* [1940] 2 KB 99 Atkinson J said direct damage is that which flows naturally from the breach without other intervening cause and independently of special circumstances while indirect damage does not so flow. Consequential has come to mean "not direct" and refers to something which is not the direct or natural result of the breach. It would seem to follow from this that:

(a) "indirect" and "consequential" are synonymous;
(b) damage is not direct if it is attributable to a new intervening cause; and
(c) damage is direct if it is the natural result of a breach.

It is submitted that there is an inconsistency between (b) and (c) above. Something may well be a natural result even though it involves the intervention of a new third party event. In *London Joint Stock Bank* v *MacMillan* [1918] AC 777 a customer of the plaintiff bank, in breach of his duty of care not to draw cheques so as to facilitate fraud, signed a cheque drawn by a clerk of his in such a way as to enable the clerk to alter the amount from £2 to £120. The clerk cashed the cheque and absconded. The House of Lords held that the customer was liable to the bank for the forged increase, Lord Finley LC saying that the fact that an *intervening* crime was necessary to bring about the loss did not prevent the loss being the natural consequences of the carelessness. Does this mean that the loss resulting from the intervening third party crime should be regarded as loss flowing directly from the customer's duty of care so as not to be rendered irrecoverable by a (hypothetical) clause excluding liability for indirect loss? The writers believe so but there appears to be no conclusive authority on this subject.

(d) Mitigation of loss

It is an established principle in contract law that a plaintiff must mitigate his loss—ie he must take reasonable steps to avoid loss. If he does not and could have avoided loss by so doing, he will not recover damages. But a plaintiff is not obliged to take every conceivable step to minimise his loss. The onus of proof rests with the defendant to show that the plaintiff, as a reasonable man, ought to have taken a particular step. What is, or is not, reasonable will depend upon the particular circumstances of each case but it is easy to conceive circumstances in which a holiday maker clearly has a duty to mitigate his loss. If, for example, an operator incorrectly details a flight time as a result of which the holiday maker misses his flight but the operator is able to arrange a flight to the same destination from the same airport some two hours later, the holiday maker must be under a duty to mitigate his loss and take that flight. If he does not but instead returns home, the only compensation to which he should be entitled is a nominal sum for the inconvenience of a two hour wait to catch the alternative flight. It is patently unreasonable not to accept the alternative flight and so is clearly a breach of the holiday maker's duty to mitigate his loss.

There are certain other points regarding mitigation which should be borne in mind:

(a) If a plaintiff succeeds in mitigating his loss wholly, he cannot recover for such avoided loss.

(b) If the plaintiff incurs loss or expense in taking reasonable steps to mitigate, the defendant will be liable to compensate him in damages for such loss or expense. Thus, in the example above, if the alternative flight is from another airport, the tour operator is liable to compensate the holiday maker in damages for the cost of travelling to the other airport.

(c) A plaintiff's inability to mitigate his loss due to his impecuniosity should not reduce the damages to which he is entitled. This was specifically stated in *Clippens Oil Co* v *Edinburgh and District Water Trustees* [1907] AC 291, and appears to have been accepted in *Leisbosch Dredger* v *SS Edison* [1933] AC 449. If, for example, a holiday maker is accommodated in a hotel abroad which is totally unsatisfactory and the tour operator refuses to relocate him or return him to the UK straightaway, the holiday maker's damages will not be reduced merely because he did not have the funds to relocate himself or arrange his own immediate flight to the UK.

Regulation 15(9) provides that the contract terms must specifically detail a holiday maker's duty to complain at the time of dissatisfaction. If there is no contract term to this effect, the obligation does not arise.

An obligation to complain at the time is, of course, one step to be taken in seeking to mitigate loss. If there is no contract term to this effect, Regulation 15(9) will operate to prevent a tour operator from arguing failure to complain. In all other aspects, however, the duty to mitigate is unaffected.

(e) Special and general damages

Damages are usually divided into special and general damages. The former are those "out of pocket" expenses which have arisen as a result of the breach of contract. The remaining items of general damage—for example loss of enjoyment of a holiday—are not amenable to precise monetary quantification by the holiday maker. Their assessment is left to the courts and it is submitted that there are three main questions which a court will bear in mind when assessing a claim for general damages:

(i) What is the value of that part of the holiday package which the holiday maker has not received? This is the head of general damages known as diminution of contract value. If a package holiday to Greece at a cost of £600 per person was supposed to include the services of the operator's courier to take the holiday makers to various sites of antiquity and explain the history, architecture, etc but the courier was not available, the court would assess the extent to which such services were reflected in the price of the holiday and make an appropriate award. If, in a two week period, there would only have been two excursions to sites of antiquity, the reduction in the value of the contract would be minimal—say £50— but, if daily excursions had been contracted for, a judge might assess it at £250.

(ii) Did the holiday maker suffer any physical inconvenience and discomfort as a result of the operator's breach? If so, damages will be awarded. Cases such as *Hobbs* v *LSW Ry* (1875) LR 10 QB 111, *Stedman* v *Swan's Tours* (1951) 95 SJ 727, and *Feldman* v *Allways Travel Service* [1957] CLY 934, have established that damages are recoverable for physical inconvenience and discomfort. If, in the example in (i), the non-availability of a courier had resulted in holiday makers becoming stranded, and having to spend one night by the ancient temple of Corinth without any accommodation, food etc, damages would be awarded for that physical inconvenience and discomfort.

(iii) Did the holiday maker suffer mental distress, annoyance and disappointment because of the breach? If so, damages will be awarded to compensate him. This head of damages has only been available since the historic decision of the Court of Appeal in *Jarvis* v *Swan Tours* [1973] 1 All ER 71, the facts of which are set out on page 163. It is a rule in contract law that damages will not be awarded for mental distress, annoyance and disappointment unless the contract is of a type to make such damages appropriate. In *Jarvis* v *Swan Tours* the court held that holiday contracts were of such a type. It is occasionally submitted that the decision in *Jarvis* creates an exception to the rule that damages for mental distress etc will normally not be awarded. The writers disagree. The rule is that such damages will not be awarded unless the mental distress is of a kind which the defendant, when he made the contract, ought to have realised was not unlikely to result from a breach such as that

> which occurred. Tour operators, in effect, peddle dreams, and broken dreams are bound to produce mental distress, annoyance and disappointment.

The court can at its discretion add interest to any damages awarded. The amount of interest will reflect current commercial rates. In the High Court interest is awarded under the Supreme Court Act 1981 and in the County Court under s.69, County Courts Act 1984.

3. Damages in tort

At the start of this chapter, mention was made of the basic distinction between the measures of damages in contract and in tort. The purpose of damages in tort is to restore the plaintiff, so far as money can, to the position that he would have been in had the tort never been committed. The succeeding paragraphs give a broad statement of the relevant principles, but lawyers advising about a particular case should also consult textbooks such as *McGregor on Damages.*

A plaintiff will recover damages for a particular loss if he can show that the defendant's tort caused it—whether directly or indirectly—and that the loss was reasonably foreseeable. As in contract, this incorporates elements of causation and remoteness. The Judicial Committee of the Privy Council in *Overseas Tankship (UK)* v *Morts Dock and Engineering Co, The Wagon Mound* [1961] AC 388 (PC) purported to make foreseeability the sole test of the extent of liability in an action for negligence, since when the subject has been much litigated. However *McGregor on Damages* (20th edition) suggests that elements of causation cannot be easily excluded and will, at least in some cases, be a valid consideration.

There are two points of difference with contract law which must be mentioned:

(a) The provisions of the Law Reform (Contributory Negligence) Act 1945 apply to an assessment of damages in tort.

(b) In contract, if there are circumstances peculiar to a plaintiff which would result in him suffering abnormal damage in the event of a breach, the plaintiff must disclose those circumstances if he seeks to recover compensation for the abnormal damage. This is not so in tort. A defendant must take a plaintiff as he finds him.

Under contract law, a holiday maker can recover damages, for physical inconvenience, mental anguish, distress and disappointment. It is submitted that in cases where they are "reasonably foreseeable" these are also material considerations in tort.

Whether damages for misrepresentation under common law or the Misrepresentation Act 1967 should be assessed under tortious or contractual principles is a difficult question which can only be dealt with properly by reference to the various types of misrepresentation. A detailed examination is beyond the scope of this book and what follows is no more than a brief synopsis:

(a) The Court of Appeal in *Doyle* v *Olby (Ironmongers)* [1969] 2 QB 158 unreservedly held that tortious principles should apply in the event of fraudulent misrepresentation.

(b) *McGregor on Damages* suggests that, at common law, damages for negligent misrepresentation, where no contract results, should be assessed on tortious principles but that, where a contract results, both contractual and tortious principles may be applicable.

(c) Despite the decision of Graham J in *Watts* v *Spence* [1976] Ch 165 that by virtue of s.2(1) of the Misrepresentation Act 1967 the plaintiff was entitled to damages for loss of bargain where he had suffered loss as a result of the defendant's negligent misrepresentation, it is suggested that tortious principles should apply in the event of negligent misrepresentation under s.2(1) of the 1967 Act.

(d) The assessment of damages for an innocent misrepresentation under s.2(2) of the Misrepresentation Act 1967 creates a more difficult problem. Section 2(3) of the 1967 Act states:

"Damages may be awarded against a person under subsection (2) of this section whether or not he is liable to damages under subsection (1) thereof, but where he is so liable any award under the said subsection (2) shall be taken into account in assessing his liability under the said subsection (1)"

This provides a clear indication that damages under s.2(2) can be less than under s.2(1). *McGregor* suggests that the purpose of damages under s.2(2) should be to put the plaintiff into the same position as he would have been if a decree of rescission had been granted.

4. The leading cases

In recent years there have been five major Court of Appeal decisions regarding the damages to be awarded to justifiably aggrieved holiday makers. These will now be considered in detail.

(a) *Jarvis v Swan Tours Ltd* [*1973*] *1 All ER 71*

The facts: The defendants' 1969/70 winter sports brochure described one of their holidays as a "house-party in Morlialp", Switzerland, with "special resident host". The brochure stated that the price of the holiday included the following house-party arrangements:

> "Welcome party on arrival. Afternoon tea and cake . . . Swiss dinner by candlelight. Fondue party. Yodller evening . . . farewell party".

It also stated that there was a wide variety of ski runs at Morlialp, ski packs could be hired there, the hotel was chosen because of its comfort, the hotel owner spoke English and the hotel bar would be open several evenings a week. The brochure added . . . "you will be in for a great time when you book this house-party holiday". The plaintiff booked a fifteen-day holiday between 20.12.1969 and 3.1.1970 for a cost of £63.45. In the first week of the holiday, the house party consisted of only 13 people, and for the second week he was the only person there. There was no welcome party, the ski runs were some distance away and no full length skis were available except on two days in the second week. The hotel owner did not speak English. The cake for tea was only potato crisps and dry nut cake. There was not much entertainment at night – the yodller was a local man in his working clothes singing a few songs quickly and the hotel bar was an annexe open only on one evening. During the second week there was no representative at the hotel.

In the first instance, the trial judge held that the plaintiff was entitled to damages for breach of contract. He assessed these as being worth £31.72 (half the holiday price), on the basis that the contractual measure of damages was the difference between what the plaintiff had paid for the holiday and what he had got. The plaintiff appealed.

Held: In a proper case damages for mental distress could be recovered in an action for breach of contract. The plaintiff was not necessarily restricted to damages for physical inconvenience suffered by the breach. Breach of a contract to provide a holiday or entertainment and enjoyment was a proper case in which to award damages for mental distress, or inconvenience, because in such a contract it was foreseeable that a material breach might well cause frustration, annoyance and disappointment, and damages could be awarded for such inconvenience. The measure of the damages to which the plaintiff was entitled was not restricted to compensation for the loss of entertainment and enjoyment which he had been promised and did not get. He was also entitled to be compensated for the vexation and disappointment which he had suffered. On a broad view of the case, the plaintiff was awarded £125 and, accordingly, his appeal was allowed.

The following *dicta* in particular should be noted. *Per* Lord Denning MR:

> "If the contracting party breaks his contract, damages can be given for the disappointment, the distress, the upset and frustration caused by the

> breach . . . A good example was given by Edmund Davies LJ in the course of the argument. He put the case of a man who has taken a ticket for Glyndbourne. It is the only night on which he can get there. He hires a car to take him. The car does not turn up. His damages are not limited to the mere cost of the ticket. He is entitled to general damages for the disappointment he has suffered and the loss of the entertainment which he should have had . . . He (Mr Jarvis) is entitled to damages for the loss of those facilities and/or his loss of enjoyment . . . The right measure of damages is to compensate him for the loss of entertainment and enjoyment which he was promised, and which he did not get."

Per Edmund Davies LJ:

> "The court is entitled, and indeed bound, to contrast the overall quality of the holiday so enticingly promised with that which the defendants in fact provided . . . I am of the opinion that . . . vexation and being disappointed in a particular thing which you have set your mind upon are relevant considerations which afford the court a guide in arriving at a proper figure".

(b) Jackson v Horizon Holidays [*1975*] *3 All ER 92*

The facts: The plaintiff booked a package holiday with the defendants for four weeks for himself, his wife and two children at a hotel in Ceylon at a total cost of £1,200. The plaintiff told the defendants that he wanted everything at the hotel to be of the highest standard and requested a communicating door between his children's room and his and his wife's room. The defendant's brochure described the hotel as having all facilities for an enjoyable holiday, including mini golf, excellent restaurant, swimming pool, beauty and hairdressing salon. It also described the bedrooms as well furnished, each having a private bath, shower and w.c. The plaintiff and his wife were very disappointed with the hotel. There was no connecting door with the children's room and in any event the room was unusable because of mildew and fungus on the walls; there was no private bath, and the shower and w.c. were dirty; the food was distasteful; there was no mini golf; no swimming pool and no beauty or hairdressing salons. After a fortnight at the hotel the plaintiff and his wife moved to another hotel which was somewhat better but building work was still taking place there. The plaintiff brought an action against the defendants for breach of contract claiming damages in respect of the loss of the holiday for himself, his wife and children. The defendants admitted liability. The judge awarded total damages of £1,100 against which the defendants appealed.

Held: Where a person had entered into a contract for the benefit of himself and others who were not parties to the contract, he could sue on the contract for damages for the loss suffered not only by himself but also by the others in consequence of a breach of contract even though he was not a trustee for the others. It followed that the plaintiff was entitled to damages not only for the diminution in the value of the holiday and the discomfort, vexation and disappointment which he himself had suffered by reason of the defendant's breach of contract but also for the discomfort, vexation and disappointment suffered by his wife and children. On that basis the damages awarded by the judge were not excessive and the appeal would be dismissed.

The following *dicta* in particular should be noted:

Per Lord Denning MR:

> "The judge did not divide up the £1,100 . . . Counsel for Mr Jackson suggested that the judge gave £600 for the diminution in value and £500 for the mental distress. If I were inclined myself to speculate, I think the suggestion of counsel for Mr Jackson may well be right. The judge took the cost of the holiday at £1,200. The family only had about half the value of it. Divide it by two and you get £600. Then add £500 for the mental distress . . . I think that the figure of £1,100 was about right. It would, I think, have been excessive if it had been awarded only for the damage suffered by Mr Jackson himself. But when extended to his wife and children, I do not

think it is excessive. People look forward to a holiday. They expect the promises to be fulfilled. When it fails, they are greatly disappointed and upset. It is difficult to assess in terms of money; but it is the task of the judges to do the best they can".

(c) Adcock v Blue Sky Holidays [*Unreported 13 May 1980*]

The facts: The plaintiff booked with the defendants a ski-ing holiday in Italy for himself and friends at a cost of £98 per person plus £42 insurance. The complaints about the holiday, as summarised by the Court of Appeal, were—"The hotel was said to be dirty; the hot water supply was inadequate (to say the least), at times non-existent; the cold water supply was not always available; the central heating did not work properly and was only available for part of the holiday; the rooms were in consequence cold; the blankets and the bedding were inadequate; the beds were themselves uncomfortable; and there was no warm and friendly atmosphere in the place; indeed there were no public rooms in which such an atmosphere could develop". Further, the cistern of the lavatory in the bathroom overflowed, and the bedside lighting was weak. The judge awarded the plaintiff damages of £75, the plaintiff's son £20, the plaintiff's friend £75, the friend's son £20 and the friend's daughter £10. The plaintiff appealed.

Held: In the original award not enough attention had been paid to the inconvenience and distress caused to the holiday makers. Adopting a broad approach, damages would be increased from £200 to £500 on the basis of the difference between what was expected and what was obtained. A lump sum was awarded since there was no question of the parties disagreeing about the division of the sum. Accordingly, the appeal was allowed.

The following *dicta* in particular should be noted:

Per Eveleigh LJ:

"The trial judge had applied the correct principle in assessing damages, namely that the plaintiff was 'entitled to compensation for the diminution of the value of the holiday, discomfort and inconvenience and diminution of enjoyment which resulted therefrom and for mental distress caused by disappointment' . . . The plaintiff and his party had suffered a lower standard of enjoyment of the holiday than they were entitled to expect and the lower standard of material comforts in fact positively induced not enjoyment but irritation, frustration and depression which all derogated from the holiday atmosphere . . . Although the boys in the party had at all times found the funny side of events, the defendant could not in response to a claim for damages say that the boys themselves showed enough fortitude to put up with it, or indeed to be able to joke about it. They were entitled to a holiday of a certain standard, a standard very much higher than that which they received; and it is for that which compensation, in my opinion, should be paid".

Per Cumming-Bruce LJ:

"I cannot find in those cases (ie *Jarvis* and *Jackson*) anything that really indicates a scale of damages which can readily be applied to the facts of the instant case".

(d) Chesneau v Interhome Ltd [*1983*] *CLY 988*

The facts: The plaintiff rented from the defendants a house in Grasse, France for three weeks commencing on 13 September 1980 at a total cost of £385, for himself, his wife and three year old child. The defendants, so it was held, represented that the house was in a quiet location near the woods, that it had a garden and swimming pool, that it was approximately thirty-five square metres in floor area, that it had an open gallery with a double bed and that it was not part of a complex. Upon arrival the plaintiffs discovered that the house was one of a complex, the swimming pool was shared by the complex, there was no privacy in the house, which had no bed but a double mattress taking up most of the floor space and the plaintiffs, accordingly, decided not to stay. They contacted the defendants who agreed that the contract should be rescinded and the plaintiffs refunded the costs. The plaintiffs spent £11.40 on telephone calls and found alternative accommodation in St. Tropez two days later at a cost of £209 over and above the original contract price. The plaintiff claimed, on behalf of himself and his family, the sums of £209 and £11.40 and damages for disappointment, stress and vexation under s.2(1) of the Misrepresentation Act 1967.

Held: An Assistant Recorder sitting at Wandsworth County Court held that the defendant's representations entitled the plaintiffs to damages under s.2(1) of the Misrepresentation Act 1967 but that, in view of the fact that they had recovered the cost of the holiday for which they had contracted with the defendants, they were entitled to damages for inconvenience only for the two days during which they were making alternative arrangements. He assessed these damages at £30 and also awarded £50 for the plaintiff's loss of opportunity to obtain a villa that suited their requirements.

The plaintiffs appealed. The Court of Appeal awarded them £200 compensation for inconvenience and mental distress, the return of the £209 (the difference between the cost of the original villa and that which they subsequently arranged) and £11.40 for telephone calls.

The following *dicta*, in particular, should be noted:

Per Eveleigh LJ:

> "On both sides, but for different reasons or with a different object in view, counsel have argued that damages awarded are, strictly speaking, damages in tort. For myself, I think that that is probably correct. Indeed, they should be assessed in a case like the present on the same principles as damages are assessed in tort . .. One has to see the position they were in back in England before they started off and then compare it with the position which they found themselves in as a result of this misrepresentation. They found themselves in the position where they were about to face a disastrous holiday, disastrous from their point of view from that which they had arranged and were entitled to expect . .. So the

> plaintiff was in a position where he would have to say: 'I will go home, regard the holiday as lost and sue for that'. Alternatively, he could have stayed at Grasse, decided to put up with it and sue for whatever damages he might then get on a chance basis. Or, mindful of the fact that he might have been criticised if he did not do so, he could seek to mitigate the overall position by finding somewhere else that would give him the kind of holiday to which he was, as I see it, entitled . . . In my judgment, had they not taken the house in Grasse, they would have been entitled to damages in excess of £209 . . . So one really is concerned with what they would have received on the general heading, damages such as the courts now award in this kind of case. It seems to me that, for the distress of the initial period, taking into account also the fact that the holiday they in fact enjoyed was less than they would have had, a figure of £200 would be appropriate to reflect the loss sustained for that. As I say, I think that a greater figure for the general loss of the amenity of the holiday would be attracted for the ensuing three weeks, or just under three weeks, and a figure greater than £209. But, as they have chosen properly to mitigate their loss by the expenditure of that sum of money, I think they are entitled to that amount".

Per O'Connor LJ:

> "When one is considering the head of damage of inconvenience, discomfort, annoyance and disturbance to what had been planned, in my judgment all those factors can be taken into consideration. For that head the learned judge awarded £30. In my judgment it was a wholly erroneous assessment of damages. It was so far too little that this court is entitled to, and indeed is bound to, interfere and I agree that under that head the award should be increased to £200".

(e) Kemp v Intasun Holidays Limited [*1987*] *2 FTLR 234*

The facts: On 2 February 1984 Mrs Kemp and her daughter called at a branch of Thomas Cook in Worcester to choose a summer holiday. There was a conversation between Mrs Kemp and one of the assistants at Thomas Cook. In it Mrs Kemp referred to the fact that her husband suffered from asthma. The finding of the judge in the Worcester County Court about the conversation was:

> "Mrs Kemp explained to Thomas Cook that she was sorry her husband could not be there but he was ill. I am satisfied that she said he was suffering an asthmatic and a bronchial attack, as he sometimes did."

The judge also found that Mrs Kemp said that, because of her husband's health, some special insurance was required. But he did not base his conclusions on anything concerning the desirable insurance cover. Following the discussions between Mrs Kemp and Thomas Cook, the plaintiff decided to choose a fourteen day holiday in August 1984 at a hotel called "America I" at Callas de Mallorca at a cost of about £828. The relevant booking form for that holiday, which was included in the defendants' brochure, was taken away by Mrs Kemp as well as a proposal form for an insurance policy. On 6 February Mrs Kemp came back with her daughter and paid the insurance premium of some £29. By 29 February the Kemps had completed and returned the booking form and it was accepted by Intasun.

On 4 August 1984 the family departed on their holiday and for the first thirty hours it proved to be disastrous. They arrived at Palma at about 6.30 on a Sunday morning and were taken in a minibus with other travellers to their hotel, the America I, but found it was full up. The judge awarded £400 for the general inconvenience and disappointment resulting from this.

The plaintiffs were given alternative accommodation in a hotel called Las Chihuahuas which was of substantially lower quality than America I. The judge described the new accommodation as

> "a room in the staff or service quarter of the hotel. This was not a part of the normal hotel accommodation. There was a broken window, filled in with

> lattice work of bricks, and there was glass on the floor. Mrs Kemp said that the room was filthy, very dirty, very dusty. The toilet had no door, the shower did not work and there was no bath. There were two single beds and a portable bed which they could not make work."

The dirty and dusty condition of this accommodation had a particular effect on Mr Kemp's asthmatic condition. Because of this Mr Kemp, who, as shown by a medical report, suffered from chronic bronchitis and emphysema, had an attack of asthma which caused him and the other members of the family considerable distress. The judge found that Mr Kemp suffered from this throughout the thirty hours that the plaintiffs spent in the alternative accommodation. The judge awarded £800 compensation for this, and the defendants appealed.

Held: A tour operator is liable for consequences which flow naturally from his breach of contract, and for any additional consequences which should reasonably have been within his contemplation when entering into the contract. Information which is not part of the booking arrangements but is given to the travel agent in casual conversation is not sufficiently with the tour operator's knowledge to give rise to contractual consequences. Accordingly, the Court of Appeal allowed the defendants' appeal against the award of £800 damages in favour of the plaintiff.

The following *dicta* in particular should be noted:

Per Kerr LJ:

> "He (a tour operator) must also accept liability for any other consequences which should have been in the reasonable contemplation of the parties if these flowed naturally from his breach and caused additional foreseeable loss or damage ... For instance, if the consequence of not providing the contractual accommodation is not merely the loss of its enjoyment and so forth, but also the fact that the plaintiffs had to sleep out on the beach, with the result that their health suffered in a natural and ordinarily foreseeable way because they caught

colds or even pneumonia, then that would be a natural and foreseeable additional consequence which would equally flow from the tour operator's breach."

Per Parker LJ:

> "I cannot accept that a casual conversation in February that the plaintiff was an asthmatic sufferer and because of his health required extra insurance is sufficient to bring it within the contemplation of the parties that, in the event of a breach in August consisting of putting the plaintiff in a disgusting room, an asthmatic attack was not unlikely to occur. I use the words 'not unlikely' because they were among the words used by their Lordships in *Koufos* v *Czarnikow*."

(f) Conclusions

The above five cases deal with damages for breach of contract and misrepresentation, and various important points are to be elicited from them:

(i) It is now established law that a holiday maker who proves breach of contract is entitled to recover general damages for diminution in the value of the contract and also for loss of enjoyment, disappointment, mental anguish and inconvenience. This unites the categories of physical and mental distress mentioned previously. This is, of course, in addition to special damages (ie out of pocket expenses which he has incurred as a result of the breach).

(ii) A holiday maker who enters into a contract with a tour operator can sue on it for damages for loss suffered not only by him but also by any others who went on the holiday under cover of the contract.

(iii) None of the cases, despite the extent of the plaintiffs' claims, decided that there was total failure of performance of the contract by the defendants.

(iv) None of the cases provide any definite indication of the sort of sum which should be awarded for disappointment etc. There is, though, something of a discrepancy between the *Jarvis* and *Horizon* cases. In the latter, although the decision was not made on this basis, Lord Denning suggested that the £1,100 be split as to £600 for diminution of value of contract and £500 for loss of enjoyment. In *Jarvis* there seems to have been agreement that the diminution of value of the contract was half (approximately £30) so that the damages for disappointment etc were approximately three times that. Perhaps what the cases establish is that, when assessing disappointment, the facilities affected must be carefully considered to establish whether they go to the heart of the holiday. For instance, on a skiing holiday a lack of skis is a most material source of disappointment whereas on a holiday in a continuously hot and sunny climate the absence of electric heaters at the hotel is not a major cause for concern.

The courts have given some very broad outlines of the factors to be taken into consideration when evaluating damages. The factors set out below are ones which the writers consider should be taken into account on all occasions, although one or two of these have been specifically rejected by county courts:

(i) What proportion of the holiday was affected by the events complained of? Damages will encompass not only the amount for which an allowance in reduction of the holiday price should be made but also compensation for disappointment etc. To evaluate the allowance referred to above, it is necessary to break down, at least approximately, the overall cost of the holiday so that the cost of the item(s) complained of may be determined and a satisfactory reduction evaluated depending upon the gravity of the breach. This may only provide a nominal sum but it may be increased by damages for disappointment etc.

(ii) What amount of enjoyment did the holiday maker obtain from the holiday? It can be seen that in the *Jarvis* case Mr Jarvis recovered almost twice the cost of his holiday and in the *Adcock* case Mr Adcock and party recovered a sum slightly in excess of the holiday price whereas Mr Jackson in his claim did not recover the holiday price. The reason must be that Mr Jackson, despite the breaches, still obtained enjoyment from his holiday whereas Mr Jarvis did not and, despite the attitude of the minors, neither did Mr Adcock and his party. Aside from flagrant breaches it is unlikely that a holiday maker can allege that no enjoyment whatsoever was obtained from the holiday. An unsatisfactory bedroom in a hotel, for example, does not prevent a holiday maker from enjoying other facilities offered by the hotel or from enjoying normal outdoor activities. As has already been stated, what must be decided is whether or not the matters complained of go to the heart of the holiday.

(iii) Whether or not the holiday maker has made any effort to mitigate his loss? In the event that a bedroom in a hotel is unsatisfactory a holiday maker should not relocate himself in a more expensive hotel of a higher standard and be allowed to reclaim this sum. He should first comply with any contractual obligation to complain to the hotelier or the tour operator's representative (see Regulation 15(9)). In many cases, the representative will be able to arrange satisfactory relocation within the actual hotel or transfer to another hotel at no extra cost. Tour operators will need to explain that there is an obligation so to complain, and to do so also to the relevant supplier.

(iv) What was the price of the holiday? It is suggested that the standards to be expected from cut price holidays should not be as high as in full price holidays. The old maxim "you get what you pay for" should be applied. This does seem an equitable consideration to take into account when assessing damages, although the Westminster County Court rejected it in the *Levine* v *Metropolitan Travel* case (see Appendix D).

(v) What was the exact wording in the brochure? If, for example, a hotel is described as "simple and unpretentious" it should not be interpreted as meaning anything other than that the facilities will be fairly basic. It is appreciated that holiday makers expect to enjoy their holiday but their expectations should be realistic. Although tour operators are "peddling dreams", this is merely an unavoidable consequence of the product being sold. It should not be a reason for imposing what are in reality punitive damages.

(vi) Did the holiday maker make any effort to enjoy his holiday? The fact that a holiday maker puts on a brave front in the face of adversity should not constitute a defence to a claim for damages. But courts should be aware that there are some holiday makers who seek to find and magnify faults, perhaps with a view to trying to fund next year's holiday. This should be borne in mind under the heading of mitigation.

(vii) Were there children on the holiday? The county court judge in the *Adcock* case accepted that matters which affect an adult's enjoyment of a holiday will not necessarily affect a child's. If, for example, in breach of contract there is no discotheque this is not something which will cause a child disquiet. Unfortunately, the Court of Appeal in *Adcock* did not go into this point and did not even split up their increased award of £500. It is suggested that this consideration might be taken even further so that if one member of a holiday party enjoyed a holiday despite breaches this should be taken into account when assessing damages.

5. County court cases

A major difficulty in advising about damages is that the vast majority of cases are county court cases which are in the main unreported. Different county courts have adopted different criteria. These are, to a certain extent, inconsistent with each other and with the above-mentioned cases, although in law the principles enunciated by the Court of Appeal take precedence over contrary county court decisions.

It is, though, instructive and necessary to consider county court decisions because, as the county court is the most common forum for deciding a dissatisfied holiday maker's claim, they provide practical illustrations of likely awards at first instance. Recent years have seen an increase in the number of county court cases to such an extent that it is impractical, in this book, to comment on each one. Reports of various cases not mentioned elsewhere in the text are contained in Appendix D.

There are two cases which need particularly to be mentioned. The first is *Glover* v *Kuoni* [1987] CLY 1151 in which Mr and Mrs Glover booked a package holiday with Kuoni, to include sixteen days' accommodation in the Maldives. The flight on which they travelled lost their luggage which contained valuable photographic equipment. One of their purposes in visiting the Maldives was for underwater photography. They had no clothes or items whatsoever of their own for the duration of the holiday; there were no available places to purchase replacements and they had to borrow from other holiday makers. For the first week Kuoni's on-the-spot representative did nothing to help and was abrasively dismissive. It was held that the holiday was a total disaster. Kuoni were held liable, not because of the loss of luggage but because of their representative's attitude. Mr and Mrs Glover, aside from interest, costs and special damages recovered the cost of the holiday (approximately £2,200) and £50 per person per day for loss of enjoyment.

This case is significant for two reasons. The first is that the judge did make an effort to make specific awards for each type of damage, and awarded a daily sum for loss of enjoyment. The second is the amount of the daily sum. At the time, it sent shockwaves through the travel industry. Looked at in the cold light of day, what the daily sum equates to is approximately £2 for every hour where it was found as a matter of fact that the plaintiffs obtained no enjoyment whatsoever from the holiday.

In *Skrakowski* v *Airtours* [1990] CLY 1543 the plaintiff bought a package holiday from the defendant for himself and his wife. The defendant's brochure gave the accommodation a rating of 3 palm trees (maximum 4) and referred to "huge gardens with orange and mimosa groves". The price (2 people, 14 nights) was £710. The bungalow in which they were staying and the hotel of which it was a part were tatty and dilapidated; there was a large hole in the door to the bungalow through which countless insects entered; the cover of their lavatory cistern was split in two; on their terrace, there was no light bulb and one of the two chairs was rusty and dilapidated. There were other defects too. "It was clear that the accommodation was nowhere near 3 star by anyone's standard". The grounds were barren and deserted; unlike nearby hotels, they were not irrigated. Food was poor. The defendant's representative did not visit their bungalow until half-way through their holiday. The plaintiff's wife was five months pregnant with their first child, so it was to be their last holiday "as free spirits".

The plaintiffs were awarded damages: firstly, £355 being half the price of the holiday to represent diminution in value; secondly, special damages of £100; thirdly, £1,250 for loss of enjoyment and, fourthly, interest. The loss of enjoyment figure equates to a daily sum per person of approximately £45. On its face, this directly follows on from the *Glover* case with a generous mark-up for inflation given that the holiday was not said to be a total disaster.

The judge's reasoning in making the award was rather novel. He concluded that, since the cost of the holiday was twenty times more than the cost in *Jarvis* v *Swan Tours*, he would multiply the loss of enjoyment award in that case by approximately twenty. This is, in the authors' view, an inherently flawed approach. Such an approach could only be justified where the holiday arrangements were the same, the level of disappointment the same and the multiplier an accepted inflation multiplier.

6. Limitation of damages

As discussed in Chapter 3, Regulation 15(4) allows a tour operator to include in his terms of contract a term limiting the amount of compensation provided that it does not apply to personal injury claims and that the limitation is "not unreasonable". From a tour operator's point of view the key issue is to identify what is "not unreasonable". There is little point in having a limitation of damages clause upon which reliance cannot be placed in dealing with holiday makers' complaints – unless, of course, a tour operator takes a robust view that the clause will have a deterrent effect.

There is a number of formulae which can be used which, in the writers' opinion, would be considered "not unreasonable" by the courts. The first is an application of limits contained in international conventions (see pages 218–226). These limits apply to delay and loss of baggage. Given that they are generally enforced, it seems clear that they would also be valid within the context of Regulation 15(4).

Convention limits, however, will not enable the tour operator to deal with the majority of complaints which relate to dissatisfaction with some or all of the package holiday. One approach to them is to set out the maximum sum which will be awarded in the worst case – this will, of course, be where the package holiday was a total "disaster" – and then provide that in any other case proportionate sums would be awarded at the operator's discretion.

How should the maximum sum be calculated? As can be seen from the preceding sections, the courts, in awarding damages, take into account three factors, namely the diminution of value, special damages and loss of enjoyment etc. A limitation could be stipulated applying this formula. To do this the contract term would state that in the worst case the holiday maker would receive a refund of holiday monies, payment of all special damages and a daily sum to cater for loss of enjoyment etc.

The difficult question in the above formula is the amount of the daily sum. The most which has been awarded in any case to date is the £50 per person per day in *Glover* v *Kuoni* (see above). That case was in 1987 so that, if it is to be used as a precedent, the current figure would be slightly higher. It would clearly be reasonable to pick a daily sum of around £50. In choosing a daily sum, there is merit in making it divisible by 24. This means that an hourly figure can be calculated, and enables compensation to be assessed in a reasonably precise manner.

An alternative is to assess a maximum sum by reference to a multiple of the holiday cost. This is, however, illogical since its inevitable implication is that loss of enjoyment will depend upon the amount paid for the holiday. The extent of loss of enjoyment is more likely to depend upon the significance of the cost to the person paying, the purpose of the holiday, the numbers of holidays taken by the holiday maker in any one year and any other relevant personal circumstances which have been communicated to the operator before the making of the contract. For example, if the holiday was for a honeymoon the holiday maker will be entitled to damages which take that into account only if the tour operator was told of the honeymoon before the contract was made.

In deciding whether or not to include a clause limiting damages, tour operators will need to take into account their general policy. Additionally, they will need to review amounts paid out in previous cases to clients that have been accepted without quibble by those clients. The facts of those cases should then be applied to a proposed damage limitation clause. If the result would have been payment of a higher sum, clearly there is no point in having the clause. If there would have been payment of a lower sum, clearly there is point. In general, it does seem that, from the tour operator's point of view, the worth of a damage limitation clause depends upon the average package holiday cost. The higher that cost the more it is worthwhile having a damage limitation clause.

Chapter 8

Claims

A holiday maker who is dissatisfied with any aspect of his holiday and who fails to obtain satisfaction from the tour operator concerned, must decide whether to pursue matters further and, if so, how. The purpose of this chapter is to consider the two basic alternatives available to him—ABTA (or AITO) arbitration or court proceedings—and to give guidance regarding both making and defending claims.

1. Preliminary considerations

In essence a holiday maker will have to consider the same basic criteria in deciding whether to pursue a claim as a travel company will in deciding whether to resist it. These are—

(a) the likelihood of success;

(b) the costs involved in pursuing/defending the claim if successful;

(c) the costs involved in pursuing/defending the claim if unsuccessful.

Apart from forums in which a successful party will not be awarded costs, such as county court arbitration, the normal rule is that a successful party (be he plaintiff or defendant) will recover what are called standard basis costs. These are costs reasonably incurred in taking the action to trial—this excludes, though, costs in respect of such aspects as discussions with legal advisers about general matters. As a rule of thumb they will be in the region of one-half to two-thirds of his total legal costs. This leaves a successful party with a costs liability to his own legal advisers which in the case of a claimant can all too easily absorb the bulk of the damages which he is awarded. An unsuccessful party will be responsible for not only his own legal costs but the standard basis costs of the other side.

In pursuing a claim a holiday maker has certain built-in advantages. In general, the sympathies of the court are likely to be with a dissatisfied holiday maker. Any publicity resulting from a claim is likely to be adverse to the travel company. The costs which travel companies are likely to face in defending most claims will be substantially higher than those faced by holiday makers since the travel companies will, in all probability, require as witnesses persons normally resident abroad. In practice, therefore, the odds are very much in the holiday maker's favour. After all, to allege disappointment and loss of enjoyment he merely has to give evidence himself which can be very difficult for the travel company to shake no matter how minor the default in respect of which proceedings have been issued.

One of the basic points which this book seeks to emphasize is that a holiday maker's contract for a package holiday is with the tour operator who arranges it and, *prima facie,* any liability for defects in the holiday will attach to the tour operator. Thus, a dissatisfied holiday maker should address his complaints to the tour operator, either directly or through the travel agent with whom the booking was made. In cases of obvious default there is merit in using the travel agent's services since he may be able to exert pressure upon the operator to offer satisfactory compensation but the holiday maker should not expect compensation from the agent in respect of matters which are clearly the operator's responsibility. The effect of Regulation 4, however, is that, in the event of any "descriptive matter" about a package being "misleading", a holiday maker has the option of claiming against the travel agent which supplied the descriptive matter—in addition to having a claim against the tour operator. The holiday maker is given the option of whom to sue. Also, a holiday maker may have a claim against a travel agent if the agent misrepresented the facilities available, failed to process the booking satisfactorily or gave unsatisfactory advice.

Consider the following example:

> Mr Jones books a fortnight's holiday for himself and his wife at the Hotel Luxury, Greece at a cost of £800. The operator with whom the contract is made and whose brochure details the facilities available is Utopian Tours Limited, an ABTA member, and the agent through whom the booking is made is Good Advice Limited, also an ABTA member. The Hotel Luxury, a well known hotel in a well known resort, is described in the operator's brochure as having an Olympic size swimming pool. This is of particular importance to Mr Jones since both he and his wife are keen swimmers but do not like swimming in the sea—something which he emphasized to Good Advice who, on the basis of Utopian Tours Limited's brochure, recommended the Hotel Luxury. Upon arrival Mr and Mrs Jones discover that the pool is closed.

In this situation, leaving aside the question of actual liability, which will depend upon the circumstances and date of closure of the pool and whether or not Utopian Tours passed on any information available to it about closure of the pool to Good Advice, Mr and Mrs Jones could have claims against—

(a) Utopian Tours for failure to perform the contract under Regulation 15, breach of contract under the general law, breach of Regulation 4 and misrepresentation; and

(b) Good Advice for breach of Regulation 4, misrepresentation, breach of duty of care and negligent advice.

2. Making a claim

When Mr and Mrs Jones make their claim, they should stress to Utopian Tours and Good Advice that both are being held liable. If each claims that the other is responsible (say, with the operator alleging that errata letters about closure of the pool had been sent to the agent who had failed to warn the Joneses and the agent denying ever having received them), how do the Joneses proceed?

Although both Utopian Tours and Good Advice are ABTA members, it will not be possible for the Joneses to avail themselves of ABTA's arbitration scheme. This is because it does not extend to commercial disputes between its members, and this includes members alleging each other to be responsible. Although Regulation 4 does not permit a defence, the sole criterion being whether or not descriptive matter was misleading, Utopian Tours will no doubt claim that the descriptive matter they supplied was the brochure and errata, and, therefore, it was not misleading. Proceedings in the courts will, thus, be necessary.

(a) Limitation of claim

Generally, most holiday claims in respect of which court proceedings are issued are brought in the county court. The amounts which can be claimed in the county court are presently determined by the High Court and County Courts Jurisdiction Order 1991. Its general effect is that any breach of contract claim for less than £25,000, and any personal injury claim for less than £50,000, should be brought in the county court. If a claim for less than these amounts is commenced in the High Court, the High Court, pursuant to s.40 of the County Courts Act 1984, may transfer the proceedings to the county court, taking into account the following criteria –

(i) the financial substance of the action;

(ii) whether the action is otherwise important and, in particular, whether it raises issues of general importance;

(iii) the complexity of the facts, legal issues, remedies or procedures involved;

(iv) whether the transfer is likely to result in a more speedy trial.

In the writers' view, it is more than likely that package holiday claims would be transferred by the High Court to the county court. If a new point of law is involved which arises from the Regulations it is just conceivable that the claim would be retained in the High Court, but the point of law would need to be particularly complex and of general import.

Returning to our example, the Joneses' claim should be for damages limited to £5,000, depending upon whether or not any special damages are claimed—say, for the expense of travelling daily to another Olympic sized swimming pool in the area and the cost of using it. The rationale behind this limitation is that the Joneses would claim—

(a) A refund of a portion of the £800 holiday price for the lack of a material facility;

(b) Damages for loss of enjoyment and disappointment. The holiday is unlikely to be found to be a complete disaster so that these damages will not come within the levels envisaged by *Glover* v *Kuoni* (see page 177).

(c) Any special damages.

(b) *Small claims court*

If the Joneses were prepared to limit their claim to £1,000 or less, it would come within the county court's automatic reference to arbitration ("the small claims court"). There are several advantages for a holiday maker if he feels able to confine his claim to £1,000 or less:

(a) The proceedings are much more informal than full county court/High Court proceedings both leading up to and during the hearing of the action. It is, therefore, much easier for a holiday maker to conduct his own claim without seeking legal assistance and incurring the resultant legal costs. In fact, at the pre-trial review the registrar, when giving directions to enable the matter to proceed to hearing, will frequently give an inexperienced party procedural advice.

(b) No orders as to costs are normally made save that a successful plaintiff will recover the costs stated on the Summons (Order 19 rule 6, County Court Rules 1981). This assists a holiday maker conducting his claim in person since the tour operator, even if confident of successfully defending a claim, runs the risk of incurring legal costs in excess of the sum which the plaintiff is claiming. An unfortunate result of this, from a travel company's point of view, is that it renders inapplicable the normal court rules whereby costs are awarded in favour of a defendant, if at an early stage of the proceedings he makes a payment into court which exceeds what is subsequently awarded by the judge (who is not told about the payment until after he has reached his decision). It is, therefore, most difficult for travel companies to protect their costs position and thereby encourage the holiday maker to negotiate a reasonable settlement.

(c) If the registrar certifies that there are costs which have been incurred through the unreasonable conduct of a party in relation to the proceedings that party will be ordered to be responsible to the other parties to the proceedings for those costs (Order 19 rule 6(c)). Such a decision is totally at the registrar's discretion which is only exercised in exceptional circumstances.

(d) The normal rules of evidence are relaxed, to enable a more informal hearing. Although, in theory, this could make it easier for the tour operator to rely upon written statements adduced as evidence under the Civil Evidence Act (this is covered in greater detail at a later stage) rather than produce witnesses, in practice the registrar will be more inclined to accept the evidence given by the holiday maker.

(e) The hearing date for arbitration is likely to be much earlier than that for a full county court trial.

Theoretically, it is possible for any party to proceedings involving claims for £1,000 or less to make an application to the county court registrar under Order 19 rule 2 of the County Court Rules 1981 for an order rescinding the reference to arbitration on the grounds that:

"(a) a difficult question of law or a question of fact of exceptional complexity is involved; or

(b) a charge of fraud is in issue; or

(c) the parties are agreed that the dispute should be tried in court; or

(d) it would be unreasonable for the claim to proceed to arbitration having regard to its subject matter, the circumstances of the parties or the interests of any other person likely to be affected by the award."

Unless application is made on the grounds of (b) or (c) above it is unlikely to be successful for two reasons. Firstly, most registrars will by now have heard at least several holiday cases and will not regard it as unusual for them to hear it. Secondly, it is always difficult to advise a registrar who is likely to conduct the arbitration that it is too complicated for him. If the application is unsuccessful it does not bode well for the applicant for the actual arbitration.

(c) Issue of proceedings

Mr and Mrs Jones determine that they will issue proceedings in the county court. It was, of course, Mr Jones who made the booking and in accordance with *Jackson* v *Horizon Holidays* (see pages 165-167) he is entitled to sue on it on behalf of both himself and his wife. The importance of this decision was that it overcame any difficulties for holiday makers in respect of allegations by a tour operator that those who were in the holiday party but who did not sign the booking form were not parties to the contract and therefore could not claim damages for breach of contract.

The conclusions reached by the Court of Appeal, and in particular by Denning LJ, in *Jackson* v *Horizon Holidays* were disapproved of by the House of Lords in *Woodar Investment Development* v *Wimpey Construction UK* [1980] 1 WLR 277. Lord Wilberforce said, *inter alia*:

> "I am not prepared to dissent from the actual decision in that case (ie *Jackson* v *Horizon Holidays*). It may be supported either as a broad decision on the measure of damages or possibly as an example of a type of contract–examples of which are persons contracting for family holidays, ordering meals in restaurants for a party, hiring a taxi for a group–calling for special treatment . . . there are many situations of daily life which do not fit neatly into conceptual analyses, but which require some flexibility in the law of contract. *Jackson's* case may well be one. I cannot, however, agree with the basis on which Denning LJ put his position in that case . . .".

Lord Wilberforce's comments were supported by the rest of the court in the *Woodar* case. The present position, therefore, appears to be that the result of the *Jackson* case is approved, although its *ratio decidendi* is not.

Where a tour operator is bound by ABTA's present Tour Operators' Code of Conduct, that Code, at clause 2.8, provides that the obligations which ABTA tour operators have to accept when things go wrong with a package apply to all named on the booking form, irrespective of whether or not any individual actually signed the booking form. Further, Regulation 2 contains a definition of consumer. That definition makes it clear that the obligations imposed upon tour operators and travel agents by the Regulations apply to all who participate in a package holiday booking, irrespective of whether or not they sign the booking form. The relevance of the *Jackson* decision is, accordingly, limited to claims which are brought against tour operators who are not members of ABTA and where the Regulations do not apply.

If proceedings are issued against Utopian Tours and Good Advice as first and second defendants, and both intend to defend the proceedings, consideration should be given by each of them to the preparation and service of contribution notices. These are formal pleadings whereby one defendant claims an indemnity from another on the basis that any default was the other's default. If only one of the travel companies has been named as a defendant and if it considers the other to blame, it should issue a third party notice whereby the other is joined as a party to the proceedings. The third party will, though, only be a party to the proceedings to the extent that, if the defendant is held liable, the court will determine whether or not to order that the third party should recompense the defendant. Order 12 of the County Court Rules 1981 and Order 16 of the Rules of the Supreme Court set out the appropriate provisions regarding the issue, service etc., of contribution/third party notices depending upon whether proceedings are in the county or High Court.

A holiday maker faced with a defendant and a third party should consider seeking the leave of the court to convert the third party into a second defendant in the proceedings. The reason for this is that otherwise, although the holiday maker's claim against the defendant and the defendant's claim against the third party will normally be heard contemporaneously, questions of liability will be decided separately. If, therefore, the court finds in favour of the defendant in respect of the holiday maker's claim against him, the holiday maker will not be in a position to seek any order against the third party in these proceedings. That would only be possible had the holiday maker taken steps prior to the trial to convert the third party into a second defendant.

(d) Preparation for trial

To prepare for trial Utopian Tours and Good Advice will have to consider the following:

(i) The witnesses whom they intend to call and the exchange of witness statements;

(ii) The documents in their possession which are not privileged from disclosure and should therefore be placed before the court;

(iii) Whether or not a payment into court should be made;

(iv) Whether or not it will be effective to dispense with any oral evidence and rely instead upon statements adduced under the Civil Evidence Act;

(v) Any plans or photographs which they may wish to place before the court (for instance, if the pool was cracked and generally in disrepair, photographs to evidence this and the extent of disruption); and

(vi) The bundle of documents to be placed before the court.

It is beyond the purpose and scope of this book to consider in any detail the technical rules regarding discovery and payments into court but it is worthwhile to make some brief comments. However, the reader should bear in mind that what follows is not an exhaustive set of guidelines but merely an outline of certain pertinent points.

(e) Payments into court

As has already been stated, most hearings take place in county courts and are unreported. As a consequence there is little consistency in the level of damages awarded. This can make it difficult for the operator to gauge accurately an effective payment into court and for the holiday maker to decide whether to accept a payment into court.

One of the main purposes of a payment into court is to protect a defendant's position on costs. It is based on the defendant's assessment of the maximum amount the plaintiff will be able to recover at trial. It is senseless to seek to pennypinch, but it is possible to make an initial payment into court which is less than that which the defendant considers to be truly accurate and thereafter top it up.

When a payment into court is made, the plaintiff can accept it within 21 days and is entitled, if he does so, to recover his standard basis costs from the defendant. If the plaintiff does not accept a payment into court and at trial is awarded a sum equal to or less than the payment into court, the court, in awarding costs, will normally exercise its discretion to award the plaintiff his costs up to the date of the payment into court and to award the costs thereafter to the defendant.

Where a payment in is made within 21 days of a trial, these costs consequences can still apply. The notes to the Rules of the Supreme Court provide –

> "the rule (ie that for the time of acceptance of a payment in) makes no express provision as to what is the position where a payment into court is made or increased less than 21 days before the trial . . . A payment made or received less than 21 days before the trial or hearing, which remains unaccepted by the Plaintiff, is a valid payment in and may be taken into account by the court in exercising its discretion as to costs."

In calculating a payment into court, account should be taken of the interest which would be awarded on any damages which are awarded.

At trial, it is not permitted to inform the trial judge of any payment into court until after judgment has been given. However, in summing up the defendant's advocate will normally reserve a passage to deal with *quantum* in the event that the trial judge finds against the defendant. In addressing the issue of *quantum* the advocate is well advised to put forward figures less than the sum actually paid into court. Trial judges who feel sympathy for a plaintiff may consider that the figures put forward in summing up by the defendant's advocate represent the payment into court and may seek to top these up to protect the plaintiff on costs. Allowing for a "margin of error" may result in whatever damages order is made being covered by the payment into court.

(f) Discovery

The basic rule is that all relevant documents held by a party must be disclosed except for ones which are privileged from production. Privileged documents include "without prejudice" correspondence, internal memoranda for the dominant purpose of litigation, correspondence between the parties and their legal advisers, instructions to counsel, witness statements etc. It is possible for part of a document to be privileged from disclosure and part not.

Travel companies should bear in mind that, generally speaking, the bulk of their correspondence and internal memoranda written before the issue of proceedings will not be privileged from disclosure. Much of this documentation will emanate from customer relations departments and on the spot representatives. Most tour operators have a system whereby their on the spot representatives prepare weekly reports and these will normally be subject to production, as a result of the decision in *Waugh* v *British Railways Board* [1979] 2 All ER 1169. This case held, *inter alia,* that an internal memorandum was only to be accorded privilege if the dominant purpose for which it was prepared was for submission to a legal adviser for advice and use in litigation. It will only be in exceptional cases that it will be possible to allege that a representative's weekly report was prepared for the dominant purpose of use in litigation.

It is the originals of documents which must be produced and care should be taken to avoid endorsing on documents comments which could prove to be damaging to a party's case.

The authors of letters responding to complaints by dissatisfied holiday makers and of internal company reports should always keep in mind the following:

(i) Their words could, in the long run, be read out in open court. Reports, letters etc should, accordingly, be concise, accurate, simple statements of facts. Derogatory or facetious comments should be avoided. Such comments often prejudice the travel company's case and they are likely to be seized upon by reporters at a court hearing with resultant bad publicity.

(ii) The mere endorsement of "without prejudice" at the top of a letter does not automatically preclude disclosure. Only letters which constitute genuine attempts at settlement will be privileged. Statements of purported fact contained in without prejudice letters will not be privileged.

(iii) A series of letters should be consistent in their content. It is always damaging if one letter contradicts what was said in another. Sometimes this cannot be avoided but then it should be done expressly and a virtue made of necessity.

(g) Evidence

It is the question of oral evidence that can cause travel companies the most difficulty and expense. Usually for a claim to be successfully defended it will be desirable for the operator's on the spot representative and the manager of the hotel featured in the package holiday (presuming that complaint is made about the hotel) to be flown to the UK for the hearing. As well as the expense of having such people attend the hearing, there is the difficulty of taking detailed and satisfactory statements. These can really only be properly obtained by a personal interview (extra expense). Reliance upon statements prepared at a distance, say by the manager of a Greek hotel, can be a risky foundation upon which to defend a claim. Further, the tour operator depends upon the voluntary co-operation of those abroad since the English courts do not have the power to subpoena a witness beyond their jurisdiction to attend the hearing (section 36 of the Supreme Court Act 1981). The holiday maker should also bear in mind these potential costs since, if his claim is unsuccessful, he may be ordered to pay them.

It is now commonplace for the courts to order an exchange of the statements of witnesses of fact well before a trial begins. This imposes additional burdens on tour operators to arrange for statements to be prepared through personal interviews. This is because witness statements must contain all the facts about which the witness will give evidence in person. It is important for these to be prepared accurately since, if, at the trial, there is a discrepancy between the oral evidence of a witness and his/her written statement, at the very least the credibility of the witness will be reduced.

Mention has been made of the use of written statements as evidence under the Civil Evidence Act 1968. In the Joneses' case it might be helpful for Utopian Tours to produce as evidence a statement from the manager of the Hotel Luxury explaining the reasons for the closure of the hotel swimming pool or the availability and proximity of other swimming pools. The relevant provisions of the Civil Evidence Act can be summarised as follows:

(i) Section 2(1) provides that the oral or written out-of-court statements of any person, whether called as a witness in the proceedings or not, shall, "subject to this section and to rules of court", be admissible in chief as evidence of any fact stated therein of which direct oral evidence by him would be admissible.

(ii) The party wishing to adduce a statement as evidence under s.2 must serve a notice upon the other party detailing the matters contained in the statement and indicating the reasons for not calling the maker of the statement. Section 8 of the Act outlines acceptable reasons for not calling the maker of the statement as a witness (he is dead; or overseas; he is physically and/or mentally unfit to attend the hearing; despite reasonable efforts it has not been possible to locate or identify him; or he cannot reasonably be expected to have any recollection of matters pertinent to the accuracy of the statement). Order 38 of the Rules of the Supreme Court incorporates these reasons.

The party upon whom the notice is served may object to the statement if he contends that its maker should attend in person to give evidence. If this is done the court, before trial, can decide the question of admissibility on the application of either party.

(iii) Section 6 covers the matters to which the court must have regard when considering the weight to be attached to the statement. Was it made contemporaneously with the events to which it refers? Had the maker of the statement any incentive to conceal or misrepresent any facts? This is a consideration which could adversely affect the credibility attached to a statement by a manager of a foreign hotel.

(iv) Section 7 allows evidence to be called which would destroy or harm the credibility of the maker of the statement (ie evidence of bias, previous inconsistent statements etc).

The Act deals with a wide variety of statements and documents which may be admissible in evidence. It is beyond the scope of this book to consider them in detail but both plaintiffs and defendants should bear in mind the possibility of adducing evidence under the Act. However, when advising a travel company, the writers would caution that a statement from a foreign hotelier, when contradicted by oral evidence from the plaintiff holiday maker, is unlikely to be given much weight by the court. In certain circumstances it may be helpful for a tour operator to call as a witness a member of another country's tourist board who is working in the UK to give evidence about idiosyncratic legislation. In the Joneses' case, for example, the hotel swimming pool may have been closed as a result of unexpected and temporary Government legislation. However, senior members of the tourist board in question are likely to be covered by the Diplomatic Privileges Act 1964. It incorporates various articles of the 1961 Vienna Convention, Article 31 of which states that a "Diplomatic Agent" is competent to give evidence but *is not obliged to do so.* Article 1E defines a "Diplomatic Agent" as the head of a commission or member of the diplomatic staff of the mission. The Foreign Office publishes a list of those commonly regarded as being diplomatic agents. In the absence of co-operation by the particular tourist board official, the tour operator will be unable to compel him to give evidence.

In the Joneses' case, Good Advice may wish to allege that Mr Jones did not stress to their booking clerk the importance of the swimming pool. This would not establish a successful defence in respect of the actual lack of the facility but would be relevant to *quantum* in that, if Good Advice succeed on this point, the materiality of the swimming pool to the enjoyment of the holiday would be greatly reduced. What Good Advice will have to counter in court is evidence from Mr Jones that he did inform Good Advice's booking clerk (John) of the importance of the swimming pool. If John can only say that he cannot remember such a comment being made, it is almost certain that the court will accept Mr Jones's evidence. If, however, Good Advice have forms which were completed contemporaneously with the booking summarising John's conversation with Mr Jones and these contain no reference to the swimming pool, this would go some way towards supporting John's evidence.

3. ABTA and AITO arbitration schemes

It has been stated earlier in this chapter that Mr Jones cannot use ABTA's arbitration scheme because there is a commercial dispute between Utopian Holidays and Good Advice. Suppose, though, that Mr Jones is only claiming against Utopian Holidays and that there is no dispute between it and Good Advice. It will now be possible for ABTA's arbitration scheme to be used. How does it work?

(a) Principles of the ABTA scheme

The ABTA Conciliation and Arbitration Scheme came into force on 1 April 1975. Since then it has changed in format, particularly through abolition of the conciliation service. Essentially, the basic principles of the Scheme are as follows:

(i) Tour Operators are themselves supposed to take all possible steps to resolve complaints.

(ii) In the event of failure to resolve a complaint, the holiday maker can contact ABTA to seek assistance. This will result in the holiday maker being invited to make a formal application to the Chartered Institute of Arbitrators for the matter to be settled by an independent arbitrator. If he does apply, the operator must consent to arbitration, and agree to be bound by the decision.

(b) Operation of the ABTA scheme

Chapter 1 briefly mentioned disputes the nature or amount of which preclude arbitration. In general terms, ABTA states that the arbitration scheme "is not designed to accommodate disputes in which issues are unusually complicated, the proper resolution of which would be likely to require a formal hearing and oral evidence".

Several other points about the adoption of ABTA's arbitration scheme should be noted. First, application for arbitration must be made within nine months from the end of the holiday. Secondly, the holiday maker must agree to be bound by the arbitrator's decision. The Arbitration Act 1950 does provide for an appeal against an arbitrator's decision or the subsequent issue of proceedings in respect of matters arbitrated but it is beyond the scope of this book to examine these provisions. Thirdly the arbitrator will decide disputes solely upon the documentation placed before him—there will not be an oral hearing.

The basic arbitration stages are as follows:

(i) Mr Jones completes his application form and despatches it to the Institute of Chartered Arbitrators, together with an application fee. The Institute will despatch an application form to Utopian Tours to be completed and returned by them together with their application fee.

(ii) The Institute, after receipt of Utopian Tours' application form will despatch a claim form to Mr Jones. He must complete and return it within twenty-eight days of its receipt together with any supporting documents.

(iii) The claim form will be sent by the Institute to Utopian Tours who must prepare and submit their defence and any supporting documents within twenty-eight days. These will be sent by the Institute to Mr Jones who has fourteen days to submit his comments about the defence.

(iv) An arbitrator will then be appointed by the Institute. If he considers any of the documentation unclear, he can seek further details. Otherwise he prepares his award and submits it to the Institute for despatch to the parties within twenty-one days.

The award which the arbitrator forwards to the Institute comprises two documents. The first is "the Award" which sets out the brief details of the dispute (to enable identification of the matter) and the compensation, if any, which the operator must pay the holiday maker. It also sets out any costs award. The only costs which can be awarded are the application fees—the cost of preparing documents etc must be borne by the parties. If an award in excess of £200 is made, the arbitrator will usually order that the successful party's application fees be paid by the other party. The second document comprises the arbitrator's notes which give an informal indication of the rationale of his award and the matters taken into consideration.

Arbitration under the ABTA scheme is based on an examination of written statements and not upon an oral hearing of the claim. If Mr Jones considers that he cannot present his case satisfactorily in writing, he should not embark on arbitration unless he has a friend who is equipped to help him.

(c) AITO arbitration

AITO's scheme generally operates on a similar basis to that of ABTA. Perhaps the most important differences are that AITO's scheme does contain a conciliation service and that the arbitrator will not rely solely upon written submissions.

The arbitrator is at liberty to make direct contact with either the holiday maker or tour operator to seek further explanations or pose direct questions. There is no oral, contested hearing but it is envisaged that arbitrators will commonly make direct contact with the parties.

4. The outcome

But what of Mr Jones's claim? Irrespective of the forum in which it is adjudicated, should it succeed? The information set out so far is not sufficient to enable a decision to be made but various scenarios are considered below:

(a) Suppose that the closure of the pool was due to an emergency Greek Government decision taken only a few hours before Mr and Mrs Jones's arrival, and implemented contemporaneously with their arrival at the hotel. Further suppose that there had been no indications in Greece that such legislation was being considered so that neither Utopian Tours nor Good Advice could have had any advance knowledge of closure. In these circumstances, it is submitted that neither Utopian Tours nor Good Advice will incur any liability to the Joneses under either the Regulations or the general law. What conversations there were about the importance of the pool to Mr and Mrs Jones are irrelevant since their primary importance is to the assessment of damages in the event of liability existing, which it would not where the closure of the pool was an unexpected occurrence over which the travel companies had no control and of which they had no advance knowledge.

(b) Suppose, though, that the Greek Government's decision had been taken a week before the Joneses' arrival and that Utopian Tours' local representative was aware of the situation. Utopian Tours knew, or should have known, of the closure of the pool because their representatives should have reported it to head office straightaway. In any event, it is submitted that for the purposes of civil proceedings, Utopian Tours will be held to have the knowledge of their on-the-spot representatives, although, in view of the *Wings* v *Ellis* decision (see page 116 *et seq.*), this would not be so in the event of a prosecution under the Trade Descriptions Act 1968. This being so, liability will attach to Utopian Tours. They had advance knowledge of the situation and did not inform the Joneses or Good Advice of the closing of the pool so that an alteration of arrangements could be considered.

(c) Utopian Tours may admit liability but dispute *quantum*, and argue that, as the hotel has a beach with fine sand and safe water for swimming, the lack of a swimming pool was only a minor irritant. However, the Joneses allege—and it is accepted by the court—that they told Good Advice how important it was that they be able to make use of the swimming pool. Since the Olympic swimming pool was an item featured in Utopian Tours' brochures, it is submitted that Good Advice were not under a duty to notify Utopian Tours of the importance of the swimming pool to the Joneses, although it would have been better practice had they done so. Mr Jones's conversations with Good Advice prove the importance of the swimming pool to him and his wife, and Utopian Tours must accept an assessment of damages accordingly.

Damages will be awarded under two heads—diminution of contract value and loss of enjoyment (including mental distress). In the writers' opinion, the diminution of contract value in this instance is insubstantial (it being accepted that the only fault with the holiday was the lack of swimming pool)—say £75 per person—but the damages for loss of enjoyment should be considerable—say £280 per person. This represents £20 per person per day which, it is suggested, is equitable compensation for the loss of a facility proven to be important to the holiday maker.

The Joneses' case has provided a concrete background against which to discuss the various means of resolving holiday disputes, problems regarding evidence, and the relevant procedural and tactical considerations. Any claim brought by a holiday maker will have its own special factors but the basic law and general guidelines outlined in this chapter provide the basis for decisions regarding whether and how to claim and whether and how to defend.

Chapter 9

The providers of transport and accommodation

1. Contractual arrangements

In arranging the various components that make up a package holiday a tour operator enters into contracts with airlines, coach companies, hoteliers and others since it is they who actually provide the transport and accommodation which feature in the package. To discuss in any depth the legal considerations applicable to this range of contracts would require a book on its own. But an outline discussion of the subject is necessary to give readers a fuller understanding of how the package holiday industry operates.

People like hoteliers and coach companies provide services and facilities to holiday makers under contracts between themselves and tour operators. Usually nothing happens which creates a contract between an individual holiday maker and, say, the hotel at which he stays. The position as regards air transport is somewhat different. Although flights are provided under a contract between the tour operator and the airline, the holiday maker is almost invariably issued with a ticket which shows the airline as the issuer. The ticket will often be made out by the tour operator as agent for the airline whose plane it has chartered. But it clearly identifies the airline as the issuer and establishes a contractual, or quasi contractual, relationship between the holiday maker and the airline.

2. Accommodation

(a) Usual arrangements

The provider of accommodation will normally be a hotelier, villa owner, camp site owner (tents and caravans), or innkeeper and his liabilities and duties to the tour operator will be governed by the terms of the contract between them. A tour operator does not normally book a specific room for the holiday maker as and when the need arises but rather, before the commencement of the season, reserves a number of rooms to be allotted to his customers upon arrival. Whether or not an advance payment is made for such reservations is a matter for negotiation between the parties.

Allowing for the different types of accommodation that exist, the contract between a tour operator and a provider of accommodation (using a hotel as an example) should deal with the following:

(a) The part of the hotel in which the rooms reserved are situated.

(b) The number of rooms and the facilities in them (for example, some may be air conditioned apartments with a balcony, bath, shower and seaview while others may only be air conditioned with a shower).

(c) The period covered by the contract.

(d) The cost of different types of rooms, which may well vary according to the time of the year, and of any additional facilities available on request (eg cots). Also details of any reductions for young children.

(e) Details of meals included in the price quoted by the hotel and of other meals available.

(f) A clear description of all facilities (eg swimming pools, discotheques) provided by the hotel.

(g) An undertaking that the hotel complies with local sanitary, fire and safety regulations and that regular checks to ensure this will be made. Any breach should render it liable at its expense for the immediate relocation of customers of the operator to alternative accommodation of a similar graded standard, failing which the operator should be entitled to terminate the contract straightaway.

(h) An undertaking that the accommodation, food and service will be at least as good as that set out in the hotel's promotional literature and laid down by the relevant local authority for a hotel of its class. If it is not, or if the hotel does not provide the exact accommodation contracted for, it should be obliged to refund to the operator any compensation that the operator consequently has to pay to its customers.

(i) An undertaking by the operator to provide the hotel with a list of clients to be accommodated at least two weeks before their arrival, with a right for the operator to release any then unsold accommodation to the hotelier without being obliged to pay for it.

(j) An undertaking by the hotel to take out an insurance policy against the risk of any customer of the operator suffering death, personal injury, or loss of or damage to property, as a result of residence at the hotel and to indemnify the operator against any claims which may be made against it by its customers as a result of such residence. The indemnity and insurance cover should be as wide as possible given the operator's potential liabilities under Regulation 15. In practice, however, it may be difficult for an operator to persuade a hotelier to accept, in the contract, liability for anything other than the negligence of the hotel, its employees and agents.

(k) The hotel should undertake that all the facilities and services supplied by it to any customer of the operator will be of sufficient standard to avoid the risk of injury or death, failing which the operator should be entitled to serve notice requiring the defect to be rectified straightaway, failure to do which will justify immediate termination.

(l) An undertaking by the hotel to keep the grounds and facilities (eg swimming pools) clean and tidy, clean the rooms regularly, and maintain a steady and safe supply of water, gas and electricity.

The above is not meant to be exhaustive. There are many other clauses which are often inserted, such as one imposing an obligation to provide free accommodation for the operator's representatives and one whereby the operator seeks to ensure that the hotel is not charging it more than it charges other operators.

The hotel contract should identify the proprietor of the hotel so that the tour operator will know against whom legal proceedings should be issued if the occasion arises. Under English law firms or individuals who carry on business under a business name, such as the name of a hotel, are obliged to identify themselves on their business stationery and in their contracts but it appears that that is not the case in many holiday resort countries. In theory the failure of many contracts between tour operators and hoteliers to identify the legal person who owns the hotel could give rise to serious legal problems if things go wrong. In practice it seldom does.

Technically speaking, the tour operator should ensure that whoever signs the hotel contract for the hotel is empowered to do so. In practice the contract is normally signed by the ostensible proprietor or manager of the hotel and nobody ever seems to deny that the hotel is legally bound by it.

(b) Jurisdiction

The question of jurisdiction and the laws which are to govern the agreement require careful consideration. It is more expedient and economic for an English operator to issue proceedings in an English court in respect of an agreement governed by English law and, where this can be achieved, it means that the operator's legal position vis-à-vis the hotelier will be subject to the same laws as the operator's position vis-à-vis the British holiday maker. Whether or not a hotel agrees to this is a matter for negotiation.

Provided that the leave of the English courts can be obtained to issue English proceedings against someone out of the jurisdiction, and provided that the hotel is in a country with which the United Kingdom has an agreement for reciprocal enforcement of judgments, the operator should not encounter excessive difficulty in enforcing a contract which confers jurisdiction on the English courts. If the hotel is in a country with which the United Kingdom does not have such an agreement, the contract with the hotel might as well be subject to the laws and jurisdiction of that country since an English judgment will be unenforceable.

On 1 January 1987, the Civil Jurisdiction and Judgments Act 1982 came into force. It implements the 1968 Brussels Convention, the purpose of which is to standardise, *inter alia*, jurisdiction rules within the EC. Its effect, and that of the 1982 Act, are beyond the scope of this book. In general, however, they should make it considerably easier to enforce in other member states a contract conferring jurisdiction on the English courts.

The contract between hotel and tour operator should be sufficiently detailed and precise to cover all obvious situations and to avoid any need, in the event of disputes, for the operator to rely on implied terms—such as that the hotel will be fit for human habitation. In all cases where local law will or may apply, or if the hotel is in a country with which the United Kingdom has no reciprocal enforcement of judgments treaty, the operator should take steps to ascertain the local law and, ideally, have the proposed contract approved by a local lawyer.

3. Transport

Transport may be by air, sea, rail or road and the independent contractors who provide it will, therefore, include airlines, shipping companies, coach companies and train companies. Most tour operators' brochures specifically state that the holiday maker is transported subject to the carrier's conditions of carriage and that they are available for inspection.

Such a term should relate to claims between holiday maker and carrier. In many cases, particularly with air carriers, the carrier requires a tour operator to incorporate the carrier's terms into the operator's terms with its customers. But the carrier's terms may well not comply with the Regulations and any term seeking to incorporate them should expressly provide that the carrier's terms, as between operator and holiday maker, do not apply where they are inconsistent with the operator's terms.

In addition there are various international conventions which determine the liability of those who provide international carriage by air, sea or land.

(a) Air travel arrangements

Using air travel as an example, it is important to note the range of contracts whereby a tour operator can obtain transport for holiday makers. It can charter a plane from an airline. It can buy a block of seats on a plane—from the airline, or from another operator who has chartered the plane, or from another carrier who has itself bought a block of seats. It can make special arrangements whereby it obtains a provisional allocation of seats to be taken up or released not less than, say, 30 days before the date of the flight in question. It can buy tickets on scheduled flights. Chartering a plane will usually be the most economical alternative in cases where the operator can be confident of filling the whole plane. But if an operator charters a plane and finds that he can only fill 65 per cent of the seats, he may suffer a heavy loss. He will then try to sell some of his spare seats to other operators but this is not always possible. Even where it is, it often involves selling them at a substantial loss.

Airlines naturally expect to receive at least a portion of the contract price well in advance and the balance before departure. Equally naturally, operators desire to postpone the payment of the price for as long as possible. This is not only because of the cash flow advantages of late payment but also, in some cases, because there is a possibility of the airline ceasing to trade before the departure date. An operator will not contract with an airline which it considers at serious risk of failure. But if it refuses to do business with all airlines which could possibly fail, it eliminates a number of attractive cheap flight possibilities. The obvious answer from the operator's point of view is to stipulate that payment will not be made until shortly before the departure date. Whether this can be negotiated in a particular case depends upon prevailing market conditions.

In some cases it may be appropriate to provide that monies held by an operator which are payable in due course to an airline should be held by the operator as trustee for the holiday makers. This should not be necessary where the monies are payable to the airline under a contract between it and the operator because in such cases the operator is not acting as agent for the airline when it collects monies from the holiday maker. Accordingly, all monies which the operator receives from the holiday maker become the operator's money and the amounts payable by it to the airline are debts. In the event that the airline ceases trading before any such debt is paid, its liquidator cannot, it is submitted, trace any money held by the operator and claim that it is impressed with a trust. All he can do is to claim against the operator under the contract between them. But in a situation where the airline is unable to perform its part of the contract, the operator should have a perfectly adequate right of set-off.

The position is complicated by the fact that in due course the operator's customers will be issued with tickets in the airline's name. In the writers' view, this does not produce a situation in which an operator is holding monies collected from holiday makers as agent for the airline. If it is holding them as agent for anybody, it is as agent for the holiday maker. But the better view is that it is holding them as its own monies from which it must pay the debts owed by it to the airline and others who provide services in connection with a holiday.

A possible exception is where an operator is also a sales agent of the airline concerned and buys tickets on a scheduled flight. In such cases there may be grounds for saying that it is selling them to holiday makers in its capacity as a sales agent of the airline. This would appear to be the correct analysis if it reports their sales in its sales agency return and claims to be entitled to commission on them.

(b) Air charter

The situation in which a tour operator charters a plane from an airline will now be considered. In general terms the charter contract is a contract of hire. The operator does not have any proprietary rights in the plane but reserves it for its customers' use. The whole plane is reserved and it is up to the operator whether he fills all the seats. Any failure to do so will not reduce the charter price.

A charter contract may take the form of a lease of the aircraft to the charterer with or without the services of a crew. This type of charter is known as a "bare hull" or dry charter. Under it the charterer becomes for most purposes the temporary owner of the plane. The crew, whether supplied by the owner or the charterer, are the servants of the charterer and under his control.

The more normal type of agreement is the "time and voyage" or "wet" charter. It gives the charterer the right to use the aircraft and its crew for the purpose of carrying passengers or freight upon a specified flight or flights or during a specified period. The crew remain the owner's servants. The charterer may be given certain rights to decide the flights to be undertaken but not the manner in which they are to be performed. Contrary to the position under a bare hull charter the owner is the air traffic operator.

A valuable outline of the various categories of time and voyage charter is provided on page 1047 of Allan

Beaver's comprehensive manual of retail travel practice *"Mind Your Own Travel Business"*:

> "*Ad hoc* charters are single or several one-off arrangements. A time charter is where an operator charters an aircraft twenty-four hours of the day for a period of time. The operator is entitled to the exclusive use of the aircraft during the period when it is chartered from the carrier. A series charter means a carrier provides flights between specified points on a regular basis, usually weekly, so that holiday arrangements can be organised back to back. A part charter is the chartering of only part of the capacity of an aircraft. This can mean that a number of operators have shared a charter. It is more commonly used to describe the situation where an operator has chartered part of the capacity of a scheduled service. This is sometimes also known as a block-off charter".

A time and voyage charter is not as such a contract of carriage (ie a contract to transport particular passengers or goods). However, it will amount to one where it is governed by the Carriage by Air Act 1961 or the Carriage by Air Acts (Application of Provisions) Order 1967. Where this is so, the owner is the contracting carrier and there is a contract of carriage between him and each of the plane's passengers.

Time and voyage contracts normally provide that the charterer enters into the charter contract on its own behalf and as agent for all who travel on the plane pursuant to the charter agreement. This is a strange provision because at the time the charterer enters into the agreement it usually does not even know who the passengers will be.

In the case of international flights a time and voyage charter will provide for the issue of tickets to passengers as required by the Warsaw Convention (see page 216). Sometimes tickets are prepared by the airline and sent to the charterer/tour operator for onward transmission to passengers. Sometimes they are prepared and issued by the charterer/tour operator as agent for the airline.

Time and voyage charters normally provide that the owner will provide a specific plane or planes, or planes of a specified type (eg Boeing 737 in 130 seat configuration), and that they will be fit for the required purpose, properly equipped and maintained, and with a crew competent and sufficient for the duties required of them. Even if there is no express term, the owner will be under a duty to take care to provide a suitable, safe aircraft and a competent pilot (*Fosbrooke-Hobbes* v *Airwork Ltd and British-American Air Services Ltd* [1937] 1 All ER 108).

(c) *Inclusive tour flights*

For purposes of illustration let us now consider briefly the type of charter agreement whereby a tour operator contracts with an airline for it to perform all or part of the tour operator's programme of inclusive tour flights ("IT Flights") for a particular season. The time-tables, dates and stopping places constituting the programme are usually set out in a schedule to the contract and the airline undertakes to use its best endeavours to comply with any request by the tour operator to make changes in the programme.

The contract will specify the charter price for each flight. This will normally be composed of route costs (covering landing fees, handling fees, crew allowance and accommodation costs, etc) and an hourly rate charge (covering depreciation or lease charges, payroll costs of the crew, maintenance and overhaul costs etc). The former are usually specified in a schedule whereas the latter result in an hourly rate which is specified in the body of the contract. The airline is normally permitted to increase the route costs element to compensate for increases in the cost of aviation fuel and other specified items. The contract is likely to specify a minimum number of hours to be flown and provide for the tour operator to compensate the airline for any shortfall.

The contract should entitle the airline in appropriate circumstances to substitute another plane from its fleet for the designated plane or type of plane and lay down conditions governing any substitution. It should also schedule the catering requirements which the airline must meet.

Examples of common provisions regarding control of the plane are:

> "**Carrier's servants**
> All ground and operating personnel including cabin staff are authorised to take orders only from the Carrier unless specific written agreement shall have been made between the parties whereby certain defined instructions may be accepted by such personnel from the Charterer.
>
> **Captain's discretion**
> For safety reasons the Captain of the Aircraft shall have complete discretion concerning the load carried on the Aircraft including the number of passengers and the amount of their baggage and their distribution, as to whether or not any Flight should be undertaken, as to where landings should be made, and as to all other matters relating to the operation of the Aircraft, and the Charterer shall accept all such decisions of such Captain as final and binding."

The contract should include references to the issue of tickets and the Warsaw Convention, and also provisions regarding traffic regulations along the lines of:

> "The Charterer will comply and will use its best endeavours to ensure that all passengers will observe and comply with all Traffic Regulations of the Carrier and all applicable laws regulations and directions made by the Civil Aviation Authority or other relevant authority or government including but without prejudice to the generality of the foregoing all Customs Police and Public Health regulations."

The contract should also include clauses regarding termination, the serving of notices, the applicable law, and various other standard form provisions.

As has already been discussed, the Regulations impose considerable obligations and potential liabilities on tour operators. Operators are liable for the actions of air carriers, and therefore, wherever possible, should seek to obtain from carriers indemnities to cover those obligations and liabilities.

Mention should perhaps also be made of the Immigration (Carriers Liability) Act 1987. It deals with all persons seeking entry into the UK, and provides that, if a person does not have a valid passport etc to gain entry, the carrier will be fined. Carriers will require an indemnity from tour operators to cover any such possibility, and tour operators should ensure that their booking conditions require customers who do not have the relevant documents to indemnify the operator and/or carrier.

A tour operator can purchase air transport for his customers from other operators — either from one who has chartered the whole plane or from one who has reserved a block of seats. Where it does this, it will contract with the other tour operator involved and not with the airline. However, it will still provide its customers with tickets in the airline's name and will have to incorporate the airline's terms and conditions of passage into its contracts with its holiday makers. This will normally be stipulated in the agreement between the respective tour operators. Any such agreement between tour operators should be conditional upon the purchasing tour operator having a valid ATOL. It should also provide for the purchasing tour operator to be responsible for its own customers and to indemnify the selling tour operator against any claims that may be made against it by them.

(d) Other travel arrangements

Some coach holidays are provided by operators which own coaches so that there is no need for them to hire coaches. Where this is not so, the operator will normally hire a coach and crew from a coach company. In that event the contract of hire will be similar in some respects to the contract for the chartering of a plane. One difference is that the operator is able to reserve more control over matters such as departure and stoppage times than it can in an airplane charter contract. Another is that it is not normal for holiday makers to be issued with tickets in the name of the coach company. The coach company's standard conditions of carriage are almost invariably incorporated into the tour operator's contracts with its coach tour holiday makers.

It is possible for an operator to share a coach with another operator providing substantially the same holiday. In that event it will enter into contracts with the coach company or the other operator for the purchase of blocks of seats similar to the contracts for the purchase of blocks of airplane seats discussed earlier in this chapter.

Most cruise holidays are provided by shipping companies. Occasionally a tour operator will charter a boat in order to provide a cruise but it is not proposed to discuss that unusual situation. In principle a shipping charter party contract is similar to a contract for chartering a plane and its crew but it contains a number of detailed provisions which are specific to it.

Insofar as rail travel features in a package holiday, it will involve the operator in reserving compartments, or even a whole train, in much the same way as a football club or political party will do for a match or party conference. The rail company's standard conditions of carriage will apply and will be incorporated into the operator's contracts with the relevant holiday makers. Usually the holiday makers will be issued with tickets in the name of the rail company.

4. The Warsaw Convention

The Warsaw Convention of 1929 is the foundation stone of the international regulations concerning the liabilities of air carriers to their passengers. It was amended by The Hague Protocol of 1955. The Amended Convention, which has been ratified by a large number of states, was given statutory force by s.1 of the Carriage by Air Act

1961. This states that "the provisions of the Convention known as 'the Warsaw' Convention as amended at the Hague in 1955 . . . shall so far as they relate to the rights and liabilities of carriers, carriers' servants and agents, passengers, consignors, consignees and other persons, and subject to the provisions of this Act, have the force of law in the United Kingdom in relation to any carriage by air to which the Convention applies, irrespective of the nationality of the aircraft performing that carriage".

This establishes that under English law an airline's duties and liabilities are governed to a large extent by the amended Warsaw Convention. The Convention applies to all international carriage of persons, baggage or cargo performed by aircraft for reward (Article 1(1)). International carriage means "any carriage in which . . . the place of departure and the place of destination . . . are situated either within the territories of two High Contracting Parties or within the territory of a Single High Contracting Party, if there is an agreed stopping place within the territory of another State, even if that State is not a High Contracting Party". In simple terms a "High Contracting Party" means a country. Carriage between two points within the territory of a single country without an agreed stopping place within the territory of another country is not international carriage for the purposes of this Convention. This means that flights for package holidays within the United Kingdom are outside the scope of the Warsaw Convention.

(a) Tickets

Article 3(1) of the Convention provides that in respect of the carriage of passengers a ticket shall be delivered containing:

(a) an indication of the places of departure and destination;

(b) if the places of departure and destination are within the territory of a single High Contracting Party, one or more agreed stopping places being within the territory of another state, an indication of at least one such stopping place;

(c) a notice to the effect that, if the passenger's journey involves an ultimate destination or stop in a country other than the country of departure, the Warsaw Convention may be applicable and that the Convention governs and in most cases limits the liability of carriers for death or personal injury and in respect of loss of or damage to baggage.

A carrier that permits a passenger to embark without a ticket containing the notice required by subparagraph (c) will not be allowed to avail himself of the limitations of liability contained in Article 22 (see page 218).

(b) Liabilities of airlines

Article 17 provides that a carrier is liable for damage sustained in the event of death or wounding of a passenger or any other bodily injury suffered by a passenger if the accident which caused the damage took place on board the aircraft or in the course of any of the operations of embarking or disembarking. Despite its wording, it does not impose strict liability because defences are available for a carrier under Articles 20 and 21.

Article 18(1) provides that the carrier is liable for damage sustained in the event of the destruction or loss of, or damage to, any registered baggage or any cargo, if the occurrence which caused the damage so sustained took place during the carriage by air. Subparagraphs (2) and (3) of Article 18 make it clear that "carriage by air" is deemed to mean the period during which baggage is in the carrier's charge. The same defences are open to a carrier as under Article 17. In addition, the passenger's complaint must be made no later than 7 days from the date of receipt of the damaged baggage (Article 26(2)).

Under Article 19 the carrier is liable for damage occasioned by delay in the carriage by air of passengers' baggage or cargo. Article 26(2) provides that complaints in respect of such damage must be made within 21 days of embarkation.

(c) Limitations of liability

By virtue of Article 20 the carrier is not liable under Articles 17-19 if he proves that he and his servants or agents had taken all necessary measures to avoid the damage or that it was impossible for him or them to take such measures. In *Grain* v *Imperial Airways Ltd* [1937] 1 KB 50, Greer LJ said "this seems to me to amount to a promise not to injure the passenger by avoidable accident, the onus being on the carrier to prove that the accident could not have been avoided by the exercise of reasonable care". Article 21 provides that if the carrier proves that the damage was caused or contributed to by the negligence of the injured person the court may, in accordance with the provisions of its own law, exonerate the carrier wholly or partly from his liability.

Article 22 contains various limitations of liability:

(i) If a passenger is killed or injured 125,000 Gold Francs (£6,817);

(ii) For loss of or damage to hand baggage 5,000 Gold Francs (£273);

(iii) For loss of or damage to checked baggage 250 Gold Francs (£13.63) per kilogram.

The limit of 125,000 Gold Francs (£6,817) on a carrier's liability for death or personal injury was set at a time when damages awards were much lower than nowadays and when there was a general desire to protect a fledgling industry. But the wealthier developed countries, led by the USA, became increasingly dissatisfied with such a low limit. This resulted in the limitation of liability for death and personal injury being doubled by the 1955 Hague Protocol to 250,000 Gold Francs (£13,633). But this only applies to airlines based in countries which have ratified the Hague Protocol.

One of the countries which has never ratified it is the USA which considers the 250,000 Gold Francs limitation to be far too low. Its insistence on a higher limit for passengers flying to or from the USA led to the 1966 Montreal Inter-Carrier Agreement which applies to all commercial flights which start, finish, or have an intermediate stop, in the USA. It set a limit for death or personal injury of $58,000 exclusive of legal fees or $75,000 inclusive of them.

All this is briefly summarised in the tickets of UK airlines along the following lines:

> "**ADVICE TO INTERNATIONAL PASSENGERS ON LIMITATION OF LIABILITY**
>
> Passengers on a journey involving an ultimate destination or a stop in a country other than the country of origin are advised that the provisions of a treaty known as the Warsaw Convention may be applicable to the entire journey, including any portion entirely within the country of origin or destination. For such passengers on a journey to, from, or with an agreed stopping place in the United States of America, the Convention and special contracts of carriage embodied in applicable tariffs provide that the liability of certain carriers parties to such special contracts, for death of or personal injury to passengers is limited in most cases to proven damages not to exceed US Dollars 75,000 per passenger, and that this liability up to such limit shall not depend on negligence on the part of the Carrier. For such passengers travelling by a carrier not a party to such contracts or on a journey not to, from, or having an agreed stopping place in the United States of America, liability of the carrier for death of or personal injury to passengers is limited in most cases to approximately US Dollars 10,000 or US Dollars 20,000.
>
> The names of carriers parties to such special contracts are available at all ticket offices of such carriers and may be examined on request. Additional protection can usually be obtained by purchasing insurance from a private Company. Such insurance is not affected by any limitation of

the carrier's liability under the Warsaw Convention or such special contracts of carriage. For further information please consult your Airline or Insurance Company Representative.

Note: The limit of liability of US Dollars 75,000 above is inclusive of legal fees and costs except that in the case of a claim brought in a state where provision is made for separate award of legal fees and costs, the limit shall be the sum of US Dollars 58,000 exclusive of legal fees and costs."

Readers will have noted that the Warsaw/Hague limits are expressed in Gold Francs. This means the former Poincare French Gold Franc which consisted of 65½ milligrams of gold of millesimal fineness 900. This somewhat archaic unit of value needs to be converted into the national currencies of the various signatories to the Warsaw Convention. In Britain this is dealt with at periodic intervals by the publication of a Carriage by Air (Sterling Equivalents) Order. The one currently in force is Statutory Instrument No. 1778 of 1986.

The Warsaw Convention limitation in respect of death or personal injury is effectively increased in the case of British airlines by Condition H of the CAA's Standard Conditions for Air Transport Licences:

> "The licence holder shall enter into a special contract with every passenger to be carried under this licence on or after 1 April 1981, or with a person acting on behalf of such a passenger, for the increase of not less than the Sterling equivalent of 100,000 Special Drawing Rights, exclusive of costs, of the limit of the carrier's liability under Article 17 of the Warsaw Convention of 1929 and under Article 17 of that Convention as amended at the Hague in 1955."

The Sterling value of 100,000 Special Drawing Rights varies from day to day. It is published daily in the Financial Times and at 29 January 1993 was approximately £109,000.

Article 25 of the Warsaw Convention provides that the limits of liability specified in Article 22 shall not apply if it is proved that the damage resulted from an act or omission of the carrier, his servants or agents, done with intent to cause damage or recklessly and with knowledge that damage would probably result.

Article 25 was considered in *Goldman* v *Thai Airways International Ltd* [1983] 1 WLR 1186. In 1977 the plaintiff was travelling on an international flight as a passenger in an aircraft of the defendant airline. On entering an area in which moderate clear air turbulence had been forecast, the pilot did not switch on the sign ordering passengers to fasten their seat belts despite instructions to pilots in the defendant's manual to do so when turbulence could be expected. The aircraft encountered severe turbulence and the plaintiff, who was sitting with his seat belt unfastened, was thrown from his seat. He sustained serious injury to his lower spine. On his claim against the defendant for damages Chapman J gave judgment for £41,852.42 together with interest and costs, holding that, in disregarding the instructions in the manual, the pilot had acted recklessly and with knowledge that damage would probably result. Therefore Article 25 applied and liability was not limited under Article 22.

Subsequently the defendant succeeded on appeal to the Court of Appeal. It held that Article 25 was not to be construed in isolation but in its context and with the qualification that the act or omission had to have been done *both* "recklessly" *and* "with knowledge that danger would probably result." The test was subjective and, therefore, the pilot had only acted recklessly if it was proved that he had omitted to order the passengers to wear seat belts when aware that damage of the kind that did occur would probably result, or indifferent to that likelihood. It was doubtful whether the pilot had been reckless in interpreting the flight operations manual as giving him a discretion to defer switching on the seat belts sign until there was an indication of turbulence but, even if he had been, the evidence did not establish a probability of encountering clear air turbulence of a severity that would cause the kind of injury suffered by the plaintiff. Accordingly, since the pilot could not have had knowledge of the likelihood of the injury, Article 25 did not apply and the defendant's liability was limited under the terms of Article 22.

By virtue of Article 29 a passenger's right to damages under Articles 17-19 is extinguished if an action is not brought within two years reckoned from the date of arrival at the destination, or from the date on which the aircraft ought to have arrived, or from the date on which the carriage stopped.

(d) Amendments

Since the amendments made to the Warsaw Convention by the Hague Protocol, there have been other amending conventions to which the United Kingdom has been a party, but, because of their restricted number of signatories they have not yet been brought into force:

(i) The Guatemala City Protocol of 1971 sought to improve the position of passengers in the event of personal injury or loss by limiting a carrier's defence to Article 17 and by increasing the maximum liability.

(ii) An international conference in Montreal in 1975 adopted four additional Protocols, again with the aim of imposing greater liability on carriers. It should be noted that the limits of carriers' liabilities, under the Montreal Protocols, are described in terms of Special Drawing Rights (SDRs).

The amended Warsaw Convention has been applied to non-international carriage by the Carriage by Air Acts (Application of Provisions) Order 1967. The Order, which has been amended by statutory instruments in 1969, 1979 and 1981, applies the phrase "non-international" to flights not only within the UK but also between the UK and those countries which are not parties to any of the international conventions. The purpose was to harmonise the regulations for "international" and "non-international" carriage by air. The Order differs from the international conventions in three important respects:

(i) there is no need for a passenger ticket;

(ii) Articles 10-16 of the Convention are excluded; and

(iii) the upper limit on the carrier's liability for the death or wounding of, or bodily injury to, a passenger is 100,000 SDRs (approximately £109,000).

In November 1992 Japanese carriers announced a significant revision to their terms of carriage. It was an abandonment, in certain circumstances, of Warsaw Convention limits. It will be interesting to see what other carriers follow suit. Further, if many do, it raises the possibility that the English courts might regard as "not reasonable" a tour operator's attempt to limit compensation pursuant to the Warsaw Convention.

5. The Athens Convention

International carriage by sea is also regulated by an international convention, the Athens Convention 1974, the terms of which were made effective in the United Kingdom by s.14 of the Merchant Shipping Act 1979. Schedule 3 of that Act sets out the text of the Convention, the provisions of which are only applicable to "international carriage". By this is meant any carriage in which, according to the contract of carriage, the place of departure and the place of destination are situated in two different states, or in a single state if, according to the contract of carriage or the scheduled itinerary, there is an intermediate port of call in another state.

The Convention covers the carriage of passengers and their luggage by ship but not by hovercraft. Under it the shipping company is liable for damage suffered as a result of the death or personal injury of a passenger and for loss of or damage to luggage, if the incident which caused the damage occurred in the course of the carriage and was due to the fault or neglect of the shipping company or of its servants or agents acting within the scope of their employment. The burden of proving that the incident occurred in the course of carriage, and the extent of the loss or damage, lies with the claimant. If the death of or personal injury to a passenger, or the loss of or damage to cabin luggage, arose in connection with a shipwreck, collision, stranding, explosion or fire or defect in the ship, fault or neglect by the carrier is presumed unless the contrary is proved. In other cases the burden of proving fault or neglect lies with the claimant.

For carriers whose principal place of business is the UK, convention limits of compensation have been increased by the Carriage of Passengers and their Luggage by Sea (UK Carriers) Order 1987 (SI 1987/855) and the subsequent 1989 amendment Order (SI 1989/1880). They mean that the limit of damages for death or personal injury is 100,000 Special Drawing Rights (approximately £109,000), for loss of or damage to cabin luggage it is 833 Special Drawing Rights (approximately £910), and 12,000 Special Drawing Rights (approximately £1,300) for other luggage.

6. The Berne and Geneva Conventions

There are also international conventions concerning the carriage of passengers and luggage on land both by rail and road. The 1970 Berne Convention, which incorporated some of the provisions of the 1961 Berne Convention, governs carriage by rail. It is expressly incorporated into English law by the International Transport Conventions Act 1983. The text of the Convention is contained in the Schedule to that Act. The international carriage of passengers and luggage by road is governed by the 1973 Geneva Convention. The United Kingdom has not yet signed or ratified it but the Carriage of Passengers by Road Act 1974 provides for its incorporation into English law when the United Kingdom does ratify and sign.

The Berne Convention is not as far reaching as the Conventions applicable to international carriage of passengers by air and sea since it does not deal with the question of liability of the railway for death and personal injuries, nor with liability for delay. What the Convention says is that such questions must be left to the law of the state in which the incident causing death, injury, loss or damage occurs. It does contain provisions concerning loss or damage to luggage but its application is beyond the scope of this book.

The Geneva Convention provides that a carrier by road is liable for any loss or damage resulting from death or personal injury of a passenger due to an accident which occurs while the passenger is inside the vehicle, or embarking or disembarking. He is also liable for loss of or damage to luggage during the whole time that it is in the vehicle or being loaded or unloaded. However, the carrier will be able to avoid liability if he can show that the circumstances causing the accident are such that he could not have avoided it by exercising greater care. Article 12 of the Convention provides that the law of the country in which the court hearing any claim is situated determines the extent of the injury which gives rise to the claim of compensation and those persons who are entitled to sue for compensation.

The carrier by road's liability for death or personal injury under the Geneva Convention is subject to a maximum of 250,000 Francs (approximately £11,799). Liability for luggage is stated to be a maximum of 500 Francs (approximately £23.60) for each piece of luggage with a limit of 2,000 Francs (approximately £94.90) per passenger. These figures will be increased at a time to be appointed to 83,333 Special Drawing Rights (approximately £91,000), 166.67 Special Drawing Rights (approximately £182) and 666.67 Special Drawing Rights (approximately £728) respectively under the Carriage of Passengers by Air and Road Act 1979.

7. The 1962 Paris Convention on the Liability of Hotel-keepers

The UK ratified the 1962 Paris Convention in July 1963, and the Convention was given force of law in the UK in 1967. From the outset, it should be stated that this Convention appears to be little known. No mention is made of it in the leading text books on hotel law. Further, it sets out limits on the amount of compensation to be paid but they are by reference to "gold francs". When this happens, there is normally a statutory instrument setting out the relevant conversion rate. There is no such statutory instrument.

The 1962 Convention applies only to the property of those staying at "hotels" – hotel is not defined. The main thrust of the Convention is that "hotel-keepers" are liable to compensate guests for property damaged or lost while at the hotel up to a maximum of 3,000 Gold Francs. Where, however, property is specifically entrusted to a hotel-keeper, there is no limit.

8. Other contractors

This chapter has concentrated on those independent contractors who provide accommodation or transport. Services may also be provided by other persons, such as guides and skiing instructors, over whom the tour operator has no direct control. However informal the arrangements may be, tour operators should take into account their liability under the Regulations for such independent contractors.

9. Insurance

At the risk of repetition, it is worth stressing that the impact of the Regulations, and in particular Regulation 15, is that tour operators will henceforth be liable primarily for the actions of, *inter alia*, those who provide any aspect of the package holiday. Not only does this make it all the more necessary for tour operators to review their contractual arrangements with such suppliers to ensure that as wide-ranging and effective indemnities as possible have been obtained, but also tour operators need to pay particular attention to the insurance cover which they have arranged to guard against the risk of holiday makers' claims. The arrangement of such insurance is perhaps the most important step to be taken by tour operators. When arranging it, the existence of proper contracts with suppliers may have a beneficial effect on premiums.

Chapter 10

Insolvency of tour operators and travel agents

In law a contract is not automatically terminated by the bankruptcy or liquidation of one of the parties unless it so provides. Instead, the benefit of the contract passes to the insolvent party's trustee in bankruptcy or liquidator, who is entitled to disclaim contracts which he regards as unprofitable. In some cases the liquidator of an insolvent tour operator has kept uncompleted holiday contracts in being and arranged for them to be performed by another operator. But this chapter confines itself to the normal situation where that does not happen.

Where a party to a contract makes it clear before the time for his performance of the contract that he will not perform it, this amounts to an anticipatory breach, and one which is so serious that the innocent party is entitled to treat it as a repudiation of the contract. Alternatively the innocent party can stay his hand and wait to see what happens.

When a tour operator ceases trading, it makes it clear (in the absence of any indication to the contrary) that it will not perform its outstanding holiday contracts. In these circumstances a customer who has not then paid the full holiday price would be well advised to accept the operator's repudiation of the contract in which event:

(a) he will not be obliged to pay the unpaid balance of his holiday price;

(b) he will be entitled to claim repayment of all monies previously paid by him; and

(c) he may, in theory, have a claim for loss of

bargain or compensation for disappointed expectations.

The ability to claim repayment of monies paid to the operator arises because there has been a total failure of consideration. The position was summarised on page 1339 of volume 1 of the 26th edition of *Chitty on Contracts* as follows:

> "Where money has been paid under a transaction that is or becomes ineffective the payer may recover the money provided that the consideration for the payment has totally failed . . . In that context failure of consideration occurs where the payer has not enjoyed the benefit of any part of what he bargained for".

The ability to claim a refund might not be of much value to a disappointed holiday maker, who would probably be one amongst many unsecured creditors of an insolvent company. With luck he might eventually receive a dividend from the liquidator calculated as a percentage of his claim. At the worst he would receive nothing.

Before the Regulations, holiday makers who booked package holidays with tour operators, whether directly or through travel agents, which did not participate in bonding schemes were unprotected from the consequences of financial failure, unless they had paid by credit card (see pages 235–236 below). In theory, the advent of the Regulations means that no holiday makers booking a package holiday should be unprotected in the event of the operator's or agent's financial failure.

Chapter 4 discussed the financial security provisions imposed upon tour operators by Regulations 16–21. This chapter assumes that financial security has been provided by means of a bond. It considers the problems which arise in the distribution of bond monies and the competing claims made by holiday makers, tour operators or travel agents (and their receivers/liquidators) and the providers of the bond monies.

At the time of writing, the administrators of bond monies will be those connected with existing bonding schemes, that is the CAA, ABTA, TOSG, AITO, BCC or PSA.

ABTA's handbook for members contains a detailed exposition of ABTA's policies. Additionally, the CAA, the Air Travel Trust, ABTA and TOSG issue a joint policy statement on the administration of bond monies, the most up-to-date version of which is dated December 1991 ("the CAA policy statement"). By and large, in every existing scheme bond monies are administered in accordance with the CAA policy statement, as amended from time to time, and the comments in the rest of this chapter assume that this is so.

1. Collapse of a tour operator

(a) Payment of bond monies

A bond is an irrevocable obligation on the part of someone, such as a bank, to pay a stated sum to a third party, such as the TOSG Trust Fund Ltd ("TOSG Trust"), upon the happening of a certain event such as the financial failure of ILG Travel Ltd ("ILG"). The bond itself specifies the events which can lead to its being called. Normally, these would include the following:

- TOSG Trust having reasonable grounds for believing that ILG cannot carry out its obligations to its customers, or knowning that this is so;
- a petition having been presented for the compulsory winding-up of ILG;
- any company in the ILG Group of Companies convening a creditors' meeting or having a Receiver or Administrative Receiver appointed;
- an inability on the part of ILG to pay its debts within the meaning of s.123 of the Insolvency Act 1986 (this includes present and contingent liabilities).

The bond also states who is entitled to call upon the bank to make payment under the terms of the bond. That is TOSG Trust and, where the bond is also used to satisfy the requirements for obtaining an ATOL, the CAA.

The decision makers in TOSG Trust, or indeed the administrators of other bonding schemes with the exception of the CAA, are representatives of tour operators. In many cases they will be competitors of the tour operator in difficulties. Competitors will therefore be passing judgment on each other.

The provider of the bond – the bank – when it is called upon to pay, will have no option other than so to do, provided that the bond has been properly executed. But, before making payment, the bank will wish to ascertain that the travel company known or suspected to be in financial difficulties is in fact covered by the bond.

The Court of Appeal, in *Girozentrale und Bank der Österreichischen Sparkassen AG and Others* v *TOSG Trust Fund Ltd* [1992] Financial Times 5 February, on appeal from His Honour Judge Diamond, dealt with this point. The plaintiffs represented nine of the fourteen banks which provided the funds making up ILG's bond of approximately £63 million. They claimed that TOSG Trust was not entitled to use the bond monies in respect of companies within the ILG group of companies which were not named in the bond. The Court of Appeal found in favour of the banks.

On its face, this could have had the result that approximately £10 million of the bond monies was to be repaid by TOSG Trust to the banks. However, TOSG Trust maintained that almost all of the bond monies were necessary to deal with the claims of customers of ILG companies which were named in the bond. Accordingly, TOSG Trust alleged that there should be no obligation to repay the sum of approximately £10 million but only such overall balance, if any, which remained. In separate proceedings – *TOSG Trust Fund Ltd* v *Girozentrale und Bank der Österreichischen Sparkassen AG* [1992] Financial Times 10 June – the Court of Appeal upheld TOSG's stance. These proceedings were, in fact, issued by TOSG Trust in response to the bank's demand for repayment of the £10 million.

The practical result was, therefore, that TOSG Trust was able to make use of all the bond monies. These cases, however, do illustrate the need for all companies intended to be covered by the bond to be specified properly in it.

(b) Application of bond monies

A bond normally provides that the bond administrators will administer bond monies in accordance with known rules, such as the CAA policy statement. This enables the provider of the bond to be reasonably certain as to the manner in which bond monies will be administered. The CAA standard bond, however, provides that policies known at the time of provision of a bond can be altered during the currency of the bond, albeit not without the prior written consent of the provider of the bond. That consent is not to be unreasonably withheld.

The overall purpose of bond monies is that, in the event of the financial failure of the tour operator, the consequences to holiday makers are alleviated. That overall purpose is, effectively, the main restriction upon administrators of bond monies. Within it, wide discretion is given. But it is the general rule that the overall purpose is to be achieved by putting bond monies to two specific uses. They are, firstly, payment of the cost of repatriation of holiday makers stranded overseas and, secondly, payments of refunds to holiday makers who have paid the failed tour operator, either directly or through a travel agent, for holidays which will not be provided.

(c) Stranded holiday makers

Some customers will be on holiday when the collapse occurs. In cases where the operator has paid the relevant hotels and airlines in advance, the holiday may continue as planned albeit without the services of the operator's on the spot representative. The CAA policy statement, however, provides that payments may be made to local agents and, in some cases, to the operator's own representatives.

Where hotels have not been fully paid in advance, whichever of TOSG, ABTA or the CAA is administering the operator's bond will be prepared to pay whatever is still due to the hotelier but this takes time. Some hoteliers are prepared to let the holiday go ahead confident that they will be paid in due course. Others turn nasty and demand immediate payment of the balance of their charges from the stranded holiday maker.

Airlines are usually paid in advance. But TOSG, ABTA or CAA may still have to make and pay for alternative arrangements in cases where, because of the attitude of foreign hoteliers, holiday makers are forced to return early. In addition they may have to do so in cases where holiday flights are provided by the collapsed operator itself or one of its subsidiaries as was the case with ILG.

Catering for stranded holiday makers is a first call on the various bonds and predominantly gives rise to practical rather than legal problems. However, where a stranded holiday maker loses part of his holiday, he will have a claim for a partial refund of what he paid for it and in this respect the ensuing paragraphs may apply to him as well as to holiday makers whose holidays "never get off the ground". The amount of such a partial refund will *prima facie* be related to the proportion of the holiday lost so that, as a starting point, a holiday maker who loses one third of his holiday will be entitled to a refund of one third of what he paid for it. However, a customer who finds himself making long outgoing and return flights for only two days holiday, or whose holiday is abruptly terminated before its high spots occur, should be able to recover more.

Where a stranded holiday maker is unaware of repatriation arrangements, or is unable to take advantage of them, he may arrange and pay for his own repatriation. Provided that the reasons for doing so were genuine, bond monies will normally also be used to repay such expenses. These matters are discussed in section 4 of the CAA policy statement.

(d) Aborted holidays

Bond monies will be applied first to arrange for stranded holiday makers to enjoy the balance of their holiday or be repatriated. They will then be used to make refunds to customers who paid for holidays which will never take place. Within this second category, there are two possibilities. One is that the customer seeks simply to obtain a refund. The other is that the customer makes arrangements with a travel agent or another tour operator for an alternative holiday. Each is considered in turn below.

To obtain a refund, a customer will be expected to complete claim forms, providing proof of the booking and payment. Normally, the holiday maker will be expected to supply the failed tour operator's confirmation invoice, and also documentary proof of the method of payment and the amount. That will normally be by provision of the relevant cheque, credit card slip etc.

If a customer has booked his holiday through a travel agent which provides a quick money-back guarantee, the customer need only visit the shop at which he booked his holiday, sign the relevant forms, collect his refund and leave the agent to pursue his claims against the relevant bond holder. A guarantee does not require that the holiday concerned should be provided by the agent as tour operator. Indeed, that would be a meaningless guarantee because the agent would be guaranteeing itself. All that is required is that the holiday should be booked through one of the agent's retail outlets and be one that is within the ambit of the guarantee.

Rather than obtaining a refund, a passenger may wish to book an alternative package holiday. This can be done through a travel agent. The agent will make the booking with another tour operator, taking an assignment of the customer's claim on the bond in part or full payment for the alternative holiday. It is common practice for bond administrators to pay out to agents on assigned claims. However, travel agents will need to be able to supply bond administrators with full documentation in support of the assigned claim. Such alternative arrangements may also be booked directly with another tour operator who again will accept the assigned claim in full or part payment.

(e) Low deposits

From the late 1980s onwards, low deposit schemes became a popular selling tool. They work in this way. A tour operator, at the time a booking is made, might require a deposit of £65 per person to be made, but the travel agent taking the booking might accept from the holiday maker a lower sum per person – this could be as low as £5 or even nothing. The travel agent accounts to the tour operator for the full deposit in the normal way according to the credit terms which the travel agent has with the tour operator. The travel agent at the time of booking will require the holiday maker to sign an agreement acknowledging that the holiday maker is due to pay to the travel agent the balance of the deposit by a certain date. In other words, the travel agent is giving the holiday maker a form of interest free loan.

At the time of the financial failure of ILG, many travel agents operated such low deposit schemes. They made claims against TOSG Trust, the administrators of ILG's bond monies, for the amount of the deposit which they had paid to ILG. TOSG Trust initially refused to pay. They stated that the operation of low deposit schemes was a commercial decision by travel agents and that bond monies were not there to compensate travel agents for commercial risks.

Travel agents disputed TOSG's refusal to pay. The basis was that the holiday makers, by virtue of the fact that loans which had to be repaid had been made to them, would suffer a loss if the agents took action against the holiday makers for repayment of the loans. Of course, it was not practicable for the agents to do this. There were many thousands of holiday makers involved, each one of whom owed a small sum – almost invariably it was less than £65. The cost of issuing proceedings against each holiday maker would have been prohibitive.

TOSG Trust, on reflection, accepted that as a matter of principle, a holiday maker who had a legal obligation to make repayment faced a potential loss. Accordingly, they stipulated that agents would be refunded out of bond monies their low deposit payments provided that each agent operating a low deposit scheme instituted a test case against a customer. Lunn Poly was the first agent to do so. Mantell J, in *Lunn Poly Ltd* v *Gerald James Forshew* [1992] unreported, stated *inter alia* –

> "It is clear from the agreement – and if there had been no agreement the position would have been the same at common law – Lunn Poly were acting as the defendant's agent in paying the £60 to ILG. Whether one regards that transaction as one of money lent or whether one regards it as money being paid to the use of the principal matters not, the consequence is the same. In the absence of some failure to perform its part of the contract by the agent, and none is alleged here, the agent is entitled to recover that money from its principal, in other words Lunn Poly is entitled to recover the £60 from the defendant."

As a result of Lunn Poly's success, and the attitude adopted by Mantell J, no other agent was obliged to pursue a test case. The CAA policy statement, in its section on low deposits, still contains the possible requirement for a test case. Travel agents who indulge in low deposit schemes must ensure that their documentation clearly establishes the holiday maker's obligation to reimburse them.

(f) Credit card payments to operator

Another special situation is where the customer books direct with a tour operator and pays with a credit card. In the case of Barclaycard he will find that neither the relevant bondholder nor the Air Travel Reserve Trust will be willing to accept his claim. Instead, they will invoke s.75 of the Consumer Credit Act 1974 and refer him to his credit card company. Broadly speaking, what s.75 does is to render the credit card company jointly liable to the customer for any breach of contract by a supplier who has been paid by credit card. Section 75 is discussed on pages 245–246—in relation to the complex problems which arise where a customer uses a credit card to make payments to a *travel agent* to be passed on to the tour operator whose holiday is being booked. Suffice it to say here that where a credit card (as defined in the Consumer Credit Act) is used to pay a tour operator *direct*, then if the operator ceases trading, the customer should be able to recover the payment from his credit card company. If he only pays part of the price by credit card, it appears that he can recover the whole holiday price from his credit card company, not just the part which he paid by credit card.

A number of credit card companies have reached agreements with the Air Travel Trust, CAA, ABTA, TOSG etc that, if bond monies are sufficient to meet claims, they will do so. If, however, they are not, they will be used firstly for non credit card claims and afterwards for credit card claims to the extent that there is available money. A list of the credit card companies which have reached such an agreement is contained in Annexe 1 to the CAA joint policy statement.

(g) Recovery of pipeline monies

Customers of a collapsed tour operator who do not have a valid claim against a credit card company under s.75 clearly have suffered a loss. Their first move should be to contact the travel agent through whom they booked their holiday. In certain special cases they may be able to recover money from him without having to claim against the relevant bond holder or the Trust. For instance, the agent may be holding money paid shortly before the collapse for a booking which has not been confirmed by the collapsed operator. In such a case the relevant booking conditions required by the CAA and recommended by ABTA would make it clear that the monies are held by the agent as agent for the customer and so should be returned to him.

Another special case is where the agent is holding money paid by a customer who has cancelled his holiday *before* the collapse of the operator. A circular issued by ABTA in connection with the collapse of Laker advised that the agent should account for the contractual cancellation charge to the collapsed operator's liquidator and return the balance to the customer. In the writers' view, the ability of an agent to return monies to a customer in such circumstances depends on the wording of the formal agency agreement and on trade practice. If the agreement states that in the event of a cancellation the agent may, after deducting the cancellation charge, return any monies received from the customer and still in the agent's possession, or if that has been the course of dealing between the agent and the operator, it would seem that the agent should be both entitled and obliged to refund such monies to the customer. But if neither the terms of the formal agency agreement nor the course of dealing before the collapse support the return of such monies, the agent may be vulnerable to a claim by the liquidator and so find himself out of pocket.

Another special situation occurs when, at the time of an operator's collapse, a cheque drawn by the agent or the customer in favour of the operator has not been cleared. A customer in this position should immediately stop the cheque. In the somewhat unlikely event of the liquidator suing him on the cheque, the customer should set off his claim against the operator for the loss of his holiday. An agent whose cheque has not been cleared will be tempted to do the same but his position may not be so strong.

Much depends on whether the agent's cheque is paying money which has become the property of the operator (eg money paid in respect of a booking which has been confirmed before the collapse). If it is, then the better view appears to be that if the agent stops the cheque the liquidator will be successful in suing the agent on it. But if the cheque accompanies a booking form which the operator has not accepted before the collapse, then it would seem correct for the agent to stop it on the grounds that:

(i) the money belongs to the customer; and

(ii) the operator has not given the agent any consideration for the cheque.

(h) Money held by or for the tour operator

The preceding paragraphs have discussed situations in which monies are held by an agent who is, or may be, entitled—or even under an obligation—to return them to the customer. But in most cases monies paid by a customer for a holiday which has not commenced will be held either by the operator, or by the agent in circumstances where it is clear that he holds them as agent for the operator. The latter should always be the case where an agent holds monies after the confirmation of the booking in respect of which they were paid. This is because standard term 9(1) of the ATOL granted by the CAA requires all ATOL holders to notify travel agents that monies held by agents in respect of ATOL holidays are held as agents for the operator from the date of confirmation of the booking. This should be dealt with in the operator's brochure.

When does confirmation of a booking take place? On general principles of contract law, and in the absence of any contrary provision in the operator's booking conditions, it is when the confirmation, which is an acceptance of the offer contained in the holiday maker's booking form, is handed or posted to the holiday maker or his agent. In the past the confirmation of a booking was posted by the operator after the operator received the booking form from the agent.

The confirmation was normally posted to the agent who forwarded it to the customer. In these circumstances it could be argued that the contract was not concluded until the agent, whom the writers regard as the operator's booking agent, posted the confirmation to the customer. But it was generally accepted that posting by the operator to the agent concluded the contract.

Nowadays holiday bookings are often effected electronically. In such cases the booking is confirmed on the travel agent's VDU in the presence of the customer after the customer has completed the booking form and paid his deposit. The customer normally receives a computer print-out confirmation at the time, followed by a conventional confirmation-cum-invoice later. In these cases, any money which the agent collects is held by him for the operator from the moment the booking is made unless booking conditions specify a later date.

Assuming a clearcut case in which monies are held by a

tour operator, or by a travel agent as the operator's agent, in respect of an ATOL holiday which "never gets off the ground", what will happen when a holiday maker contacts the agent through whom he booked the holiday?

Some agents will immediately refund any monies which they still hold even though in law such monies should be accounted for to the liquidator. Some will go further and refund monies which they have already paid to the operator. As indicated on page 233, agents who provide money-back guarantees will often be under an obligation to do this but some other agents do it for goodwill purposes even though they are under no legal obligation to do so.

In cases where ABTA agents refund monies which have become the property of the operator, they require the customer to sign certain forms supplied by ABTA. These comprise a claim form, a form of assignment whereby the customer assigns the benefit of the customer's claim against the collapsed operator's liquidator, and an authority to the bond administrator to make payments in respect of the claim to the agent rather than to the customer himself. In cases where the agent does not itself make refunds, the customer is asked to sign the same forms—except for the one authorising payments to be made to the agent which is only appropriate in cases where the customer has received a refund from the agent.

The practical outcome will be the same in both cases, namely that the customer will obtain his refund—immediately from agents who adopt a policy of advancing refunds, or some months later from the TOSG, ABTA or the CAA if the agent through whom he booked does not operate such a policy.

Finally, reference should be made to an interesting issue which can arise in respect of the status of pipeline monies held by agents after a confirmation invoice has been issued by the failed operator. It is whether those pipeline monies simply create a debt owing from the agent to the failed operator or whether they are to be regarded as "trust monies". Trust monies are sums which should be specifically held, in a separate account, by the agent for the operator and which the agent is not entitled to use.

The particular significance for travel agents is that rights of set-off cannot, in general, be exercised against trust monies. In other words, a travel agent who is owed monies by the failed operator for commission payments etc cannot legally deduct those payments from pipeline monies which are trust monies. Therefore, upon the financial failure of a tour operator, the travel agent would be obliged to pay such trust monies in their entirety to the operator's liquidator – and to make a claim, as an unsecured creditor, for commission payments etc owed by the operator to the agent. It is unlikely that such a claim will recover an amount of any size.

Many agency agreements between tour operators and travel agents do use wording which could suggest that pipeline monies should be regarded as trust monies held by the agent for the operator. However, for monies to be regarded as trust monies, general principles of law mean that they should be kept in separate bank accounts and should not be utilised in any way by the agent. That is wholly contradictory with general practice in the travel industry. In general practice, pipeline monies are not kept in separate bank accounts but form part of a travel agent's normal working capital. They will be used, with other receipts, to pay for such diverse items as airline tickets or salaries. This practice is well known to tour operators.

Further, agency agreements normally also provide that the agent is entitled to interest earned on pipeline monies. In many cases, where a tour operator is late in paying the commission due to the agent, the agent will deduct such payments from pipeline monies before accounting to the tour operator. These practices do not lie easily with the existence of a trust.

The issue of whether pipeline monies could be regarded as trust monies on the basis of a written agency agreement arose following the financial failure of ILG. Its administrative receivers alleged the existence of a trust against a number of travel agents. The administrative receivers have issued proceedings against a number of travel agents. At the time of going to print, no hearings had taken place.

However, travel agents would be well advised to review their agency agreements. They should ensure that the agency agreements could not be construed as establishing a trust, and should also provide specifically for rights of set-off.

2. The Barclays Bank case

The operation of the bonding system was considered in the case of *Barclays Bank & Others* v *TOSG Trust Fund Limited and others* [1984] 2 WLR 650. Although the point of law decided in it can be summarised fairly briefly, it is proposed to explain the facts in some detail because they illustrate in concrete terms the way in which the ATOL bonding system works. The essential facts are clearly set out in the summary contained in the 1984 Weekly Law Reports at page 650:

> "In August 1974 the 13th defendant (C Ltd) a holiday tour operator, went into liquidation. The first defendant (TOSG), a company set up to receive and dispense at its complete discretion monies payable under bonds in the event of, *inter alia,* C Ltd being unable to fulfil its obligations to holiday makers, called up bonds given by the plaintiff banks. After repatriating holiday makers stranded abroad, TOSG expended the remaining bond money in repaying in full some of C Ltd's customers who had paid for holidays but not had them. When settling such claims, TOSG required the customers to assign their claims in the liquidation of C Ltd to the 12th defendant ("the Agency") a body established in 1975 to manage and administer a statutory fund for compensating persons losing holidays as a result of the collapse of tour operators. Pursuant to counter-indemnities obtained from C Ltd when the bonds had been executed, the banks proved in the liquidation, *inter alia,* in respect of such part of the bond moneys as had been dispensed by TOSG to the customers who had lost their holidays, and the Agency proved, *inter alia,* in respect of the claims assigned by those customers.

> The liquidators contended that the two proofs reflected the same debt and that, under the rule against double proof, one or other of them must be reduced accordingly. The banks brought an action for, *inter alia,* a declaration that they were entitled to prove to the exclusion of the Agency for the sum involved, and the Agency counterclaimed for declarations that the liquidators should reject the bank's proof and admit the Agency's proof".

C Ltd was Clarksons, a member of TOSG. By virtue of s.26 of the Civil Aviation Act 1971 and Regulation 3 of the Civil Aviation (Air Travel Organiser's Licensing) Regulations 1972 it could not act as an air travel organiser without a licence from the CAA. The CAA granted a licence subject to Clarksons obtaining bonds totalling £2,225,850 from substantial financial institutions.

One of the institutions which agreed to provide a bond in favour of TOSG was Barclays Bank. Clarksons and Barclays entered into a formal counter-indemnity agreement in which Clarksons requested and authorised Barclays to provide a £500,000 bond to TOSG and undertook to indemnify Barclays:

> "against all payments actions . . . which you may make suffer incur or sustain by reason or on account of you (Barclays) having executed the bond".

The bond stated that Barclays was "held and firmly bound unto TOSG in the sum of £500,000 . . ." and it was declared to be void unless during the period of 12 calendar months commencing 1 October 1973 Clarksons should cease trading. The bond imposed certain obligations on TOSG one of them being that:

> "upon payment of the said sum of £500,000 . . . (TOSG) will . . . repay to (Barclays) on demand such part of the said sum as shall not be expended or required by (TOSG) in the performance and execution of its rights duties, powers and discretions as set out in (TOSG's) memorandum and articles of association and that such memorandum and articles will not be altered during the currency of this bond without the prior written consent of (Barclays)

> (which shall not be unreasonably withheld) first obtained".

During the period of the bond Clarksons ceased trading. Immediately TOSG required Barclays and the other banks involved to pay the aggregate sum of £2,226,000 secured by the various bonds. Subsequently a winding-up order was made against Clarksons as a result of which Barclays' right to repayment under the counter-indemnity given by Clarksons became a right to prove as a creditor in Clarksons' liquidation. TOSG spent £958,000 of the total bond monies in assisting and repatriating stranded Clarksons holiday makers. The balance was devoted to making refunds to customers who in the event never received the Clarksons' holidays for which they had paid.

The role of the Air Travel Reserve Fund Agency ("the Agency") the predecessor of the Air Travel Reserve Trust has already been mentioned, and the mechanics of its operation are described in the following passage from Templeman LJ's judgment in the Barclays Bank case:

> "By an agreement ('the assignment agreement') dated 23 July 1975 and made between TOSG and the Agency, but to which the banks were not parties, it was agreed that TOSG would, subject to the retention of certain reserves and expenses, employ all the moneys remaining in the hands of TOSG and applicable for the purpose of alleviating the consequences of the business failure of Clarksons in repaying in full, so far as the moneys would go, deposits and advance payments made by Clarksons' customers who never, in the event, enjoyed the holidays for which they had paid. The Agency agreed to pay the claims of all Clarksons' customers remaining outstanding after the moneys available to TOSG to reimburse Clarksons' customers were exhausted. TOSG agreed that before paying any customer of Clarksons, TOSG 'will obtain an assignment in favour of the Agency from the payee of his right to prove in the liquidation of Clarksons . . . for the full amount of his claim'. TOSG paid £1,268,000, part of the aggregate sum of £2,226,000 provided by

> the banks pursuant to their bonds to Clarksons' customers. Each customer who received part of the sum of £1,268,000 lodged a claim with the joint liquidators of Clarksons, and assigned in writing to the Agency 'all my . . . rights against (Clarksons) under my . . . claims against (Clarksons) in respect of overseas holidays which I . . . have lodged with the joint liquidators' ".

The dispute between Barclays and the other banks providing bonds on the one hand and the Agency on the other arose because both claimed in Clarksons' liquidation for the sum of £1,268,000, being the total monies paid by TOSG in making refunds to Clarksons' customers. The banks' claims were made under the counter-indemnities given by Clarksons to each of them (see *ante*). The Agency claimed on the grounds that the assignments to the Agency obtained by TOSG gave the Agency the right to prove for £1,268,000.

The House of Lords held that:

> "Upon the true and simple construction of the bond and the indemnity, when TOSG paid £1,000 of Barclays' money to a customer whose claim against Clarksons amounted to £1,000, the claim of that customer against Clarksons was extinguished and there became vested in Barclays an indisputable claim against Clarksons for £1,000 under the indemnity. If TOSG paid £200 to a customer whose claim was £1,000, then the customer could thereafter only claim and prove for the balance of £800 and Barclays could claim and prove under its indemnity for £200. By the indemnity Clarksons agreed to repay to the banks every penny that the banks paid under the bond and that TOSG paid to the customers".

In arriving at its decision the House of Lords rejected the argument that the payment of refunds by TOSG entitled it to direct the customers concerned to assign the benefit of their claims to the Agency. This was because TOSG's memorandum of association meant that TOSG were "only authorised agents for the distribution to customers of monies provided by the bonds". The House of Lords held that there were originally two mutually exclusive debts, "namely the debt which Clarksons owed the customers under the contracts and the debt which Clarksons owed the banks under their indemnities". The payments by TOSG reduced the customers' debts by £1,268,000, leaving them with nothing to assign to the Agency, and increased by the like sum the amount owed by Clarksons to the various banks.

3. Credit card payments

(a) Section 75, Consumer Credit Act

A situation which has given rise to considerable disagreement is where a holiday maker uses a credit card to make payments to the *travel agent* through whom he books his holiday. The problem concerns the application of s.75(1) of the Consumer Credit Act 1974 which provides that:

> "If the debtor under a debtor-creditor-supplier agreement falling within section 12(b) or (c) has, in relation to a transaction financed by the agreement, any claim against the supplier in respect of a misrepresentation or breach of contract, he shall have a like claim against the creditor, who, with the supplier, shall accordingly be jointly and severally liable to the debtor".

Section 189 of the 1974 Act defines terms used throughout the Act, some of which must be mentioned to appreciate the significance of s.75. A debtor is defined as "the individual receiving credit under a consumer credit agreement" and a creditor as "the person providing credit under a consumer credit agreement". Consumer credit agreements include *inter alia*, debtor-creditor-supplier agreements (see next paragraph) which can be either restricted use credit agreements or unrestricted use credit agreements. The former are, in general terms, the types of agreement under which credit cards are issued. Thus, the creditor referred to in s.75 can be the issuer of a credit card.

A supplier is someone other than the creditor with whom the debtor comes to an arrangement to purchase goods, services or land. The definition of "debtor-creditor-supplier agreement" contained in s.12 of the 1974 Act is extremely abstract and the authors quote instead the explanation given in the OFT Booklet *"Regulated and Exempt Agreements"*:

> "Generally, a debtor-creditor-supplier agreement will arise when the creditor is connected in some way with the transaction to be financed by the credit advanced: for example where the creditor and the supplier of the goods, services or whatever is financed by the credit, are one and the same person. Thus a retailer offering his own credit or a finance house making a hire purchase transaction will be entering into a debtor-creditor-supplier agreement. If the creditor and the supplier are different people, the agreement will be a debtor-creditor-supplier agreement only if there are arrangements between them under which the creditor is prepared to finance the transaction between the supplier and the customer. An example of what would normally be debtor-creditor-supplier credit is a high street shop arranging a personal loan with a finance house for its customers to finance their purchases in the shop. A credit card or trading check for use in certain shops will also usually involve debtor-creditor-supplier credit".

Under s.189 the verb "to finance" means to finance "wholly or partly". Accordingly, it appears not to be necessary in order for s.75 to apply for the creditor to have provided the total funds needed by the debtor to make his purchase from the supplier but merely some of them. In other words, although this may not be accepted by all credit card companies, where a customer uses his credit card to pay the initial deposit but not the subsequent final balance (or *vice versa*) s.75 applies if it would apply if the whole price had been paid by credit card.

(b) Rights against a credit card company

One of the effects of s.75 is that a customer who purchases goods from a supplier and pays for them by credit card will, in the event that the supplier is liable in law to the customer for misrepresentation or breach of contract, be able to make a claim against the credit card company identical to that which he can make against the supplier. Although the Act permits the creditor to seek an indemnity from the supplier, it does not allow him to seek to exclude this liability to the customer. This is so even where the debtor, by entering into the transaction in question, exceeds his credit limit or in any other way breaks the terms of the credit agreement. However, in such an event, it may be possible for the creditor to counterclaim against the debtor.

There are certain limitations to the credit agreements and types of purchase to which s.75 applies, namely:

(a) The cost of the item being purchased must be more than £100 and not more than £30,000 (including VAT).

(b) The credit agreement must be "regulated" within the meaning of the 1974 Act. This means, amongst other things, that the borrower must not be a corporation and the credit made available must not exceed £15,000.

(c) The credit agreement must not have been made before 1 July 1977.

(d) The number of payments to be made by the debtor in repayment of the whole amount of credit provided in any period must exceed one.

The latter is especially important since it creates a distinction between charge cards, such as American Express, which are *not* subject to the Act and credit cards, such as Access and Barclaycard, which are.

It is possible for a holiday maker to pay direct by credit card to the tour operator providing the holiday. In this event, it is easy to see s.75's application. The holiday maker is the debtor, the tour operator the supplier and the credit card company the creditor. If the tour operator commits a breach of contract or misrepresentation, the holiday maker can direct his claim against either the tour operator or the credit card company or both. The credit card company, provided that the tour operator is liable in law for breach of contract or misrepresentation, will be liable to compensate the holiday maker and cannot seek to avoid liability by claiming that it was not responsible for making the holiday arrangements.

Payments to the travel agents through whom holidays have been booked have however, created difficulties. Following the collapse of Laker, it was unable to supply holidays which it had contracted to supply and was therefore in breach of contract. Some of Laker's customers, who had paid by credit card the travel agents through whom the holidays were booked, claimed under s.75 against the credit card companies for the refund of the purchase price. When these claims were made against Barclaycard and Access, they rejected liability on the grounds that the relevant supplier for the purposes of s.75 was not Laker but the travel agent to whom the holiday maker effected payment. They maintained that the collapse of the tour operator, Laker, did not involve any breach of contract by the travel agent so s.75 did not apply. Holiday makers in this position then found that the Air Travel Reserve Fund Agency maintained that the credit card companies were liable under s.75 and that therefore the holiday makers had not suffered any loss in law.

In the event, Barclaycard and Access reached agreement with the Agency regarding the apportionment of responsibility for claims from Laker customers. The actions taken by Access and Barclaycard mean that the question of whether a credit card company can be held liable under s.75 where a credit card is used to pay the *travel agent* for a holiday may never be litigated.

The CAA policy statement provides that claims in respect of which payment was made by credit card to an agent will be reimbursed from bond monies.

4. Collapse of a travel agent

The collapse of a tour operator is a traumatic event for

customers who have booked holidays with it. The collapse of a travel agent creates far fewer ripples but does generate some legal problems which require consideration. In relation to package holidays these arise where the agent holds monies which have been paid by customers for onward transmission to tour operators.

If the agent holds monies on behalf of a tour operator, there is no problem so far as the customer is concerned. This is because—certainly in cases involving ATOL holidays and probably in other cases—the agent will not be holding a sum on behalf of the operator unless the customer's booking has been accepted by the operator. In that event there is a firm contract between the operator and the customer which is not affected by the collapse of the agent who helped to bring it into being.

There will of course be a problem for the operator because it is owed money by an insolvent company. But that in no way relieves the operator of its obligations to the customers concerned. They have paid their deposit or balance of holiday price to the operator's agent who holds it on the operator's behalf and they are entitled to the full benefit of their contracts with the operator. The operator will have to prove as an unsecured creditor in the agent's liquidation and hope that the agent's net assets will be sufficient to enable the liquidator to pay a substantial dividend. Any shortfall will not be recoverable from the customers.

What is the position where the agent holds monies which belong to the customer? The most likely instance of that is where at the time of the agent's collapse a booking has been taken but not yet accepted by the operator. The operator may be reluctant to accept the booking if he knows that the deposit for it is held by an insolvent agent—and even more reluctant if the booking is a late one in respect of which the customer has paid the whole holiday price to the agent.

The initial presumption is that in this situation the operator is under no obligation to accept the booking and provide the holiday unless the customer sends him another cheque, and that the customer will be left with the thankless task of proving in the agent's liquidation in the hope of recovering some of what he paid to the agent. This would seem to follow from the basic fact that the money held by the agent belongs to the customer. However this may not be the case if, as is submitted in Chapter 5, the agent when taking bookings, is acting as booking agent for the operator. If that is so, the courts might imply a collateral contract between the operator and the customer whereby, in return for the customer effecting the booking through the operator's agent, the operator warrants that monies can safely be paid to the agent. There are no decided cases regarding this but the explanation of collateral contracts on page 97 suggests that one may exist in the circumstances outlined in this paragraph.

But do the financial security provisions of the Regulations affect this situation? Regulation 16(1) provides that "the other party to the contract shall at all times be able to provide sufficient evidence of security for the refund of money paid over . . .", and Regulation 16(2) provides that "the other party to the contract" must ensure that there are either bonding or insurance or trust monies arrangements in place. These requirements have been discussed in some detail in Chapter 4.

"The other party to the contract" is defined in Regulation 2 as meaning "the party, other than the consumer, to the contract, that is, the organiser or the retailer, or both, as the case may be". Regulation 2 also defines the contract, and the definition is "the agreement linking the consumer to the organiser or to the retailer, or to both, as the case may be".

The definitions are rather obscurely worded and not particularly helpful. The contract for the package holiday is between the tour operator and the holiday maker. On its face, therefore, this suggests that the other party to the contract should be regarded as the tour operator. However, the authors understand that the DTI regards the definition as extending in certain circumstances to the travel agent and considers that in the circumstances outlined above the travel agent is under an obligation to have security for such monies paid by the holiday maker to the agent. If that is right, this will of course protect the holiday maker.

Another case where a collapsed travel agent may be holding money which belongs to the customer is where a customer has cancelled his holiday. But for its collapse the agent would have refunded any monies held by it to the customer after deducting the appropriate cancellation charges. But the insolvency of the agent will limit the customer's rights against it to proving for his debt in the agent's liquidation. However, in the writers' opinion, the customer will also have a good claim against the operator because the customer's right to a partial refund on cancellation is part of the contract between the customer and the operator. This right should not be prejudiced because of a failure to perform on the part of the operator's appointed booking agent. Technically, the customer's claim against the operator will be for the shortfall of what he recovers in the liquidation of the agent but in practice the operator may well be prepared to pay in full and take over the customer's claim against the agent.

If the collapsed agent was a member of ABTA, much of the preceding paragraphs may be primarily of academic interest. This is because ABTA Travel Agent's Fund will make good losses sustained by members of the travelling public as a result of the collapse of an ABTA travel agent. In addition it will usually make good any such losses sustained by ABTA tour operators.

Appendix A

Extracts from the Tour Operators' Code of Conduct and ABTA's Standards on Brochures

CONDUCT BETWEEN TOUR OPERATORS AND MEMBERS OF THE PUBLIC

2.1 Minimum Standards on Brochures

A Tour Operator shall ensure that his brochure complies with the spirit as well as the principles, rules and procedures contained in "ABTA Standards on Brochures" as published by the Association from time to time.

2.2 Statutory Requirements for Brochures

Every brochure published by or in the name of a tour operator shall observe the requirements of the Trade Description Act 1968, the Misrepresentation Act 1967, the Civil Aviation Act 1971 (including any regulations made thereunder), the Unfair Contract Terms Act 1977, the Control of Misleading Advertisements Regulations 1988 and the Consumer Protection Act 1987, or any amendment or re-enactment thereof in accordance with the second principle of this Code.

2.3 Cancellation of Tours, Holidays or other Travel Arrangements by the Tour Operator

(i) A tour operator shall not cancel a tour, holiday or other travel arrangements after the date when payment of the balance of the price becomes due unless it is necessary to do so as a result of force majeure, or unless the client defaults in payment of such balance.

(ii) If a tour operator cancels a previously confirmed tour, holiday or other travel arrangements

(a) for any reason whatsoever prior to the date on which payment of the balance of the price becomes due or

(b) for reasons of force majeure at any time prior to departure he shall inform agents and direct clients without delay and shall offer clients the choice of an alternative holiday, if available, or a full refund of all monies paid. Such refund shall be sent to agents within 10 clear days and to direct clients within 14 clear days of the client's decision being notified to the tour operator.

(iii) Notwithstanding Clause 2.3 (i), if the cancellation is made for reasons *other than force majeure* on or after the date when payment of the balance of the tour price is due the tour operator shall also offer clients reasonable compensation. Such compensation shall be in accordance with a rising scale of payments geared to the length of time prior to departure at which the cancellation is made, i.e. the nearer to departure, the higher the level of compensation.

2.4 Material Alterations to Tours, Holidays and other Travel Arrangements by Tour Operators

(i) Except for reasons of force majeure, a tour operator shall not make a material alteration to a previously confirmed tour, holiday or other travel arrangements unless he does so in time to inform agents and direct clients not less than 14 days before the departure date of the tour, holiday or other travel arrangements.

(ii) If a tour operator makes a material alteration to a previously confirmed tour, holiday or other travel arrangements

(a) for any reason whatsoever prior to the date on which payment of the balance of the price becomes due or

(b) for reasons of force majeure at any time prior to departure

he shall inform agents and direct clients without delay and shall offer clients the choice of either accepting the alteration or of cancelling the tour, holiday or other travel arrangements and receiving a full refund of all monies paid. Such refund shall be sent to agents within 10 clear days and to direct clients within 14 clear days of receipt of the notification to cancel.

(iii) Notwithstanding Clause 2.4 (i), if the material alteration is made for reasons *other than force majeure* on or after the date on which payment of the balance of the price becomes due, the tour operator shall also offer clients reasonable compensation. Such compensation shall be in accordance with a rising scale of payments geared to the length of time prior to departure at which the material alteration is made, i.e. the nearer to departure, the higher the level of compensation.

2.5 Cancellation of Tours, Holidays or Other Travel Arrangements by Clients

A tour operator shall clearly state in his booking conditions the amount of, or the basis for calculating, the cancellation fees which the client shall be liable to incur, as well as the terms and conditions under which the client shall be liable to incur such fees.

2.6 Overbooked Hotels

(i) A tour operator shall exercise reasonable care and skill to ensure that tours, holidays or other travel arrangements are not cancelled or altered as a result of overbooking.

(ii) Where tours, holidays or other travel arrangements, are cancelled or altered as a result of overbooking by a hotel, a tour operator shall only be deemed to have exercised reasonable care and skill to prevent the cancellation or alteration if he can show that the overbooking occurred for reasons beyond his control.

(iii) If, despite sub-paragraphs (i) and (ii) above, a hotel is overbooked and a tour operator knows this before the departure of the affected clients, he shall immediately inform those clients and shall offer them the choice of an alternative holiday of at least comparable standard, if available, or a full and prompt refund of all money paid.

(iv) If, despite sub-paragraphs (i) and (ii) above, a hotel is overbooked and a tour operator does not know this before the departure of affected clients, such clients shall on arrival at their destination be offered alternative accommodation and shall also be offered reasonable compensation for "disturbance" where the location and/or facilities of the alternative accommodation can reasonably be regarded as inferior to that originally booked.

(v) For the purpose of the above sub-paragraphs, hotels include accommodation of other kinds such as apartments, villas, guest houses and camping sites.

2.7 Building Works

Where a tour operator becomes aware of building works which may reasonably be considered to seriously impair the enjoyment of a holiday he must, without undue delay, notify clients of the situation and afford them an opportunity to transfer to an alternative holiday at the price pertaining to that holiday or to cancel without penalty. Furthermore he must ensure that all prospective clients are alerted to the situation.

2.8 Tour Operator's Liability

(i) Tour operators shall include as a term of any contract for the sale of their foreign inclusive holidays or tours a provision accepting responsibility for acts and/or omissions of their employees, agents, sub-contractors and suppliers. In addition, tour operators shall indicate acceptance of responsibility should the services which the tour operator is contractually obliged to provide prove deficient or are not of reasonable standard save that tour operators shall not be responsible nor accept liability for death, bodily injury or illness caused to the signatory to the contract and/or any other named person on the booking form except as provided by Clause 2.8 (ii) below. Where the services in question consist of carriage by air or by sea, the tour operator shall be entitled to limit his obligations and liabilities in the manner provided by international conventions in respect of air or sea carriers.

(ii) A tour operator shall include, as a term of any contract for the sale of foreign inclusive holidays or tours, a provision accepting responsibility for the negligent acts and/or omissions of:

(a) his employees or agents,

(b) his suppliers and sub-contractors, servants and/or agents of the same whilst acting within the scope of, or in the course of their employment (other than air and sea carriers performing any domestic, internal or international carriage of whatsoever kind)

in respect of claims arising as a result of death, bodily injury or illness caused to the signatory to the contract and/or any other of the named persons on the booking form.

(iii) A tour operator shall include as a term of any contract for the sale of a foreign inclusive holiday provisions stating that, where appropriate and subject to the tour operator's reasonable discretion:-

(a) general assistance shall be afforded to clients who, through misadventure, suffer illness, personal injury or death during the period of their holiday arising out of an activity which does not form part of the foreign inclusive holiday nor of an excursion offered through the tour operator.

(b) where legal action is undertaken by the client, with the prior agreement of the tour operator, initial legal costs associated therewith shall be met by the tour operator, always provided clients request such assistance within 90 days from date of misadventure.

(c) the aggregate costs for the tour operator in respect of Clause 2.8 (iii) (a) and (b) above shall not exceed £5,000 per booking form. Furthermore, in the event either of there being a successful claim for costs against a third party or there being suitable insurance policy/ies in force, costs actually incurred by the tour operator shall be recoverable from the clients.

(iv) A tour operator shall ensure that he obtains adequate liability insurance to cover claims made by clients under Clause 2.8(ii) of this Code.

(v) A tour operator shall not include as a term of any contract relating to the sale of any travel arrangement, clauses which purport to:

(a) exclude or limit liability for misleading statements made by the tour operator, his employees or agents; and

(b) exclude or limit liability for the tour operators contractual duty to exercise care and skill in making arrangements for a package holiday; and

(c) exclude liability for any alleged cause of dissatisfaction by stipulating that such cause must be made known to the tour operator within a fixed period unless that period is at least 28 days from completion of holiday.

(vi) A tour operator shall indicate that claims under Clause 2.8 shall in respect of both liability and quantum fall within the exclusive jurisdiction of the courts in the country in which the contract was entered into.

2.9 Complaints and Correspondence from Clients

In the event of the dispute between a client and a tour operator all correspondence relating to clients' complaints shall be dealt with by the tour operator within the following time limits:

(i) not later than 14 days from receipt for an acknowledgement to be sent and;

(ii) not later than 28 days from receipt for a full reply to be sent or a reply containing a detailed explanation for the delay;

(iii) the final date for dealing in full with the aforesaid correspondence shall be 56 days;

2.10 Correspondence from the Association

All correspondence from the Association about complaints and compliance with the Articles of Association and this Code shall be dealt with within the same time limits shown in paragraph 2.9 above.

2.11 Arbitration

(i) A tour operator shall include as a term of any contract relating to the sale of his inclusive holidays or tours a provision whereby any dispute arising out of, or in connection with, such sale which is not amicably settled, may be referred to arbitration under a special scheme devised for the travel industry by the Chartered Institute of Arbitrators.

It shall also be stated that:-

(a) the scheme provides for a simple and inexpensive

method of arbitration on documents alone with restricted liability of the client in respect of costs;

(b) the scheme does not apply to claims for an amount greater than £1,500 per person or £7,500 per booking form or to claims which are solely or mainly in respect of physical injury or illness or the consequences of such injury or illness;

(c) details of the scheme will be supplied on request.

(ii) Where a client indicates in writing that he wishes to refer an unresolved dispute to arbitration, the tour operator shall reply to the Association within 21 days enclosing payment and documents and shall comply with the terms of the Arbitration Scheme referred to in sub-paragraph (i) above and in particular with all the relevant rules and regulations of the Chartered Institute of Arbitrators for the time being in force.

Note: A recommended clause for inclusion in booking conditions is set out in the ABTA Standards on Brochures.

2.12 Advertising

(i) All advertising by tour operators shall observe the requirements of all such Acts of Parliament as may be enacted from time to time and in particular, with the Trade Descriptions Act 1968, the Misrepresentation Act 1967, the Civil Aviation Act 1971, the Control of Misleading Advertisements Regulations 1988, and the Consumer Protection Act 1987 (including any regulations made thereunder) and of any amendment or re-enactment thereof.

(ii) Where a tour operator is convicted of an offence or judgement is entered against him in respect of a proven breach of any of the statutory provisions as contained in paragraph 2.12(i) above he shall be deemed to be in breach of this Code.

(iii) All advertising by a tour operator shall comply with the Codes or Regulations of the recognised organisations or associations. Where a tour operator is reported to have breached such Codes or Regulations, the Code of Conduct Committee retains the right to reconsider the alleged complaint and to decide in their view if the tour operator has or has not breached this Code.

(iv) A tour operator shall not advertise in such a manner as to suggest that other members of the Association are or may become insolvent.

(v) A tour operator shall show his ABTA number in all his press advertisements for travel business, but shall not be obliged to do so where these advertisements are in classified run-on form unless such advertisements contain any reference to ABTA.

2.13 Surcharges – ABTA Standards

A tour operator shall ensure that his conduct complies with the principles, rules and procedures contained in 'ABTA Standards on Surcharges' as published by the Association from time to time. (See Appendix C).

2.14 Airport and Seaport Taxes

A tour operator shall include airport and seaport taxes in the prices quoted in brochures and advertisements for all inclusive holidays except in respect of taxes which cannot be paid in advance by the tour operator.

2.15 Misleading Use of ABTA Symbol

A tour operator shall not, directly or indirectly cause, permit, assist or encourage a company or firm trading as a tour operator or travel agent which is not a member of the Association to represent itself as a member by the use of the ABTA symbol or by any ABTA number on brochures or other documents or by any other means which may give the false impression to the public that such company or firm is a member of the Association, or in relation to travel business be connected to or associated in any way (including through any of its proprietors, shareholders, officers or personnel) with any such company or firm which so misrepresents itself.

2.16 Representatives

A tour operator shall ensure that all his representatives can communicate clearly in English and are familiar with their company policies in order that they can comprehend and perform within written procedures.

ABTA'S STANDARDS ON BROCHURES

This document forms part of the Tour Operators' Code of Conduct.

Every brochure published by or in the name of any ABTA member Tour Operator or Travel Agent shall contain clear, legible, comprehensive and accurate information to enable the client to exercise an informed judgement in making his choice. The brochure must contain as a minimum the following information:-

1. Governmental/Statutory Licensing Authority

All information necessary to comply with the regulations for the time being of the Civil Aviation Authority and any other governmental or statutory licensing authority.

2. Legal Identity

The legal identity of the Tour Operator responsible for publishing the brochure containing the tour, holiday or travel arrangement offered including their ABTA number and ATOL number where applicable.

3. Means of Travel

The means of travel (eg ship, train, coach, motor vehicle, charter or scheduled airline).

4. Destination and/or Itinerary

The destination and/or itinerary as appropriate.

5. Date, Place and Time of Departure and Return

The date, place and approximate time of departure and return. Where any or all of these items are subject to alteration by a regulatory body (e.g. Airport Scheduling Committee) reference must be made to same.

6. Nature of Accommodation and the Meal Facilities

The nature of accommodation and the meal facilities included in the price.

7. Additional Facilities

Any additional facilities or special arrangements included in price.

8. Booking Conditions

The procedures for booking and the contractual conditions under which the booking is made must conform with all relevant provisions of this Code. Information must be given in relation to each of the following items.

(i) Payment of deposit and balance due.

(ii) Confirmation of the booking.

(iii) Price policy in accordance with paragraph 10 below.

(iv) An alteration to a confirmed booking made by the client.

(v) An alteration to a confirmed booking made by the Tour Operator having regard to the provisions of clause 2.4 of this Code.

(vi) Cancellation made by a client to a confirmed booking having regard to the provisions of clause 2.5 of this Code.

(vii) Cancellation to a confirmed booking made by the Tour Operator having regard to the provisions of clause 2.3 of this Code.

(viii) Handling of any complaint made by a client having regard to the provisions of clauses 2.10 and 2.11 of this Code and paragraph 12 below. Booking conditions shall not deny to clients the option of taking action in the courts if they so wish.

(ix) The Tour Operators' liability to the client.

(x) The existence of conditions of carriage of the carrier.

Furthermore a Tour Operator shall not print his booking conditions or insurance details on the front or on the back of booking forms unless all such conditions and/or insurance details are provided separately to the signatory of the booking form on or before confirmation of the booking.

9. Insurance Details

If a tour operator offers holiday insurance, an accurate and sufficiently detailed summary of the cover provided and the premiums associated therewith must be shown in the brochure. Furthermore it is necessary for the tour operator to indicate close to the basic price, the location of such summary and premiums in the brochure.

Where the purchase of the tour operators own insurance is compulsory, the relevant premium must be included in the basic price.

10. Price Policy

The total price, or the means of arriving at the total price, together with a precise statement of the services included therein must be shown in the brochure. Where a Tour Operator offers a variety of prices to give the client a choice the Tour Operator must make clear in the brochure (or any other material pertaining to price indication) what the basic price is and what it covers.

The base date by reference to which prices were calculated and the relevant exchange rates published in the Financial Times "Guide to World Currencies" on that date must also be shown in the brochure. In this regard compliance with H.M. Customs & Excise regulations on VAT is required.

If a Tour Operator reserves the right to levy a surcharge, a statement to that effect must appear close to the basic price with an indication of where further information may be found within the brochure.

If a price indication becomes misleading while the brochure is still current the Tour Operator shall inform all travel agents to whom the brochure has been distributed. Where the Tour Operator sells direct to the public and the price becomes misleading in the advertisements and/or brochure the Operator must ensure that prospective clients are informed of the correct price prior to a booking being made.

The following information regarding additional charges is intended solely for the guidance of tour operators. No liability in respect of such information can be accepted by ABTA.

(i) *Non Optional additional charges of fixed amount (except taxes payable locally overseas)*:-
shall be included in the basic price and not shown as additions unless they are payable by some clients only. In that case the Operator should specify near to the details of the basic price either what the amounts are and the

circumstances in which they are payable or where in the brochure the information is given. All price indications must include VAT.

(ii) *Non Optional additional charges of variable amount*:-
together with details of what is included in such charges shall be made clear to the clients near to the basic price or a reference made close to the basic price of where the information is given in the brochure.

(iii) *Optional additional charges*:-
ie, those additional optional charges which are directly related to the cost of the holiday eg, rooming/board supplement. The details of what is included in such charges shall be made clear to the clients near to the basic price or a reference made close to the basic price of where the information is given in the brochure.

(iv) *Charges for additional services*:-
ie, those additional services which are not directly related to the package, eg, car hire. As such charges have nothing to do with the basic price they need not be made clear to clients near to the basic price nor is it necessary to make a reference close to the basic price of where the information is given in the brochure.

11. Health Matters

The brochure must contain adequate information pertaining to health requirements of countries featured or a reference to the D.o.H. leaflet *Protect your Health Abroad*, available from their ABTA travel agent or the Department of Health. Clients should also be advised to check with their own doctor before their departure as to which innoculations are available and necessary for specific areas.

12. Arbitration

It is recommended that the following clause is included in booking conditions:

"Disputes arising out of, or in connection with, this contract which cannot be amicably settled may be referred to arbitration, if the customer so wishes, under a special Scheme which, although devised by arrangement with the Association of British Travel Agents, is administered quite independently by the Chartered Institute of Arbitrators.

The Scheme provides for a simple and inexpensive method of arbitration on documents alone with restricted liability on the customer in respect of costs. Full details will be provided on request. The Scheme does not apply to claims for an amount greater than £1,500 per person. There is also a limit of £7,500 per booking form. Neither does it apply to claims which are solely or mainly in respect of physical injury or illness or the consequences of such injury or illness. The rules of the Scheme provide that the application for arbitration must be made within nine months of the date of return from the holiday but in special circumstances it may still be offered outside the period."

13. Noise

Brochures which feature resort-based holidays shall contain adequate information relating to all known sources of noise which exist or might be expected to exist at resorts and which may reasonably be considered to cause offence to clients. Such sources of noise include, but are not limited to, night clubs, bars, discos, amusement parks, and airports.

14. Building Works

Where it is known, or can reasonably be expected, that building works which are likely to adversely affect the enjoyment of a holiday, will take place during the period covered by the brochure all specific information must be published on the relevant page in the brochure.

15. Publication Date

The month and year of publication must be printed in the brochure.

16. Delays at points of Departure

Brochures must state clearly and unambiguously the tour operator's policy on the handling of clients who are delayed at the outward and/or homeward points of departure. Tour operators are encouraged, but not obliged, to provide refreshments/meals appropriate to the time of day and overnight accommodation dependent upon the length of delay and nature of holiday. Furthermore the brochure must state what action will be taken in the event that circumstances prevent the policy referred to above being carried out.

Appendix B

Air Travel Organisers' Licence Schedule of Standard Terms

Standard Term 1

(i) The licence holder shall quote legibly:—

(a) the licence number stated at the head of the licence and his name on all publicity material in which he holds himself out as a person who does or may make available accommodation for the carriage of persons on flights and which is published between the date on which the licence is issued and the date on which it expires;

(b) his name and licence number on every booking form or other document forming or evidencing the formation of a contract for the carriage of persons on flights which he issues during the currency of his licence.

(ii) Where the licence holder has authorised an agent to act on his behalf he shall ensure that the agent states that he is acting as agent for the licence holder and quotes clearly and legibly the licence holder's name and licence number on all publicity material in which the agent holds himself out as a person who does or may make available accommodation for the carriage of persons on flights as agent for the licence holder and on any booking form or other document forming or evidencing the formation of a contract for the carriage of persons on flights which the agent issues on behalf of the licence holder.

(iii) For the purposes of Standard Term 1 where the licence holder is a company the licence holder's name shall be the registered name of the company.

Standard Term 2 A

The licence holder shall keep in force for the period stated in the licence a Bond of the amount so stated, being a Bond entered into by a person approved for that purpose by the Authority, which Bond shall be deposited with the Authority and shall, where the licence holder is a limited company, be in the terms set out in Part 1 of

Schedule 3 published in the Civil Aviation Authority Official Record Series 3 — Part I Air Travel Organisers' Licensing, and where the licence holder is not a limited company, be in the terms set out in Part 2 of the said Schedule 3.

Standard Term 2 B

The licence holder shall throughout the period of the licence comply with the bonding requirements of the Tour Operators' Study Group from time to time in force, and in pursuance thereof shall obtain and keep in force a bond or other security of the amount stated in the licence; provided that, if at any time those bonding requirements are not such as to ensure that in the event of the bond or other security being realised the said amount (after deduction of the costs of administration) will be used for the benefit of persons who have paid for but have not received accommodation for carriage by air to be provided by the licence holder under the authority of the licence (except insofar as the said amount exceeds what is required for this purpose), the holder shall comply with Standard Term 2 A.

Standard Term 3

1 Not later than one month after the end of each period ending 31 March, 30 June, 30 September and 31 December during which the licence is in force, the licence holder shall furnish to the Authority in a manner set out in Annex A hereto a statement of the number of passengers carried on flights during that period whose accommodation on the flight was made available to them by him pursuant to the licence, showing the number of such passengers carried by each airline.

For the purposes of Standard Term 3 a flight shall be deemed to have taken place on the date on which it ends.

2 Not later than one month after the end of each period ending 31 March, 30 June, 30 September and 31 December during which the licence is in force, the licence holder shall furnish to the Authority in a manner set out in Annex B hereto a certificate of his turnover during the period.

3 The licence holder shall annually furnish to the Authority in a manner set out in Annex C hereto a report by auditors appointed by the licence holder on his turnover during each period ending 31 March, 30 June, 30 September and 31 December during which the licence is in force. For the purposes of Standard Term 3 the auditors who furnish the report shall be the same auditors as those who sign the licence holder's audited accounts for the year in question or such other auditors as may be approved by the Authority for the purpose.

Standard Term 4 A

The licence holder shall furnish to the Authority a copy of any brochure in which he or any agent acting on his behalf quotes the prices at which he is prepared to make available accommodation for the carriage of persons on flights or to provide an inclusive tour which includes carriage by air and a copy of any booking form relating to any such brochure. A copy shall be furnished as soon as the brochure has been published.

Standard Term 4 B

The licence holder shall furnish to the Authority a copy of any brochure, leaflet, or other printed matter in which he or any agent acting on his behalf quotes the prices at which he is prepared to make available accommodation for the carriage of persons on flights or to provide an inclusive tour which includes carriage by air and a copy of any booking form relating to any such brochure, leaflet or other printed matter. A copy shall be furnished as soon as the brochure, leaflet or other printed matter has been published.

Standard Term 5

The licence holder shall inform the Authority within 21 days of the occurrence of any change in the following information provided in his application for an Air Travel Organiser's Licence:

- (a) the business address or address of registered office
- (b) the status of the licence holder (eg by his becoming a limited company or change of name)
- (c) the parent, holding, associated or subsidiary company or companies
- (d) the directors, company secretary or managerial staff
- (e) the partners
- (f) the authorised or issued share capital
- (g) the names and addresses of any shareholders owning 15% or more of the shares in the company
- (h) the auditors
- (i) any trading name or names.

Standard Term 6

The licence holder shall

- (a) in the case of a body corporate incorporated under the Companies Act 1985 furnish the Authority with a copy of the Annual Statement of Accounts and Directors Report at the same time as the Statement of Accounts and Directors Report are published to the shareholders in the company or as soon as possible thereafter, and
- (b) in all other cases furnish certified statements of annual accounts to the Authority at the end of the licence holder's financial year or as soon as possible thereafter and in no case later than four months thereafter.

Standard Term 7

The licence holder shall not sub-charter accommodation on a flight except to a person who holds an Air Travel Organiser's Licence authorising him to make available accommodation for the carriage of persons on that flight.

Standard Term 8

Passengers shall be informed (by means of advertisement or otherwise) before entering into a contract for carriage on any flight made pursuant to the licence of:

(a) the name of the operator of the aircraft on which the passenger is to be carried, the type of aircraft which he intends to operate, and the airport of destination at which it is intended to set down the passengers or

(b) the fact that the licence holder is not in a position to state the operator, the aircraft type or the destination.

Where passengers are informed of the operator, aircraft type or destination they shall at the same time be informed whether they can or cannot cancel their contract without penalty in the event of any subsequent change of operator, aircraft type or destination.

Standard Term 9

1. The licence holder shall not enter into a contract through the intervention of an agent, being a contract for accommodation to be made available pursuant to the licence, unless he has made it clear in writing to the agent and to the customer that any money paid by the customer to the agent under or in contemplation of the contract is held by the agent as agent for the licence holder from the date on which confirmation of the customer's booking is despatched by the licence holder until the date on which the agent pays the money to the licence holder.
2. The licence holder shall not enter into a contract through the intervention of an agent, being a contract for accommodation to be made available pursuant to the licence, unless he has made it clear in writing to the agent and, so far as is practicable, to the customer, whether or not any money paid by the customer to the agent under or in contemplation of contract is held by the agent as agent for the licence holder from the date on which the money is paid by the customer to the agent until the date on which confirmation of the customer's booking is despatched by the licence holder.

Standard Term 10

Where passengers are carried pursuant to this licence for the common purpose of attending a football match, each passenger shall have been provided with a valid ticket of admission to the match and before the date of any such flight the licence holder shall provide the Authority with details of the operator of the flight concerned, of its point and time of departure, of the football match to be attended, and the numbers of passengers to be carried for this purpose.

Standard Term 11

The licence holder shall not make available accommodation for the carriage of persons on flights whether forming part of any inclusive tour or not unless he has, within 14 days of his receiving notification of the booking and in any event before the flight, ensured that the customer has received a document containing the following information which shall be provided on the form set out in Annex D hereto, or by way of another form giving the same information which has been approved by the Authority:—

(a) confirmation of the name of the customer and of the number of passengers included in that booking with in each case details of:—

(i) the date and flight numbers of the outward and return flights on which the licence holder has undertaken to provide accommodation for the carriage of passengers and the airports of arrival and departure; if the flight numbers are not known at the time the document is issued, this should be indicated on the document;

(ii) any additional goods, services or other benefits (eg surface accommodation, car hire) which the licence holder has undertaken to provide;

(iii) the total amount payable in respect of the passengers included in the booking, with, if appropriate, an indication that surcharges may be payable;

(iv) the name of the agent (if applicable);

(b) the name and principal place of business or the registered office of the licence holder, and

(c) the number of the Air Travel Organiser's Licence issued to the licence holder.

Standard Term 12

The licence holder (and no other person on his behalf) shall retain either copies of every document issued pursuant to Standard Term 11 and every other document forming or evidencing the formation of a contract to make available accommodation on a flight pursuant to the licence (including booking forms and similar documents and any documents accepting bookings) or an electronic record of the information contained in such documents for a period of three months from the date of the latest flight to be provided under the contract and the licence holder shall furnish to the Authority any or all of such contracts and forms by which bookings are confirmed or copies thereof or a print out of information kept by electronic means within fifteen days of the same being demanded by the Authority.

Appendix C

Extract from ABTA Standards on Surcharges

2. BASIC PRINCIPLES

The basic principles are:-

– A surcharge by a tour operator in respect of currency rates, fuel or aviation cost variations or as a result of government action shall in all cases only be made if the tour operator can show that it is necessary for him to do so for reasons beyond his control.

– Tour operators must absorb increased costs up to an amount equivalent to 2% of the original holiday price. In this context the "holiday price" does not include separately itemised insurance premiums and amendment charges (eg, those that arise on name changes or as a result of part cancellation) and is by reference to the invoice total and not an individual client's price. Furthermore, if the total surcharge levied exceeds 10% of the holiday price after absorption of the 2% referred to above, the client has the right to cancel within 14 days from the issue date printed on his surcharge invoice and to be re-imbursed any monies paid towards the holiday price, excluding amendment and insurance fees.

– A tour operator who levies a surcharge shall give written notice to the client of the additional charge detailing the main cost headings. He shall also provide, or have available to provide on request, a reasonable written explanation of the reasons and calculations of the additional charge by reference to each main cost heading.

– Tour operators shall not surcharge a client less than 30 clear days before the date of the commencement of such clients holiday, tour or other travel arrangements. Tour operators shall ensure that, at least within 30 clear days before the date of commencement of the holiday, prices quoted to prospective holiday makers include any surcharge payable.

3. DEFINITIONS

For the purposes of these Standards, a surcharge is defined as a supplementary amount requested from clients after the booking has been confirmed by the operator and which is levied in addition to the originally confirmed holiday price.

5. AUTHORISATION TO SURCHARGE

Members are reminded that, until authorisation is received from ABTA, they cannot pass on any surcharges. ABTA is empowered to require any member to withdraw or reduce any proposed surcharge where the member has failed to demonstrate the surcharge is due to a verifiable cost increase or where the surcharge calculation is inconsistent with information previously submitted on Form A. Any member who attempts to pass on surcharges without prior authorisation will be in breach of these Standards and automatically referred to the Code of Conduct Committee. A list showing all operators who have been given permission to surcharge, with dates and routes, is normally available on Prestel. It should be noted that as soon as departure dates shown on Form B expire, the member's company name and details is withdrawn.

6. MONITORING OF SURCHARGES

Surchargeable Items

Surcharges may be imposed in respect of cost increases related to the following items, which arise after publication of the relevant brochure.

Fuel	Airport Security
Currency	Airport/Seaport Charges
UK or foreign government action	Overflying Charges
Scheduled fares	Road tolls.

Surcharges may not be imposed in respect of the following items unless the increase in cost arises directly as a result of government action:

Escorts*	Camp/Safari Parks*
Accommodation*	Camp Rates*
Group Size	Visas
Force Majeure	Ground Arrangements*
Late Payment	Entrance fees where part of package*

Operators may surcharge for currency fluctuation in respect of items marked with an asterisk(*) above. The Surcharge Monitoring Committee may wish to see original costings/invoices showing the price at which these elements were purchased.

7. MISCELLANEOUS

Consumer Protection Act

Part III of the above Act came into force in March 1989. Members are reminded that it is now a criminal offence to give a customer a misleading price indication. It is encumbent on each operator to ensure that a customer *is informed at the time of booking* of any possible price increases that may occur.

Travel Agents Packaging Foreign Inclusive Holidays

Where a travel agent assembles the component parts of a foreign inclusive holiday as defined in the Code of Conduct and issues his own invoice, he must comply with these Standards on Surcharges. If, however, the travel agent passes on invoices from individual suppliers direct to the client, these Standards on Surcharges do not apply.

Seat Only Arrangements

It is a government stipulation that seat-only arrangements on charter flights within Europe must include accommodation for the duration of the overseas stay. Consequently these Standards on Surcharges apply.

Seat-only arrangements on scheduled services do not normally constitute a foreign inclusive holiday. However, where land arrangements and/or ancillary services are provided in connection with such arrangements and thereby constitute a foreign inclusive package as defined in the Code of Conduct, these Standards on Surcharges apply.

Tailor Made Holidays

These Standards apply not only to brochured holidays but also to tailor made holidays that are not brochured, provided that the arrangements confirmed to the client constitute a foreign inclusive holiday as defined in the Code of Conduct.

Special Offers

For special offers (other than those published in members brochures) made to the public where all monies due are payable at the time of booking, prices must be quoted "all inclusive" with no surcharge being leviable.

Optional Extras

For the purpose of these Standards, optional extras are defined as items which are not costed into the basic holiday price, eg Ski Packs. As such they are deemed to "stand alone" and tour operators must absorb increased costs up to an amount equivalent to 2% of the original price of the optional extra. In all other respects surcharges related to these items must conform with these Standards on Surcharges.

ADMINISTRATION CHARGE AND AGENTS' COMMISSION FOR SURCHARGES

Members must state in their brochures the level of administration fee per passenger actually made in respect of surcharges. The maximum administration fee is 50p per person. Where applicable, reference must also be made to Agents' commission.

8. MANDATORY PARAGRAPHS

Any *one* of the paragraphs set out below must be shown in all brochures.

(a) *Full Price Guarantee*

"The price of your holiday is fully guaranteed and will not be subject to any surcharges."

A full price guarantee is the only situation where terms such as "No Surcharges" or "Guaranteed no Surcharges" or "Full Price Guarantee" or similar phrases may be used.

(b) *Partial Price Guarantee*

(i) "We guarantee that the price of your holiday will not be subject to any surcharges except for those resulting from governmental action. Even in this case, we will absorb an amount equivalent of 2% of the holiday price which excludes insurance premiums and any amendment charges. Only amounts in excess of this 2% will be surcharged, but where a surcharge is payable there will be an administration charge of *p together with an amount to cover agents' commission.

If this means paying more than 10% on the holiday price, you will be entitled to cancel your holiday with a full refund of all money paid except for any premium paid to us for holiday insurance and amendment charges.

Should you decide to cancel because of this, you must exercise your right to do so within 14 days from the issue date printed on the invoice."

*the amount must be inserted together with the words "per person" where applicable.

This paragraph should be used where prices are guaranteed except for governmental action.

(ii) "Whatever happens to the value of the Pound, the price of your holiday will not be subject to any currency surcharges. The price of your holiday is, however, subject to surcharges on the following items: (a full list of surchargeable items must be included in this sentence, eg governmental action, aircraft fuel, overflying charges, and airport charges).

Even in this case, we will absorb an amount equivalent to 2% of the holiday price which excludes insurance premiums and any amendment charges. Only amounts in excess of this 2% will be surcharged but where a surcharge is payable there will be an administration charge of *p together with an amount to cover agents' commission.

If this means paying more than 10% on the holiday price, you will be entitled to cancel your holiday with a full refund of all money paid except for any premium paid to us for holiday insurance and amendment charges. Should you decide to cancel because of this, you must exercise your right to do so within 14 days from the issue date printed on the invoice."

*the amount must be inserted together with, if applicable, the words "per person".

This paragraph should be used where no surcharges will be levied in respect of currency movements but other elements may be liable to surcharge. Brochures must not contain statements to the effect that "No surcharges except for . . .".

(c) *No Price Guarantee* (ie any or all permissible elements may be surcharged)

"The price of your holiday is subject to surcharges on the following items: governmental action, currency, aircraft fuel, overflying charges, airport charges and increases in scheduled air fares. Even in this case, we will absorb an amount equivalent to 2% of the holiday price which excludes insurance premiums and any amendment charges. Only amounts in excess of this 2% will be surcharged but where a surcharge is payable there will be an administration charge of *p together with an amount to cover agents' commission.

If this means paying more than 10% on the holiday price, you will be entitled to cancel your holiday with a full refund of all money paid except for any premium paid to us for holiday insurance and amendment charges. Should you decide to cancel because of this, you must exercise your right to do so within 14 days from the issue date printed on the invoice."

As the heading suggests, this paragraph should be used where any or all of the stated elements (government action, etc) may be liable to surcharge.

Appendix D

County court cases

The cases reported below are not discussed in the body of this book.

Askew v *Intasun North*

(Ashby-de-la-Zouch County Court – [1980] CLY 637)

The plaintiff, who had booked a holiday in Puerto de la Cruz for himself and his wife, was told on arrival that he would not be staying at the hotel which he had booked but in a hotel of a different type. The defendants knew this before the plaintiff's departure but made no effort to inform the plaintiff. The change caused the plaintiff's wife considerable distress.

It was held that the holiday was a complete disaster and that the family derived no benefit, although they did try to make the best of it. Damages of £943.23 (the cost of the holiday) plus £80 for car hire were awarded for breach of contract, and damages of £300 for "assault on feelings".

Levine v *Metropolitan Travel*

(Westminster County Court – [1980] CLY 638)

The plaintiffs paid £323.50 for a seven-day package holiday in Tel Aviv. The hotel was found to be totally unsatisfactory and the defendants admitted liability.

The judge rejected the submission that the holiday was a cheap one and that the value to be expected was therefore less. The proper test was to see the value of the loss sustained which was assessed at £200. In addition, damages for "assault on feelings" in the total sum of £200 (£100 per plaintiff) were awarded.

Bragg v *Yugotours*

(Westminster County Court – [1982] CLY 777)

The plaintiff paid £326.80 for a two-week holiday for herself and her daughter in Yugoslavia. On arrival at the hotel, the Yugotour representative was "unforgivably rude" and "did everything possible to ruin the plaintiff's holiday". The plaintiff was initially allocated a room with fungus and slime on the walls and was then moved to a room with damp bedding, shabby decor, exposed wires and a defective toilet. For the second night the plaintiff was moved to a single room with a camp bed for her daughter. Beetles later emerged from the floor. On the third day the plaintiff was moved to an alternative hotel without a sandy beach or children's facilities, and the plaintiff and her daughter contracted chills from damp bedding. The plaintiff asked to return home but was told that this was impossible. Yugotours offered to return the cost of the holiday plus £80 compensation.

It was held that there had been serious breaches of contract but that the plaintiff had not lost the whole value of the holiday. She was awarded £550 to cover diminution of the value of the contract and compensation for loss of enjoyment.

Hunt v *Hourmont*

(Neath and Port Talbot County Court – [1983] CLY 983)

The plaintiff booked and paid for a seven-day, two-centre holiday for a school party, comprising forty-three pupils and five teachers. Each pupil paid £98. The plaintiff complained that in Paris the food provided was uninteresting and insufficient in quantity and that the coach which was supposed to be available for evening use was not available one evening and on another could only be used for a short time. At the second centre, the plaintiff alleged that the party could not stay at the hotel which they had booked. The substitute was, it was alleged, dirty, cold and had inadequate heating. The toilets were so dirty that the female teachers had to clean and disinfect them before they could be used; the bedrooms were damp and musty with peeling papers and mould on the walls; the beds and bedding were so damp that the party slept fully clothed on the beds, not in them; the food was served almost cold, was of poor quality and insufficient in quantity. The pupils therefore bought food elsewhere and the party leader spent considerable time telephoning the defendant's representative and complaining to the hotel proprietor who told them that they should leave if they did not like it.

It was held that it would be an exaggeration to describe the holiday as a complete disaster but it was held that the second centre was inadequate in every conceivable respect. Pupils were awarded damages of £60 each for diminution in value and loss of enjoyment. The teachers were awarded £110 for extra worry and responsibility, and the leading teacher was awarded £210 because of extra worry, responsibility, work and unpleasantness in dealing with complaints.

Rhodes v *Sunspot Tours*

(Preston County Court – [1983] CLY 984)

The plaintiff paid the defendants £777 for a holiday in a Maltese self-catering apartment for himself, his wife and three children. Upon arrival at 2 am, the apartment key could not be found and they were housed in a hotel, the arrangements for which were unsatisfactory. The following day they were shown into the apartment but found that it had not been cleaned, and that the toilet had broken away from the wall creating an unwholesome smell. A bed mattress was stained with blood and urine and the cot mattress was torn. An independent witness described the flat as "grotty, grimy and horrible". After five days the plaintiff was offered an alternative apartment. Upon an inspection, green mould was found in the fridge. The plaintiff stayed in the first flat for the remainder of the holiday but ate out for all meals including breakfast, due to the unclean kitchen. The plaintiff's wife was very upset by the experience and she and the plaintiff each lost about twelve pounds in weight during the fortnight.

It was held that:

- (i) the defendants were in breach of contract providing a "disastrous" holiday; and
- (ii) the plaintiff reasonably refused the alternative accommodation offered, since by then an "atmosphere of mistrust" existed between the plaintiff and the defendant; and
- (iii) damages of £1,000 included the total waste of the price of the holiday, the discomfort and distress of the first night and the upset to all the family for the balance of the holiday.

Harvey v *Tracks Travel*

(West London County Court – [1984] CLY 1006)

The plaintiff booked a place on a trans-African expedition tour organised by the defendants at a cost of £870 plus a further £100 towards a food kitty. The trip was scheduled to take fourteen weeks from London to Dar-es-Salaam. The defendants informed the plaintiff that they could arrange a return flight from there for £210, or from Nairobi for approximately £180. The expedition left London on 19 April 1981 and ten days later the truck broke down in Tunis. It took three weeks to repair. On arrival in Nigeria the expedition was unable to purchase food as the defendants had failed to warn the truck driver of extremely high prices, which meant that he was not carrying sufficient money. On 8 July 1981 the truck crashed in Zaire and, despite efforts by the tour leader to contact the defendants and request a back-up truck, nothing was done. Miss Harvey and the others were stranded in the bush for some 27 days at the end of which they were running short of food and water, the food kitty had been exhausted and the tour leader was borrowing money from the group members to purchase food. By 4 August 1981 no news had been received and the group decided to hitchhike to Nairobi. The plaintiff had hitched some 150 kilometres when, on 6 August 1981, she met a relief truck sent by the defendants. She was told by the driver that there was no information as to what should happen to the passengers, that the broken-down truck would be towed away, that it should be available in twelve days or so and that she could rejoin it later. She booked a ticket to the nearest town but was unable to return to England as she could not afford the fare of £550 and, accordingly, flew at a cost of some £70 to meet the truck and journey with it to Nairobi. The plaintiff waited until 13 September 1981 by which time the truck had still not arrived. Distressed and frightened, she flew to Nairobi and found that tickets to England could not be purchased for less than £487. She obtained this sum from home, returning to the UK on 19 September 1981 whereas she had intended to return at the end of July. She missed eight weeks off work, losing £752 in wages. The defendants' attitude throughout was unhelpful, and on return the plaintiff was advised by them "to chalk it up to experience". The plaintiff claimed damages limited to £3,000 and obtained judgment in default.

It was held that the plaintiff should receive special damages of £1,995, including a full refund of the holiday price as there had been a total failure of consideration; general damages should be assessed at £1,005; the Registrar stated that £1,005 represented ordinary general damages for a young girl stranded in Africa for five months, instead of on a fourteen-week escorted tour, and that a claim for aggravated damages could have received sympathetic consideration had the claim not been limited.

Bagley v *Intourist Moscow*

(Westminster County Court – [1984] CLY 1024)

The defendants agreed to act as travel agents for the plaintiff and make the necessary arrangements for him to go by rail and sea from London to Eastern Siberia and thence by air to Japan. The plaintiff signed the booking form incorporating some terms and conditions but not expressly specifying what the defendants' obligations were under the contract.

The defendants informed the plaintiff, in the brochure containing the booking form, of the entry requirements for all countries except Japan. The plaintiff did not know he needed a visa to enter Japan, did not obtain one and was refused entry. He was confined to a hotel for six days and then deported by air to the UK. He paid £154 for hotel expenses in Japan and settled litigation over his return fare for a total of £488. He lost the opportunity to spend a few weeks in Japan and to travel back to the UK overland via India.

It was held that:

(i) there was an implied term that the defendants were obliged to inform the plaintiff of entry requirements for Japan or to warn the plaintiff that they were not able so to advise him. It was a relevant factor that the plaintiff was a private individual without expert knowledge; and

(ii) general damages of £1,500 were awarded, the plaintiff having wasted £324 for the journey out and £488 on the journey back; and

(iii) loss of the benefit of the overland journey back was irrecoverable as being outside the contemplation of the party as the defendant had not been informed of it; and

(iv) special damages of £154 were awarded but the return air fare was not awarded since the plaintiff would always have had to travel back.

Taylor v *International Travel Services*

(West London County Court – [1984] CLY 1023)

The plaintiff paid the defendants £1,306.52 for a three-week holiday for himself, his wife and their child in a self-contained villa of exceptional quality in an exclusive estate in Marbella, Spain. The price was stated to include flight and car hire. Three days before they were due to leave, the defendants cancelled the booking, stating that the villa had been double-booked by its owners. The defendants returned the money, as an alternative villa was not available. The defendants had, however, failed to arrange flights or car hire which prevented the plaintiff from renting an alternative villa in Marbella. The plaintiff found an alternative villa for two weeks in Spain in a less attractive location for £1,206 inclusive. Prior to payment to the defendants, the plaintiff had informed the defendants that the plaintiff's wife, a professional singer, had been invited to perform at a concert during the first week of the holiday which she wished to accept as the booking was not confirmed. The defendants assured the plaintiff that arrangements for the villa had been confirmed and in reliance of this misrepresentation the plaintiff's wife declined the concert engagements. The plaintiff claimed damages including the lost concert fees.

Judgment was entered in default and the defendants did not, in fact, appear at the hearing for the assessment of damages before the Registrar. The Registrar held as follows on the assessment of damages hearing:

(i) the plaintiff could recover special damages of £787.50 for the concert fee which the plaintiff's wife had lost as a result of the defendants' representation; and

(ii) the plaintiff would recover general damages in the sum of £1,150. The plaintiff was entitled to £250 in respect of the cost of travelling to Manchester instead of Gatwick, parking and associated inconvenience as well as the loss of pay for one week's additional holiday justifiably taken by the plaintiff. For loss of enjoyment of the wasted first week of the holiday, the plaintiff was entitled to recover double the average weekly cost of the promised quality villa at a lost bargain price of £900. For loss of enjoyment over the last two weeks the plaintiff was entitled to 50 per cent of the cost of the alternative holiday averaged out over three weeks which was £400; and

(iii) the claim for loss of enjoyment of the plaintiff's infant child was ignored.

Abbatt v *Sunquest Holidays*

(Canterbury County Court – [1984] CLY 1025)

The plaintiff booked and paid for a fourteen-day package holiday in Romania, the price for two adults and two young children in a hotel suite being £769. The defendants' brochure represented, *inter alia*, that there was a fine beach at the resort and that there was a swimming pool, nanny service and meals provided on a full board basis at the hotel. Additionally, it represented that the resort and hotel were ideal for children. Upon arrival at the hotel, the plaintiff discovered the suite to be cramped with broken tiles and a broken shower. The swimming pool contained dirty, untreated water and was unsuitable for children, and the nanny service had not been available for two years. Meals were of a very poor choice and quality and were long in duration as a result of which the children ate little. Untreated sewage had been deposited on the beach which needed clearing before the children could play. The effect of the condition of the resort and the hotel was that the family returned to England after six days.

It was held that:

(i) the plaintiff was entitled to expect a reasonable standard of facilities. There were substantial and relevant breaches of representations; and

(ii) there was no defined formula for assessing damages, and damages of £1,000 were awarded for diminution in value and loss of enjoyment.

Harris v *Torchgrove Limited*

(Manchester District Registry – [1985] CLY 944)

The plaintiff booked a holiday for himself, his wife and three teenage children in an apartment in France, selecting an apartment from the defendants' brochure. It was stated to be in "a quieter part of town". The total cost for four weeks was £1,400. When the plaintiff and family arrived, they were taken to a different apartment which was over a restaurant. It generated much noise and smell and adjoined a fruit-machine parlour. The apartment only had accommodation for four although on the second day of the holiday, a portable bed was supplied.

It was held that the defendants were liable, and damages totalling £2,157.83 were awarded against them. This sum included damages for loss of enjoyment, special damages and interest.

In the course of the judgment, it was said:

> "A tour operator sells a dream. If he sells a dream he must make it come true. This is fragile; therefore it imposes a great obligation on him to take care."

Scott & Scott v *Blue Sky Holidays*

(Willesden County Court – [1985] CLY 943)

The plaintiffs paid the defendants £512 for a seven-night holiday at a four-star hotel in Tenerife. Upon arrival they were placed in a cramped and noisy room without twin beds (as required). They complained and were transferred to another room, but not until the following afternoon. The evening meals were lukewarm and greasy. After the first of the evening meals, the plaintiffs ate out for the rest of the holiday, spending £41.

It was held that:

(i) the holiday had not been an unmitigated disaster but complaints regarding the food and the first night's accommodation were well cited and the plaintiffs were entitled to expect better conditions at an internationally classified four-star hotel; and

(ii) damages are at large and not to be determined by reference to the sums spent on the holiday; and

(iii) the plaintiffs' failure to seek to mitigate their loss by complaining to the defendants' representative at the hotel operated to reduce what would otherwise have been "substantial" damages to £400.

Powell v *Arrowsmith Holidays*

(Liverpool County Court – [1985] CLY 945)

The plaintiff was three months pregnant. She booked a holiday for herself and her husband for fourteen days in a Spanish hotel. It was a written term in the contract that they would be provided with twin beds, a bath, separate toilet and a balcony. They requested a room on the ground or first floor because of the plaintiff's pregnancy. On the day before departure the defendants attempted to vary the contract because of overbooking on behalf of the hoteliers. They offered the plaintiff's husband an apartment. He refused. No alternative accommodation was offered. The plaintiff and her husband flew out the next morning. They were kept waiting for five to six hours. The plaintiff was extremely upset. They were given eventually a single cramped room with two single beds and a shower. After the fifth night they were given a double room on the fourth floor. The defendants argued (i) that the plaintiff had accepted variation of the contract via her husband, (ii) that the terms in the standard booking form excluded breaches of overbooking by hoteliers and their failure to provide alternative accommodation, and (iii) that there were no breaches of contract. After four hours of evidence the defendants withdrew their defence and submitted to judgment. General damages for inconvenience etc were assessed at £750.

Tucker v *O.T.A. Travel*
(Salisbury County Court – [1986] CLY 383)

The plaintiff booked a holiday for himself, his wife and four-year-old daughter in a three-star hotel in Majorca, having chosen it from the defendants' brochure. The hotel was described as very reliable with a reputation for good service and cuisine, tasteful decor and a friendly atmosphere. The plaintiff chose the defendants' holiday because the brochure indicated that flights were scheduled ones, daytime and direct to the airport of destination. His daughter was shy and insecure and would be difficult if travelling at night. The plane was overbooked and he was offered a non-direct flight with no guarantees that he would make his connection at the other end. The plaintiff refused this offer and re-booked the first direct flight available. He attempted to telex the hotel, and returned home losing two days of his holiday. The plaintiff flew out two days later to find the hotel overbooked. He had to spend two nights in an apartment with a defective toilet, peeling wallpaper, beds with no springs and a dirty, rusty wash-basin. The defendants argued that (i) the contract with the plaintiff was only to use their best endeavours to arrange the flight and hotel, and that (ii) if there was a breach due to the overbooking, the plaintiff had failed to mitigate his loss by not accepting the alternative flight.

It was held that:

(i) the contract with the plaintiff was to provide the flight and hotel accommodation; and

(ii) the plaintiff had not failed to mitigate his loss as the defendants had not proved that he had failed to be reasonable within the meaning of the law; and

(iii) the plaintiff was entitled to out-of-pocket expenses of £100 and a sum attributable to a notional rebate in respect of four days' lost hotel accommodation (£129.29) and £300 for general damages for inconvenience, which would have been more had the plaintiff not exaggerated the problems. Total award: £529.29.

Carter v *Thomson Travel*
(Oldham County Court – [1986] CLY 976)

The plaintiff paid the defendants £859 for a two-week holiday for herself, her husband and three children in a self-contained exclusive villa in Majorca. It was discovered on arrival that the villa had been built very recently and the plumber was still carrying out repairs in the bathroom. The inside of the villa was damp and cold — the plaster work had not dried out prior to the plaintiff's arrival. The family's clothing and bedding became damp and they slept in sweatshirts and socks. The swimming pool could not be used and the plaintiff felt unable to allow her children to play around the villa because a vicious dog on a long chain from a nearby farm was able to encroach upon the property. The villa was burgled on the tenth day as a result of which the plaintiff's family moved to a hotel.

It was held that the facilities at the villa fell below what a reasonable person could anticipate. For diminution in the value of the holiday, special damages of £259 were awarded, and for mental distress, inconvenience and disappointment general damages of £1,000 were awarded.

Jacobs v *Thomson Travel*

(Bloomsbury County Court – [1986] CLY 975)

In January 1985 the plaintiff purchased a holiday for himself, his wife, mother and son at a five-star hotel in Israel from the defendants for £2,455. The holiday was for seven days in April 1985. The plaintiff wished to spend passover at the hotel, but did not advise the defendants of this. The day before departure, the defendants told the plaintiff that he could not stay at the five-star hotel contracted for and offered him an inferior hotel at the same resort. The plaintiff refused the offer, the holiday was cancelled and the defendants returned the price to the plaintiff. The plaintiff claimed damages for inconvenience and disappointment, including that suffered because the family had to spend passover at home.

It was held that:

(i) the plaintiff was entitled to general damages for disappointment etc and was not obliged to accept an alternative holiday. In assessing compensation for the disappointment, the court took into account that the plaintiff and his family had another holiday in Israel in May 1985 and frequently took foreign holidays; and

(ii) the plaintiff was not entitled to extra damages because it was passover since that was too remote in view of the fact that the plaintiff had not told the defendants that he was religious and the passage was important; and

(iii) general damages were assessed at £250 and special damages in respect of loss of earnings and telephone calls at £210.

McLeod v *Hunter*

(Westminster County Court – [1987] CLY 1162)

The plaintiff booked a holiday with the defendant in May 1986 for a luxury villa in St Jean Cap Ferrat. He paid £1,030 for accommodation

for the week commencing 2 August. The villa was described as being "a quality villa" with spectacular views. It had an elegant interior with accommodation for eight. The plaintiff intended the stay as the highpoint and rest-over after a touring holiday with his wife and three children. Immediately before the family set off, the defendant cancelled the booked accommodation, and the plaintiff agreed to take an alternative which the defendant assured him would be found. This turned out to be sub-standard. It was an apartment rather than a house; it was cramped and very uncomfortable. It did not provide the luxurious rest which the plaintiff had bargained for. On arrival, it was too late to change elsewhere.
It was held that:

(i) damages for diminution in value of the holiday provided: £439; and

(ii) general damages for inconvenience and disappointment: £500; and

(iii) interest at 12.5 per cent from 9 August 1986 to 8 January 1987.

Baldwin v *Tameside Travel*

(Manchester County Court – [1987] CLY 1148)

The plaintiff booked a flight to Tenerife for himself, two other adults and three children. The plaintiff had assured his children the flight would be on a Tristar aircraft. The plaintiff considered the Tristar superior to the Boeing 727. On 20 March 1985, the plaintiff duly booked the seats at a total cost of £1,161. The booking form referred to the flight being with British Airtours. A few days before departure, the plaintiff received the tickets and discovered they were in respect of a Dan Air Boeing 727. Furthermore, the departure time was at 7.30am (instead of 10.10am). The plaintiff gave evidence that with young children this caused considerable inconvenience. The plaintiff boarded the aircraft but found his family was split up in the seating arrangements. The plaintiff sued for special damages of £147, being his loss caused by being given a flight he could have obtained for £147 cheaper from another travel agent. He claimed further general damages for inconvenience.

The judge found that as the booking form referred to a British Airtours aircraft and the plaintiff was put on a Dan Air Boeing, this was in breach of contract. The plaintiff was awarded £147 in special damages and £150 in general damages for stress and inconvenience.

Hartley v *Intasun Holidays*

(Ellesmere Port County Court – [1987] CLY 1149)

The plaintiff booked a package holiday with the defendants in Majorca at a price of £270. The plaintiff, through his own error, arrived at Manchester airport a day late and missed his flight. A representative of the defendants at Manchester airport indicated that it would be possible to accommodate him on a flight later that day to Ibiza from where he could obtain a local flight to Majorca, and the representative telexed the resort to request them to keep his hotel room available. On arrival at the resort, the plaintiff found that the hotelier had re-let his room, and the plaintiff was accommodated in inferior accommodation in a different resort. The plaintiff claimed damages against the defendants for failure to supply the accommodation which had been booked.

It was held that the change of departure date by the plaintiff constituted a cancellation by him of his holiday, which attracted 100 per cent cancellation charges and this was in accordance with the defendants' booking conditions. The defendants were entitled to retain the whole purchase price and do nothing to make alternative arrangements for the plaintiff. They should not be penalised in damages for making an attempt, without charge, to patch up some form of holiday for the plaintiff. Claim dismissed.

Sage v *Bladon Lines Travel Limited*

(Wandsworth County Court 3 November 1987)

In November 1984, the plaintiff, on behalf of himself and three other families, booked a package holiday with the defendants to commence on 22 December, including accommodation at the Chalet Lamastra. The total cost of the holiday was £4,863, and the holiday was to include food and the services of two chalet girls. The plaintiff alleged that the chalet girls did not keep the kitchen in the chalet clean, that the steps to the chalet were not cleared properly, that there were insufficient chairs for the party to sit on, that there were no chest of drawers or mirrors in the bathroom and livingroom, that the chalet was inaccessible by coach and that the oven did not work for some of the holiday. Further, there were particular problems concerning heating on New Year's eve.

The judge said:

> "I have made findings of fact in some detail. I am left with the final matter, to decide, in view of all these facts, whether the defendants did not provide services and accommodation to a reasonable standard in accordance with all the circumstances and particulars in the brochure. One or two matters trouble me, ie the number of towels, which were not in accordance with the manual. It troubles me that the rep and the two chalet girls were new to the job and that Mr. Sage and party were their first customers. I cannot help remarking that the plaintiffs had a raw deal but substantially they got what the brochure said. If one looks at the brochure, there is no promise that they provide chalet girls with experience, it only refers to their training. Chalet girls do not do the work for many seasons; it is a hard life.

> I am troubled with the question of whether the travel company promises fundamental things will be provided, ie that they guarantee the working of a heating system in a cold climate. I am afraid, in seeking to find a breach of duty on the part of the defendants, I look in vain. I take no pleasure in coming to that conclusion, because the plaintiff and his party had a raw deal. They were disappointed by their holiday, but I bear in mind that nothing could be done in the circumstances. I make the highest criticism that Anita did not ring on New Year's Day and that there was a lack of communication.
>
> I am bound to find that there is not misrepresentation . . . . I therefore must dismiss the claim."

Toubi v *Intasun Holidays Limited*

(Sheffield County Court – [1988] CLY 1060)

The plaintiff booked a holiday with the defendants, six months in advance. She chose a four-star hotel and flight timings convenient for her daughter's health. Some three days before the plaintiff's departure, the defendants learnt that the hotel was overbooked and could not accommodate the plaintiff. The plaintiff rejected the alternative of a three-star hotel which the defendants offered. Since the defendants could not arrange an alternative four-star hotel they refunded the plaintiff's cost of the holiday. The plaintiff sued for damages for distress, loss of enjoyment etc.

It was held that the contract between the plaintiff and the defendants was subject to booking conditions which covered this subject. The defendants had been let down themselves by the hotel and had done their best to offer alternatives. The defendants, however, were not in breach of contract and, accordingly, the plaintiff's claim failed.

Jones & Jones v *Villa Ramos (Algarve)*

(Redditch County Court – [1988] CLY 1061)

The plaintiffs booked with the defendants a holiday in the Algarve for May 1987. The defendants' brochure described the apartment complex as having "a very large pool facility with bar, restaurant, sun lounging equipment and kiddies' pool". On arrival, the plaintiffs were told that due to a dispute they would not be allowed to use any of the facilities. This stance was maintained despite an offer by the plaintiffs to pay for the use of the facilities. The plaintiffs were forced to travel by hired car to beaches to swim but the weather did not always make such swimming possible or safe. The plaintiffs accepted that the apartment itself was entirely satisfactory.

It was held that the defendants were liable for breach of contract. The plaintiffs were awarded £750 for diminution in the value of the holiday provided, £1,000 for general damages for inconvenience and disappointment and interest at 12 per cent.

Wilson v *Pegasus Holidays (London)*
(T/A Pegasus Student Travel)

([1988] CLY 1059)

The plaintiff, a teacher, booked a one-week skiing holiday in Italy, acting as agent for thirty-one pupils. Each pupil paid £249. The plaintiff and another teacher went free as party leaders. The children were aged 12–13. The plaintiff, one month before departure, discovered that her booking was not confirmed. She was told by the defendants that she could have her money back or accept a holiday at a different resort in a different hotel. The defendants' representative made representations to the plaintiff about the alternative holiday based on "very little" investigation which turned out to be material misrepresentations. The hotel was described in the defendants' brochure as offering a "superb standard of accommodation". In fact it had inadequate toilet and bathing facilities, exposed electric wiring and was in very poor decorative order. The skiing slopes were some distance from the hotel and the bus service was erratic. Consequently, skiing time was lost and young children were forced to walk to the slopes carrying their ski equipment.

It was held that the defects in the holiday amounted to breaches of implied terms in the contract as well as founding a claim in misrepresentation. Each child was awarded £125 for loss of enjoyment and diminution in the value of the holiday. The plaintiff as the party leader was awarded £400 because of extra stress, worry and responsibility and, for the same reasons, the other teacher was awarded £200.

Duthie v *Thomson Holidays*

(Bridgwater County Court – [1988] CLY 1058)

The plaintiff booked with the defendants a fourteen-day package holiday including hostel accommodation. On arrival, the defendants alleged that the plaintiff had booked for flight only, but subsequently provided one night's accommodation. The following night the plaintiff had to sleep rough on the beach and she spent the remaining nights either in a cheap hotel or sleeping in the open on camp sites. The plaintiff claimed damages for breach of contract.

It was held that there had been breach of contract by the defendants. The plaintiff was awarded £250 for general damages for mental distress, inconvenience and loss of enjoyment, and £44 for special damages in respect of the cost of camp sites and hotel charges.

[NOTE: Charter flight passengers to Greece are required to have an accommodation arrangement — it is a Greek requirement. Many brochures which are intended to sell charter flight seats only, to circumvent this requirement, state that hostel accommodation is also arranged. Tour operators, and most customers, know that there is no intention on either side to seek to make use of any accommodation "arrangements". This case is an example of a holiday maker either not knowing or not playing by "the rules of the game"!]

Spencer v *Cosmos Air Holidays*

(Court of Appeal, on appeal from Wigan County Court [1990] CLY 635)

The plaintiff booked a two-week holiday in Spain for herself and two friends. On the ninth day of the holiday, the plaintiff and her friends were instructed by a representative of the management of the hotel to leave the hotel, allegations having been made that they had acted in a thoroughly objectionable way and upset the other guests. The plaintiff and her friends spent the next two nights sleeping on the beach until, on the third day following their expulsion from the hotel, a representative of the defendants arranged a room for them at another less pleasing resort, fifteen miles from their original resort. There they completed their holiday.

In the county court, it was held that the plaintiff's claim would fail because the management of the hotel had good reason to believe that certain guests had misbehaved and it was probable that the management believed that it was the plaintiff and her friends. It was possible, however, that the hotel had been mistaken in the identification of the guests who had misbehaved and had unreasonably excluded the plaintiff and her friends. The judge in the county court held that even if there had been such a case of mistaken identity, the defendants were entitled to rely on an exclusion clause in the Booking Conditions which stated that the defendants would not be liable for a breach of contract over which they had no control.

The county court judge held, however, that if the plaintiff's claim on liability had succeeded, the appropriate sum to be awarded was £2,000.

In the Court of Appeal, the case was referred back to the county court for re-trial because the judge in the county court had failed to make a finding one way or the other on whether the girls had misbehaved in the manner alleged. It was accepted by both parties that if, at the re-trial, the judge found that the girls were guilty of the conduct alleged, their claim would fail due to an implied term in the contract that the plaintiff and her friends would not conduct themselves in a manner which would cause discomfort or make themselves objectionable to other guests and/or the hotel staff.

The Court of Appeal held, in relation to the clause in the Booking Conditions excluding liability, that it did not need to consider whether or not the clause was unreasonable under the Unfair Contract Terms Act 1977 since the Booking Conditions seeking to exclude liability did not relate to the type of alleged breach of contract with which the court was concerned.

The Court of Appeal also considered the damages awarded by the county court. It was held that, if the plaintiff succeeded on the question of liability, the award would be reduced to a figure of £1,000 from the £2,000 awarded in the county court.

McMillan and Others v *MacLaine Holidays and Another* (1989)

The plaintiffs booked a two-week holiday with the defendants in the Algarve for the price of £115 per person, to include accommodation in a bungalow. The brochure described the properties which included the bungalow as "excellent properties". In evidence, it was admitted by the defendant that although the bungalow could be described as reasonable, it did fall short of excellence. There were a number of defects in the property, namely the patio window could not be properly secured, there was a shortage of light bulbs, a front bedroom shutter was broken and there was only a minimum amount of crockery and plates. Although complaints were made, nothing was done to remedy the defects for a period of six days – when the plaintiffs were moved to alternative accommodation in a next-door bungalow.

It was held that the condition of the bungalow constituted a breach of the contract between the plaintiffs and the defendants. A sum of £100 was awarded to each of the four plaintiffs for diminution in the value of the holiday. For the disappointment and the distress and inconvenience of being in a bungalow which fell short of their expectations for a period of six days, a sum of £50 per person per day was awarded.

Love v *Arrowsmith*

(Before H.H. Judge Pickles – [1989] CLY 1187)

The plaintiff booked a holiday in Menorca with the defendants. Through no fault of the defendants, the hotel manager failed to enter the reservation on the computer and the error was discovered by the defendants only the night before the plaintiffs were due to fly. The plaintiffs were subsequently accommodated for three nights in a self-catering apartment close to the hotel but were able to use all the hotel facilities. After three nights, the plaintiffs were accommodated in the hotel itself.

It was held that the defendants were not liable because their Booking Conditions excluded liability where the fault was not that of the tour operator. Further, the change in accommodation was not sufficiently major to require advance notice, since the alternative accommodation was of an equivalent standard. The court also held that the defendant's Booking Conditions were reasonable and would not be struck down under the Unfair Contract Terms Act 1977. His Honour Judge Pickles commented that in the event that he was wrong on liability, damages would only have been assessed at £30.

Clark and Noonan v *ILG Travel Limited*

(Bromley County Court – [1989] CLY 1188)

The plaintiffs booked and paid for a package holiday in Menorca with the defendant. Included in the price was the sum of £85 for flight supplements to travel on a flight particularly convenient to them. The day before departure, the plaintiffs were told that because of maintenance problems the aircraft would not depart until seven and a half hours after the scheduled time. Had they known this would happen, they would have booked a different flight which was not subject to supplements. They claimed back the £85.

It was held that the flight supplement related solely to the negotiated price which the defendants had to pay the airline in question, not to the time of travel. The Booking Conditions made clear that alterations in flight times were possible, and that compensation was payable only if the delay was over twelve hours. Therefore the claim was dismissed.

Graham v *Sunsetridge*

(Sunderland County Court – [1989] CLY 1189)

In March 1987 the plaintiff asked the defendant to arrange return tickets on flights to Hong Kong from London for the plaintiff, his wife and daughter. The plaintiff informed the defendant that the flight should be so arranged that the family would arrive back in London by 26 April (in time for work and school). The defendant agreed. Whilst in Hong Kong the plaintiff enquired as to the time of departure and was told the reservations were "wait listed" and not "OK" status, and seats were not guaranteed. The plaintiff telephoned the defendant to enlist his help but the defendant was uncooperative. On 25 April, the family had to book out of their holiday flat. They went to the airport. After waiting all day, they were unsuccessful in securing seats. They were given overnight accommodation in a council flat which was infested with cockroaches. Six days later they were able to return to London. The plaintiff was disciplined at work as a result and his daughter lost an opportunity to attend a guides' camp with the possibility of being selected for a trip to Moscow. Special damages (accommodation, telephone calls, meals and lost wages) were assessed at £632. General damages for annoyance, distress, frustration and inconvenience were assessed at £900.

Corbett v *Top Hat Tours*

(Bow County Court – [1989] CLY 1194)

The plaintiff, who had a heart condition, booked a twelve-week winter holiday for himself and his wife at an apartment complex in the Algarve, at a cost of £910. On the 23rd day of the holiday a power cut at the complex left the plaintiff with no light, heating or hot water. On the 26th day the plaintiff was given an apartment on a lower floor which had power. Within one hour of the move all the power failed, and the plaintiff and his wife moved back to the original apartment. After the further move, the plaintiff felt palpitations and pain in his left arm and on the 28th day he demanded to be flown home as he was feeling ill and there was still no power. The plaintiff refused an offer of alternative accommodation at another resort and flew home at his own expense, the defendant having refused to fly them back unless they signed a disclaimer. The plaintiff felt unwell for two to three months afterwards.

It was held that it was reasonable to refuse the alternative resort. Damages for diminution in the value of the holiday were awarded in the sum of £711. Damages for distress and inconvenience were awarded in the sum of £1,039 and costs of the return flight and taxi home were awarded in the sum of £290.

Compton v *ILG Travel Limited*

(Winchester County Court – [1990] CLY 625)

The plaintiff booked and paid for a package holiday in Greece with the defendant. As a result of Greek air traffic control industrial action, the plaintiff's flight home was delayed by 33 hours. As a consequence, she and her travelling companions suffered inconvenience, loss of earnings and taxi fares. The plaintiff sued the defendant for recovery of these sums.

It was held that as it was conceded that air traffic control problems could not constitute a breach of contract on the part of the defendant, the claim must be dismissed.

Booth and Ingram v *Best Travel*

(Leeds County Court – [1990] CLY 1542)

The plaintiffs booked their annual two-week holiday on the island of Rhodes at a price of £584. They reserved accommodation described in the defendant's brochure as Class A hotel accommodation. Upon arrival at the hotel the plaintiffs found that the room provided was small, had insufficient storage space and was badly lit. The electrical fittings in the room were in a dangerous condition, either hanging loose or taped to the walls and ceilings, the room was very dirty, and the bed linen was not clean. The plaintiffs registered a complaint with the defendant's company and on the following day were moved to apartment accommodation for six days. The apartment accommodation was satisfactory, but on the evening of the sixth day the plaintiffs were told that they would have to move within twelve hours to further apartment accommodation, which was described in the defendant's brochure as being Class E. Upon moving to this accommodation, the plaintiffs found it to be infested with cockroaches. Following a night during which neither plaintiff could sleep, they again complained and stated that they wished to return home; they were told that this would not be possible and were moved to further apartment accommodation, described in the brochure as being of Class C, situated in a different resort in a different part of the island, where they spent the remainder of their holiday.

It was held that the plaintiffs were entitled to the following damages:

(i) £400, being the diminution in value of the holiday;

(ii) £600 compensation to each plaintiff for distress and inconvenience;

(iii) interest of £60.

Maciak and Maciak v *Club Riviera Sales (UK) and Club Riviera Management (UK)*

(Oxford County Court – [1992] 9 CL 148)

In May 1989 the first and second plaintiffs entered into an agreement with the defendant to purchase membership of a timeshare club and the right to occupy an apartment on the Costa del Sol for the same two weeks every year from 1989 onwards, at a total cost of £4,290. In July 1989 the plaintiffs flew out to Spain with their two children for their holiday. Upon arrival they were allocated the wrong apartment, which was smaller than the one agreed upon. Contrary to statements contained in the defendant's brochure, the apartment did not have a balcony with a seaview, the beach was twice as far away as advertised and did not offer extensive water sports facilities, and a pedestrian underpass leading to the beach beneath the 6-lane Spanish coastal highway had not been completed. Later the following day the plaintiffs were offered alternative accommodation which necessitated moving three times in the course of the holiday. Instead, they moved to self catering accommodation elsewhere. Three days later they returned home after the theft of money and credit cards. Because of their experience they had not used the timeshare in the years since.

It was held that the plaintiffs were entitled to the following damages:

(i) one-third of the total price of the timeshare (£1,430) for diminution in value;

(ii) £370 special damages;

(iii) £1,050 general damages for distress and disappointment;

(iv) interest of £1,282.50 at 15 per cent per annum.

Index

page

Notes

Notes

Notes

Notes